REENGINEERING SURVIVAL GUIDE

Managing and Succeeding in the Changing Workplace

ANDREW J. DUBRIN, Ph.D.
Professor of Management
College of Business
Rochester Institute of Technology

THOMSON EXECUTIVE PRESS
A Division of South-Western College Publishing

Sponsoring Editor: Jim Sitlington
Production Editor: Holly Terry
Development: Custom Editorial Productions, Inc.
Production House: Trejo Production
Internal Design: Ellen Pettengell
Cover Design: Joseph M. Devine
Marketing Manager: Stephen E. Momper

Library of Congress Cataloging-in-Publication Data

DuBrin, Andrew J.
     Reengineering survival guide: managing and succeeding in the
     changing workplace / by Andrew J. DuBrin.
          p. cm.
     Includes bibliographical references and index.
     1. Organizational change--Management. 2. Downsizing of
     organizations. 3. Work groups. 4. Employee empowerment.
     I. Title.
     HD58.8.D83 1996
     658.4--dc20   94-43416
                                             CIP

     ISBN: 0-538-84387-X

1 2 3 4 5 MT 9 8 7 6 5

Printed in the United States of America

To my family and friends

Preface

My purpose in writing this book is to help the reader do a more effective job of leading and managing others in a reengineered, or otherwise revamped, work environment. My purpose is driven by the fact that many organizations today of all sizes are undergoing a transformation in the way they accomplish work. One major transformation is a movement away from the venerable functional structure that organized work by the various departments or functions called on to perform it. Instead, many firms are now organizing by focusing on key processes such as filling customer orders or developing a new product.

The organization of work by process is also known by such terms as reengineering, process innovation, horizontal organization structure, and "turning the organization on its side." The change to a horizontal rather than a vertical structure has even been referred to as creating "a large pipe rather than a silo."

Downsizing or "rightsizing" has been a more frequently practiced transformation than reengineering. During the last decade American companies have shed more than 6 million jobs. In the first quarter of 1993, 3,100 jobs per day were being eliminated by large employers in the United States.[1] A major target of these downsizings is middle management. Even during the recent business upturn, few organizations are as fully staffed as they used to be. Medium-sized and small firms have also maintained

trimmed-down work forces. Managers and professional survivors of downsizings have been forced to increased their workloads because their spans of control have increased and less staff
support is available. After a downsizing one middle manager
went to his boss and asked, "Who is going to type my reports
now?" His boss responded, "Get to know that friendly PC sitting on your desk."

The focus on total quality management (TQM) has also created upheavals in the workplace. Teams of individuals are empowered to make suggestions for work process improvement,
thus decreasing the authority of many managers and professional specialists. Under a system of total quality management,
managers are often required to help workers achieve feats of
imagination and work performance never previously accomplished.

Transformations in the workplace create implications for both
managers and workers that typically are glossed over in most
descriptions of reengineering, process innovation, downsizing,
and total quality management. The *Reengineering Survival
Guide* is written to help you understand how you can lead and
manage others effectively in the revamped workplace, and
meanwhile continue to survive and prosper there yourself. The
premise of the book is that for reengineering, downsizing, and
quality management to achieve the desired surges in productivity, people must relearn how to work and managers must relearn how to lead.

Accordingly, the book first explains what is meant by reengineering and then looks at the transformations created by downsizing, the horizontal organization, the virtual corporation,
focus factories, and total quality management (Chapter 1).
Chapter 2 focuses on the individual differences, personalities,
and skills of the people who fit and work best in the new organization. Creativity and how to shake it loose is the topic of
Chapter 3. This chapter describes five ways to free yourself from
traditional thinking, seven actions that managers can take to en-

hance innovation, and the value of creativity training and learning how to challenge the status quo.

The heart of the book is its discussion of change, resistance to change, and ways of implementing radical change (Chapter 4). Chapter 5 looks at the critical differences between managers and leaders and the new leadership roles and styles required today. Chapters 6 through 8 deal with a powerful new development in the workplace. These chapters explain how to build teamwork, empower team leaders and team members, and manage cross-functional teams and projects.

Chapters 9 and 10 tackle the traumatic topic of downsizing, with advice on how to downsize effectively, how to streamline work, and how to deal compassionately with victims of downsizing and nurture its survivors. Throughout the book, numerous real-world case examples are provided to support individual points. Chapter 11 is integrative, providing you with a look at CTB/Macmillan's reengineering experience noting how that experience relates to the ideas presented throughout the book.

Unlike many books written for managers and professionals, this book maintains a career-building perspective, reminding leaders and professionals to be aware of the implications of workplace revamping on their own careers. It addresses such questions as "What should I be doing differently to avoid the next hit list?" or "If teamwork is so important in the new organization, how can I be a good team player, yet still get singled out for advancement?" To this end, I present several self-examination quizzes and checklists to help keep you focused on preparing yourself to meet the challenges of the revamped workplace. My goal is to add value to every reader's leadership of others and his or her own career.

The terms *leader* and *manager*, as currently used, require some clarification. Leadership is involved with change, inspiration, motivation, and influence. Management deals more with maintaining equilibrium and the status quo. A leader is therefore someone who inspires and influences people, while a manager keeps the system running smoothly. Both skills are required in the new workplace. Managers must be leaders, but leaders must also be good managers. Employees need to be inspired and persuaded, but they also need assistance in developing and maintaining a smoothly functioning workplace.

Both terms are used throughout this book for good reason. Most managerial job titles still include the word manager, such as "manager of information systems," or "project manager." A few job titles contain the word leader, such as "team leader." In general, *leader* refers to a capability, while *manager* simply states the type of work a person is doing.

Like its subject, this book has been a team effort. My primary thanks go to my sponsoring editor, Jim Sitlington, who recognized the potential for it and encouraged me to write a book about the human consequences of reengineering. Mary Pommert, my developmental editor, contributed substantially by making both structural and content suggestions. I am also most grateful to Bill Nowlin, Associate Dean at the College of Business, Rochester Institute of Technology, who shared with me considerable information about process redesign. The members of the process mapping team at the College of Business—Peggy A. Tirrell, Mary Ann Pearl, Barbara F. Shaffer, Mary F. Murphy, Nancy L. Heuer, Mary A. Denick, and Susan B. Powell—also deserve my thanks for explaining their work to me. My thanks also to Drew DuBrin, an attorney, who described the reengineering efforts at his office to me in detail.

Andrew J. DuBrin
Rochester, New York

Contents

    Developing a Downsizing Game Plan 237
    Minimizing the Disruptions of Layoffs 247
    Managing in a Leaner Organization 252
    Managing Your Career in a Downsized
    Environment 256
    A Checklist for Effective Downsizing 261

10 Easing the Pain of Downsizing 263
    Creative Downsizing Options 264
    Offering Compensation and Support for the
    Displaced People 269
    Providing Job Security and Emotional Support
    to the Survivors 274
    A Four-Level Process for Easing the Suffering
    of Survivors 276
    A Checklist for Easing the Pain of Downsizing 286

11 Putting It All Together 289

    Appendix: Process Maps 295
    Process Mapping at a Telecommunications
    Company 295
    Process Mapping at a College 299

    Chapter Notes 303

    Index 311

The Reengineered and Downsized Workplace

I

For at least 40 years, executives, consultants, and business professors have been predicting what the workplace will be like in the year 2000. One future scenario envisaged robots dominating the workplace, with just a scattering of people to be found in most factories and warehouses. The most foreboding predictions have not yet come true. One entirely accurate prediction, however, was that information technology and worldwide competition would profoundly reshape the workplace.

To develop better products and services, and to produce them more competitively, many firms have de-emphasized the traditional method of organizing work by functional departments. Instead, they organize work by key processes, projects, or activities such as serving a customer. From this perspective, work activity cuts across functions and stays clearly focused on customer requirements.

To lower costs and speed up decision making, many middle management positions have been eliminated. Extensive use of information technology has also made it possible to jettison many intermediary positions. For example, many traditional sales jobs have been eliminated by the practice of selling and servicing products over the phone. Without advanced information technology, it would not be possible to serve clients fully and promptly in this way.

A second accurate prediction has been that both the private and public sectors would be forced to develop elaborate strategies and tactics for enhancing the quality of goods and services. A major quality driver has been international competition, which gives consumers a broader choice of products. In consequence, many companies have embarked upon formal quality programs.

As a result of these accurately predicted developments, the workplace today has a new look. Workers at all levels, and from different disciplines (such as manufacturing, accounting, and marketing), huddle together to focus on customer requirements. Ideas for improvement are likely to stem from entry-level workers in factories, mills, offices, hospitals, retail stores, and hotels.

The forces that have transformed the workplace, which include reengineering, downsizing, and total quality management (TQM), have been well publicized. Platitudes abound about how the transformed workplace will take us to exotic new heights in productivity and quality. Yet the other shoe has not been dropped, or has been dropped so softly that few people have paid attention. What do these changes mean in terms of managing people so that the workplace modifications do not become fizzled fads?

In this book I describe what managers need to know in order to lead the people who still form an essential part of the revamped workplace. Many of the failures of reengineering, downsizing, and total quality management stem directly from the mismanagement of people. The basic principles of communication, motivation, and leadership are as essential as ever. Our concern is what managers must emphasize and do differently in this overhauled—and often chaotic—work environment. A simultaneous consideration is what the reader can do to survive and prosper in the revamped workplace. Let's look more closely at six of the most significant and profound changes in the workplace today:

- Reengineering and process innovation
- Move toward horizontal organization structure
- Downsizing and the creation of flat organization structures
- Rise of the virtual corporation
- Move toward focus factories
- Continued emphasis on total quality management (or simply quality management)

CHANGE 1: REENGINEERING AND PROCESS INNOVATION

Imagine that you decide to reengineer the way you wash and wax your car. Forget about making such minor changes as using a different type of hose, detergent, and automobile wax. When you get through reengineering, you might not even need a hose, detergent, or wax. Reengineering starts from scratch and challenges everything you ordinarily do to accomplish your goal of having a clean, shiny automobile. Your reengineering might ultimately take the form of buying a car with an aluminum outer shell that requires no waxing. The same shell might be designed in such a way that it is cleaned naturally as the rain falls—much like rocks in a park. Instead of making gradual improvements in how you clean your car, you radically transform the car-cleaning process.

Reengineering in its pure form is the fundamental rethinking and radical redesign of work processes. Its goal is to achieve substantial improvements in key performance measures such as cost, quality, service, and speed.[1] As with most management innovations, reengineering carries several different labels. They include business process reengineering, process innovation, and core process redesign. All these terms imply a radical change in the actions required to accomplish significant work.

Reengineering will lead to the best results when it supports business strategy. If the strategy, for example, calls for being a low-cost producer, reengineering will dovetail that strategy.

> **REENGINEERING IN ITS PUREST FORM IS THE FUNDAMENTAL RETHINKING AND RADICAL DESIGN OF WORK PROCESSES.**

Reengineering is related to strategy in another important way. It involves such radical change that embarking upon reengineering is always a strategic decision—one with far-reaching implications.

According to organizational planning consultant Robert M. Tomasko, reengineering is a method for reinventing how to carry out a business process.[2] This stands in contrast to modifying or speeding up an existing process. Reengineering challenges conventional wisdom and the standard rules and procedures that govern the proper way to accomplish work. Beginning with a clean slate, reengineering combines breakthrough thinking assisted by information technologies in order to re-create major work processes. Flow charting and work-process mapping are standard tools of reengineering. To make our discussion more concrete, we will describe work flow associated with the key business process known as the new product development.

Reengineering is usually accomplished by a team of people from different disciplines who pool their expertise in order to overhaul the existing process. In new product development, for example, team members from research and development, marketing, finance, and manufacturing might work simultaneously on the new product. Prior to process innovation they might have waited for each other's input before taking action. This would lengthen the time it takes to develop a new product. The various functional groups now work in parallel rather than serially as in the past. Because reengineering requires such radical changes, the entire effort needs the backing of senior management.

An important aim or reengineering is to eliminate activities that do not contribute value to a process. For example, it might be found that too many budget review meetings are required. Eliminating 90 percent of these meetings might not have any adverse impact on the final cost of the product. Tomasko divides reengineering into five steps.

Step 1: Give Control of the Process to One Person

Many core processes in organizations have evolved over time with no particular thought as to whether they are the most efficient and effective choices available. Many different organizational units contribute to major processes. Each unit engages in activities that make the most sense, or are the most convenient for that particular unit. In filling a customer order, for example, a production scheduler might hold off scheduling a product until a substantial number of the same units have been ordered. Customer orders are often passed form department to department with no easy way of tracking their status. To cut short the laborious process of order fulfillment, one person is given the authority to shepherd an order through the various departments involved, such as pricing and shipping.

The person with the authority to leap over departmental walls carries a title such as *process owner* or *case manager*. A process owner is given authority to carry out the entire chain of events from customer inquiry to order fulfillment. The owner has the right to demand that the order gets appropriate attention at each step in the process. A process owner, by definition, has ownership for the whole chain of events. (The process owner can make demands because it is recognized that he or she has considerable authority granted by the organization.) This helps prevent various organizational units from hoarding inventory so that they will have ample supplies in case a surge or orders should occur.

A process owner would have the authority to tell an inventory specialist to please give him or her the spare parts required by the order right away. Similarly, the process owner would have the authority to tell the shipping department to expedite shipment.

Step 2: Map the Process

Most companies are organized in such a way that identifying key processes is difficult. Yet reengineering requires the clear identification of key processes. Hughes Aircraft put together a multidisciplinary team to analyze all the steps necessary to construct a space satellite. The group included members from design, manufacturing, marketing, and purchasing. The group discovered that hundreds of tasks were involved from the design stage to delivering the satellite for launch. Each step in the process was laid out on a lengthy flow chart. Next, the team scrutinized the chart.

The flow chart made clear what many people associated with the satellite already suspected—some steps were wasted. (In many organizations, process reengineering quickly reveals that too many approvals are required.) By eliminating those steps that did not contribute value to producing the satellite, the team reduced the time required to build a key component from 45 to 22 weeks. As a result, millions of dollars were saved. Note that reengineering is concerned with the steps involved in delivering a space satellite. In contrast, business strategy would ask whether manufacturing a space satellite is itself a meaningful activity.

After a flow chart is constructed, it must be insightfully interpreted. You must be alert for work flows that follow a route back to themselves. It is also important to reduce the number of steps that add little value to the final product or service (such as the car-wash attendant who takes a gentle swat with a towel at the blown-dry car). Closely observe how many functions or organizational units are involved in each process. It is also essential to measure the length of time required for each step, and the time intervals between steps.

Step 3: Eliminate Potential Trouble Spots in the System

The most effective reengineering efforts eliminate those steps in a process that could potentially breed trouble. Having fewer moving parts in a system means fewer parts are available to create friction. Equally, fewer people involved in a process means fewer errors and delay. A well-publicized example is how the Ford Motor Company simplified its bill-paying operation. In the early 1980s, Ford executives were searching for ways to reduce overhead and administrative costs. One place targeted for cost reduction was the accounts payable department which had more than 500 employees.

By using computers to automate some functions, Ford managers believed they could reduce the department's head count by 20 percent. A reduction of this magnitude seemed impressive until Ford managers visited the accounts payable department at Mazda. (Mazda and Ford had formed a strategic alliance, making this benchmarking foray quite acceptable. Benchmarking is the process of identifying and implementing the best practice to achieve top performance.) Ford managers observed that Mazda handled its accounts payable chores with only five people. The contrast of 500 accounts payable employees at Ford versus five at Mazda was too great to be attributed to Mazda's smaller size, *esprit de corps*, or Japanese methods of human resource management.

A reduction of the accounts payable work force by 20 percent would still not be equivalent to Mazda's low head count. Ford managers were consequently forced to rethink the entire ac-

---

HANDOFFS FROM DEPARTMENT
TO DEPARTMENT ARE ANOTHER
SOURCE OF FRICTION THAT CAN BE
ELIMINATED BY REENGINEERING.

counts payable process. Rethinking the process meant more than streamlining the accounts payable department. Reengineering focuses not on redesigning a department, but on redesigning how work is performed.

The new accounts payable process that emerged at Ford was radically different in design. Now, when a buyer in the purchasing department issues a purchase order to a vendor, the buyer simultaneously enters the order into an on-line database. As before, suppliers still send goods to the receiving dock. At point of arrival, a receiving clerk checks a computer terminal to verify whether the shipment received corresponds to an outstanding purchase order. If the shipment corresponds to an order in the database, the clerk accepts the goods. In addition, no invoices are accepted that do not perfectly fit Ford's requirements. A truck load with an imperfect invoice will be turned back. After receiving a proper invoice, the receiving clerk then pushes a button on the terminal keyboard to indicate that the goods have arrived. The computer will automatically issue and send a check when the goods are received in the department that ordered them.

Ford has reduced a number of employees in accounts payable from 500 to 125, a process that took five years from design to full implementation. Most of the reduction in personnel was possible because the receiving dock clerks have taken over most of the accounts payable work. If the former accounts payable employees are redeployed to more productive work elsewhere in the company, the human cost of reengineering has been minimized. A problem with the Ford system is that it has been much more beneficial to the company than to vendors. A consultant on the project told us that suppliers were paid very slowly.

Handoffs from department to department are another source of friction that can be eliminated by reengineering. Several insurance companies have dramatically reduced the time required to process insurance applications. A case in point is Mutual Benefit Life which now processes insurance applications in one-fifth the time it took previously. Before reengineering, processing a customer application took 30 steps handled by 19 people in five departments. It took from several days to several weeks for an insurance application to be recorded, underwritten, and investigated. Most of the application-processing time was consumed while the application sat in an in-box or was passed from one department to another. Similar bottlenecks have been uncovered in many reengineering efforts.

The president of Mutual Benefit Life spearheaded reengineering to reduce the time required to process an application. The task was accomplished through a combination of computer databases, expert systems (a computer program that simulates the judgment of an experienced underwriter), and expanded jobs. An expanded job meant that one person had the clout to bird-dog the processing of an insurance application all the way from receiving to shipping.

Step 4: Complete the Task

Tomasko emphasizes that becoming a fast-cycle company requires a change in mind-set as well as the adoption of a new technique. A common phrase used to justify an action in reengineered firms is "Life is short." This statement implies that important work should be done in a hurry.[3] It is important that reengineering not make the same mistake committed in so many organizational improvement efforts—the generation of exhaustive statistics, charts, and reports, but little change. The most justifiable studies are those that bring about constructive, needed change.

Step 5: Make Reengineering an Ongoing Process

After a reengineering program has been implemented, it is usually necessary to reengineer again in the future. New technologies may make more improvements possible, and the nature of the reengineered task itself may change. Say, for example, your customers are demanding shorter and shorter lead times between placing an order and expecting shipment. If your competitors find a more efficient way to accomplish one of your reengineered processes, you will be forced to reengineer again. Assume you are a supply company and your competition finds a way to keep on hand a vastly superior inventory. You will want to revamp your inventor control system so that you, too, can expand inventory and still maintain required profit margins.

CHANGE 2: THE HORIZONTAL ORGANIZATION STRUCTURE

As a result of reengineering or process innovation, the flow of work changes from vertical to horizontal. A vertical structure is the commonplace hierarchy in which everybody reports to somebody else at the next higher organizational level. In recent years many firms have chosen to emphasize a horizontal structure whether or not they have actually undertaken reengineering. The horizontal structure is flat, makes extensive use of cross-functional teams, and is organized around satisfying customer needs. (A flat structure has relatively few layers of authority.) In a horizontal structure, the work is divided among teams that are responsible for accomplishing a process such as order fulfillment. An important advantage of the horizontal organization is that it makes sideways transactions (such as communicating with people in other departments) easier than they are in a vertical organization.

A key person in the horizontal organization is the process owner. He or she functions as a team leader who guides the team toward the completion of a core process, as illustrated in Figure 1-1. Notice that the first set of process owners are responsible for order generation and fulfillment. The team members are selected from various disciplines, such as accounting or marketing, to form a multiskilled team. High-performing teams of this type are such an important component of the revamped

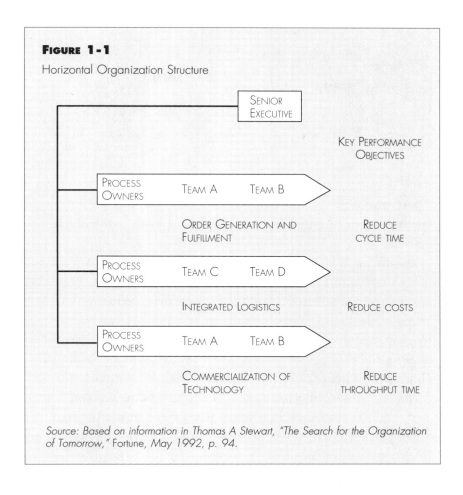

FIGURE 1-1

Horizontal Organization Structure

Source: Based on information in Thomas A Stewart, "The Search for the Organization of Tomorrow," Fortune, May 1992, p. 94.

workplace that they receive separate attention in Chapters 6 and 8.

American Express's experience with a horizontal structure provides insight into the impact it can have upon quality of service and profits.[4] Company executives began to realize that for their purposes it was ineffective to measure the work of individual departments. American Express management thought it would be more worthwhile to evaluate the total customer transaction process. To make such an evaluation, the company began to track the flow of paper and information from point of entry to exit. Next, credit card service was divided into discrete customer transactions that were visible and measurable.

> ## The process owner functions as a team leader who guides the team toward the completion of a core process.

These transactions (or business processes) included billing customers, paying retailers, and replacing lost or stolen credit cards.

American Express then developed a variety of performance measures based on these single-customer transactions. Several of these performance measures are focused on timeliness, such as speed of processing basic applications, replacing cards, and mailing customer statements. Accuracy was also measured, including the rate of errors in processing card-member address changes and processing charge-backs. A total of about 100 performance measures were used in the card business alone.

In addition to measuring individual customer satisfaction, American Express restructured its business along the lines of a horizontal organization. Raymond L. Larkin, executive vice president of operations, credit control, and quality assurance, is confident that the performance measures have profoundly affected how the company does business. Work flows have changed, with an emphasis on altering traditional reporting relationships in order to serve the customer better. Each change was cast in terms of how it would better please the customer, as, for example, reducing or eliminating bottlenecks in processing changes of address.

Follow-up customer satisfaction surveys have shown that the quality of service improved by 78 percent. Expenses per transaction decreased 21 percent. The time taken to process card-member applications was reduced by 37 percent, and over a 10-year period the savings amounted to millions of dollars.

The American Express experience with a horizontal organization includes some elements of reengineering. Many unnecessary steps were eliminated, and new procedures were created and implemented. The improvements the company achieved in quality of service and profits would not have been possible without good cooperation from its employees. Another requirement for success was creative thinking by those involved in designing performance measures and challenging existing procedures.

CHANGE 3: DOWNSIZING AND THE CREATION OF FLAT STRUCTURES

A dominant trend in the workplace is for organizations to trim down in size. Management layers are often reduced in the process. Most readers of this book know someone (possibly yourself) who has lost his or her job during a downsizing. Furthermore, some people have found themselves to be the victims of more than one downsizing. Reengineering accelerates the downsizing movement because it often eliminates many jobs from the work process.

Downsizing and creating flat organization structures (those with fewer layers) are used for several important purposes. A primary reason for eliminating one or more layers of management is to reduce personnel costs. Payroll costs are important because, on the average, they represent about 75 percent of the expense of operating an organization.

Figure 1-2 illustrates what delayering, or downsizing, looks like in practice. Two of five layers of management were eliminated, thus flattening the organization structure. The organization structure remaining after downsizing has only three layers: the CEO, the executive vice president, and the five managers reporting directly to the executive vice president. Notice that three vice president positions were eliminated, along with one executive vice president position. The executive vice president of sales

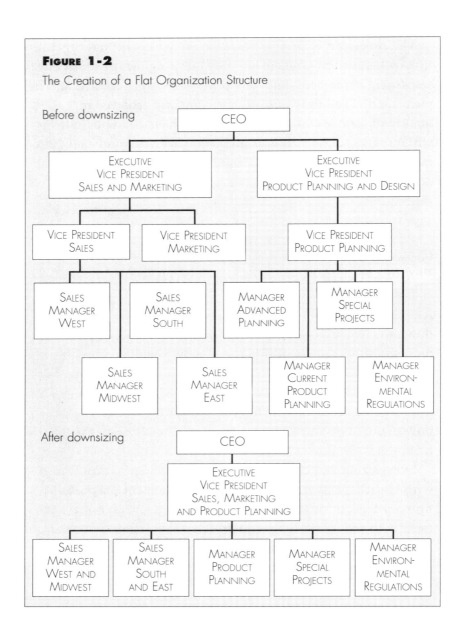

FIGURE 1-2

The Creation of a Flat Organization Structure

and marketing became the executive vice president for sales, marketing, and product planning. Notice also that four sales manager positions were consolidated into two positions; the two managers of planning positions were consolidated into one. You can imagine how busy the surviving executive vice president has become.

Cost reduction is important for American business to become more competitive with international rivals. In the public sector, cost reduction is necessary to cope with dwindling budgets. Reducing costs by decreasing the number of managerial layers, along with laying off other workers, is a favorite tactic of turnaround managers. Such people are executives who specialize in rescuing failing corporations. The slogan of turnaround managers is, "If my turnaround strategy works, one-fourth (or some other substantial fraction) of company employees will lose their jobs. If my strategy fails, everybody loses their job."

Reducing layers of management can also offer the advantage of speeding up decision making. With more layers of management, more approvals are required, thus increasing the time required to make a decision. Also, with fewer management layers, lower levels of management can communicate directly to top management instead of going through a ponderous chain of command. With rapid decision making, customer service may improve.

These reasons for downsizing are supported by a spokesperson for Xerox Corporation. In discussing a round of job cuts, he explained: "The first reason for the cuts, obviously, is the economy. The recession has been longer and deeper than we anticipated. Our second objective is to improve customer service, Xerox's stock-in-trade, by reducing management."[5] Many would not agree with the last point raised by the spokesperson. Customer service can suffer when staffing is so thin that managers are overloaded, as the following story shows.

A customer telephoned a commercial printer to inquire about a late shipment on 2,000 merchandise catalogs. The materials handling specialist replied, "I'm sorry that your shipment will be delayed a few weeks. We lost a few positions because of downsizing, and we've fallen behind on everything."

Another purpose of flat structures is to foster decentralization, as illustrated by the French company Carrefour S.A. Carrefour pioneered the concept of the hypermarket, a giant

> # DOWNSIZING SURVIVORS PLACED IN KEY POSITIONS MUST BE TALENTED AND DEDICATED PEOPLE.

store selling food and other goods such as appliances. The company stays lean by decentralizing as many functions as possible to its retail outlets. A headquarters staff of fewer than 20 employees, including secretaries, guides the business. There is only one layer of management between the central office and the stores—a group of regional managers.

The Carrefour example gives a message about the human resource requirements of downsizing. The survivors placed in key positions have to be both talented and dedicated. Asked to perform the work of several people, they must evaluate the contribution of the additional activities they are now assuming. A careful investigation sometimes reveals that the work performed by the displaced person added no value to the firm. Sometimes people work very hard, and perform well, at tasks that are meaningless in terms of achieving corporate goals.

Despite improvements in worldwide business conditions, the downsizing trend is unlikely to lose its momentum. We can anticipate that companies will regularly prune positions in order to stay competitive and enjoy large profit margins. Downsizing will also continue because it follows naturally from reengineering. By laying off employees whose work is nonessential a company can control costs and therefore remain competitive.

A well-known telecommunications company has recently implemented an unwritten policy about "rightsizing" (downsizing described from the company's perspective). Each year, managers throughout the firm are asked to identify who they think should be classified as the bottom 5 percent of performers in their area of responsibility. An employee who is ranked in the bottom

5 percent receives coaching from his or her supervisor. The employee is also assigned improvement goals, and is given the opportunity to contribute to the goal setting. Any employee who remains on the bottom 5 percent list for two consecutive years is terminated. These employees are not replaced, thus resulting in rightsizing or downsizing.

As long ago as 1987, business executive Charles Ames noted that downsizing and flat organization structures fitted the spirit of the times. His pronouncement is just as accurate today, and it reinforces the idea that downsizing appears permanent. "We are in turbulent times," Ames said, "and we must begin managing for survival in turbulent times. We must be geared to a more competitive environment, breaking apart overloaded organizational structures and streamlining, emphasizing producer people over support staff, getting our cost/profit ratio more in line. We must take the bull by the horns and do what we have to survive."[6]

CHANGE 4: RISE OF THE VIRTUAL CORPORATION

A more radical change than a downsized organization is a temporary one with permeable boundaries, the so-called virtual corporation or network firm. Many large corporations are relying on subunits that adapt readily to changing styles, technologies, and consumer demands. These smaller units can share resources with other companies in order to capitalize on opportunities. Smaller firms also can combine capabilities and

> SOMETIMES PEOPLE WORK VERY HARD,
> AND PERFORM WELL, AT TASKS
> THAT ARE MEANINGLESS IN TERMS OF
> ACHIEVING CORPORATE GOALS.

THE PURE VITAL CORPORATION
WILL HAVE NEITHER
CORPORATE HEADQUARTERS
NOR AN ORGANIZATION CHART.

resources with other firms to engage in strategic alliances (or joint ventures).

A virtual corporation is a temporary network of otherwise independent firms that are linked by technology to share expenses, employee talents, and access to each other's markets. The members of the network can be suppliers, customers, even rival firms. The pure virtual corporation will have neither corporate headquarters nor an organization chart. Hierarchy will be sacrificed to speed of decision making, and vertical integration will be supplanted by horizontal integration across company boundaries. Virtual corporations may never exist in a pure form. Larger firms, however, are likely to form units that function as virtual corporations.

To understand the workings of a virtual corporation, imagine that you worked for a company that manufactured a low-priced, sturdy athletic shoe. If you could combine resources with a company that outfitted school athletic teams, you could increase your sales and profits tenfold. To accomplish your goal you form an alliance with Champion Products. Champion has a giant market share in the school athletic uniform business. To determine how to best approach your potential customers, you exchange databases.

Proponents of the virtual corporation see it as a fluid and flexible entity taking the form of a group of collaborators who link together to capitalize upon a specific opportunity. After the opportunity has been met, the venture, typically, will disband. The virtual corporation thus shows properties similar to a project organization. Project members work together until the mission is completed. If the project is very successful, however, it spins off into a more permanent structure, such as becoming a company division.

Pushing the virtual organization concept to its extreme, each firm will stick with what it does best—its core competency. The athletic shoe manufacturer just mentioned will produce athletic shoes. Other companies will market its products and perhaps even design new products for it to manufacture. A selling point of the virtual corporation is that it limits the amount of activities one company needs to perform. The company networks with other firms whose expertise can be combined symbiotically with its own.

The growing number of strategic alliances suggests that key aspects of the virtual corporation are gaining acceptance. A representative example is MCI Communications Corporation, which forms partnerships with as many as 100 companies in order to win jumbo contracts from major customers. The partnership is justified because another firm might have a technological capability that can be combined with MCI's existing technology to satisfy a customer. For example, one firm might have an excellent call-forwarding system that MCI needs to fill the requirements of a brokerage firm.

A key advantage of the strategic alliance is that MCI does not have to fund the research and development of hardware. Instead, capital can be invested in what MCI does best—providing telecommunications service to the public. The combination of hardware and software services that the company offers its customers may well be based on the talents and resources of up to 100 other companies. MCI officials estimate that they save up to $500 million in extra expenses annually through such strategic alliances.[7]

In some strategic alliances the resources of many firms are combined to bring a product to market. TelePad Corporation of Reston, Virginia, collaborated with about 25 suppliers and partners to get its new penx-based computer to market. Working independently as a small company, TelePad would not have had the resources to bring this particular product to market.

Information technology is facilitating the growth of the virtual corporation. As computer networking becomes more advanced, more and more companies will be able to use information clearing houses to gain access to potential partners. Such access to each other's capabilities will enable companies to rapidly locate the suppliers, designers, manufacturers, or marketers they need to launch a new venture.

To implement the virtual corporation, teams of people from different companies would be working together, linked by computerized information. As in reengineering, they would work concurrently rather than sequentially, thus improving the speed of work flow. Managers will need to trust the many outside partners in any virtual corporation. It would be difficult, for instance, to prevent outsiders from purloining a company's useful ideas. Team leaders will also have to be skillful in working collaboratively with people over whom they have no formal authority.

CHANGE 5: MOVE TOWARD FOCUS FACTORIES

Profound workplace changes are also taking place in factories. A growing number of manufacturers are finding a winning combination in a small factory that has a single-product focus. Focusing a factory's activities on a narrow or single product line often yields cost savings, manufacturing efficiencies, and high quality. In the spirit of today's ideal organization, the focus factory is nimble and quick.

The concept of a focused factory is not new, but is receiving renewed emphasis. Such a place can be a free-standing manufacturing facility, or a plant within a plant. The focus factory operates as a self-contained business with its own finance, engineering, human resources, and quality maintenance staff. It manufactures narrow lines of products in small, self-contained cells in contrast to long assembly lines. The work force of a focus factory typically numbers several hundred. Such relative smallness makes it easier to identify and mull over problems, and to respond to shifting customer demands.

A flat structure is another distinguishing characteristic of the focus factory. The fact that there are few layers of management pushes decision making and accountability down to the floor level. The high efficiency of such a factory stems from manufacturing techniques that emphasize eliminating waste and improving product quality. A focus factory will have almost no finished-goods inventory. Production is restricted to making only what customers want, on a time schedule that fits customer preference.

Another distinguishing characteristic of a focus factory is its high-quality work force. A case in point is the Carrier Corporation compressor plant in Arkadelphia, Arkansas.[8] Job applicants must complete a demanding six-week course before being considered for employment there, and only one in 16 applicants receives a job offer. Production workers in this plant, as in other focus factories, have substantial authority. Following the Japanese manufacturing tradition, production workers have the authority to shut down an operation if they spot a quality or safety problem. Workers are also authorized to order some of their own supplies.

Work force members at the Arkadelphia plant experience a greater sense of freedom than do most factory operatives. Time-recording devices are not used to control attendance, nor do workers need written statements from health-care professionals to justify an absence. Workers are taught several jobs, so that they can take over for others who are out ill or resign suddenly. Multiple skills are also important in case the factory has to shift products lines on short notice.

Focus factories, requiring a small, relatively well-educated work force, are sprinkling the American workplace. A close look at a Xerox focus factory sheds insight into how these small factories operate differently from a traditional manufacturing site. Xerox Corporation had ended production of a line of small photocopiers that were manufactured in Building 209 of its Webster, New York, manufacturing facility. When an order came in for 100 copiers, however, a small factory housed within Building 209 was equal to the task of setting up to build $200,000 worth of product. This focus factory was designed by the company and the labor union.

After a year-long, step-by-step renovation, Building 209 had boosted efficiency by 30 percent. In addition, the time required to complete the manufacturing cycle was reduced. Building 209 was especially important to Xerox because the company faces intense competition from Japanese manufacturers of personal copiers. A union official said that the focus factory is helping Xerox leapfrog over the competition.

For the focus factory to move from plan to reality, the union had to permit changes in the work rules that were protected by the union-management agreement. Before bargaining began, members of the Xerox management team approached the union and sketched out the concept of the focus factory. The managers requested that the necessary changes in work rules be negotiated outside contract negotiations. Union officials cooperated because they perceived the long-range benefit of job preservation.

The union parlayed its support of focus factories into job protection concessions for local workers. Management, in turn, asked union officials to participate in planning the new, small factories. To design the factories, focus teams were formed, composed of executives, engineers, union officials, and production workers. Focus team members strived for efficiency, worker comfort, safety, job satisfaction, cost savings, and environmental friendliness.

To conserve investments in inventory, the team included just-in-time inventory methods in the factory design. With this approach to just-in-time, parts flow into one end of the building and finished copiers packed in boxes leave at the other end. In place of a long assembly line characterized by a sharp division of labor, teams of about seven workers each are responsible for building entire machines. This multitasking approach decreases boredom and injury-inducing repetition. Another contribution is that workers are more accountable for the quality and productivity of their group. Monthly bonuses are used to reward good performance.

Each manufacturing cell loops around on itself, forming an actual circle, so that team members face and help each other while assembling machines. Work stations carry only a few hours' worth of parts. When more are needed, workers run a scanner across a bar code, triggering an automatic shipment of the parts within a defined time period. Copiers are built on roller-equipped conveyors which latch together and an be quickly disassembled. This flexibility facilitates enlarging or reducing manufacturing cells in response to customer demand. Decisions about expanding or contracting cells are made at the plant level.[9]

The changes brought about by the focus factory fit the overall theme of the revamped workplace. A focus factory leads to a reduction in organizational size, greater flexibility, and a heightened demand for intelligent workers. At the same time, managers turn over more authority to workers.

CHANGE 6: CONTINUED EMPHASIS ON TOTAL QUALITY MANAGEMENT

The total quality management movement has attracted many advocates, staunch supporters, and zealots. In the past several decades only management by objectives has had so many proponents. Although the heyday of management by objectives has long passed, its legacy of goal setting and review is still used in many private and public firms. Total quality management (TQM) appears to be experiencing the same cycle. The impact of TQM has been far-reaching, yet converts to TQM appear to be declining. Nevertheless, the TQM movement has had the net effect of heightening quality awareness for workers at all levels.

Total quality management is a management system for improving performance throughout a firm by maximizing customer satisfaction and making continuous improvements. This definition underscores a major difference between reengineering and total quality management. Reengineering swings a mighty ax to bring about improvements, while TQM focuses on gradual, continuous refinements to achieve the same ends.

Total quality management as a formal system of improving organizational effectiveness may be less popular than it was, but the TQM movement has made a lasting contribution to the revamped workplace. More executives today evaluate work in terms of the value it adds for the customer. Worth mentioning here are five features of total quality management that have had the biggest impact on managing the work force, and have also influenced reengineering.

- Total commitment to quality, including commitment by top management
- Focus on customer requirements
- Emphasis on continuous improvement
- Empowerment of employees
- Recognition of employees for achieving quality goals

So far we have overviewed six major workplace changes that will have, or may already have had, a major impact on how you perform your job. The workplace innovations described in this chapter can influence both how you manage your staff and how you manage your own career. The remaining 10 chapters deal with the management of these changes, topic by topic. As a preliminary, review the box on "Facts of Life in the Revamped Workplace," and check through "Managing Your Career in the Revamped Workplace: A Survival Checklist."

FACTS OF LIFE IN THE REVAMPED WORKPLACE

Fact 1: Many organizations will continue to slim down even during prosperous times.

Fact 2: Reengineered organizations are designed with fewer layers of management. Many middle management positions are being eliminated. As a result, managers who survive reengineering will have a much wider span of control and more power and authority to accomplish work.

Fact 3: Top management will insist that only value-added activities be part of a manager's job.

Fact 4: A key person in the organization of the future will be the process owner (one who owns the process of satisfying a customer requirement).

Fact 5: The acquisition of relevant skills through training is more important than ever. Managers and other workers who fail to acquire the skills necessary to meet the demands of the revamped workplace will lose their jobs.

MANAGING YOUR CAREER IN THE REVAMPED WORKPLACE: A SURVIVAL CHECKLIST

However long the changes described in this chapter may last, without question the movement toward reengineering and a less hierarchical workplace has become dominant. Here are six suggestions to help you, as manager or professional, to cope and advance in the revamped workplace.[10]

☑ *Draw a process map of your work*. Determine who makes effective use of your output. Eliminate all activities that do not contribute value to a process. Organize your work around satisfying customer needs. Understand how the work you perform meets some customer needs, and be ready to defend its value to your boss. The Appendix on pages 300–301 will help you to get started.

☑ *Adjust to less formal structure and hierarchy*. Already many managers are being forced to operate with less formal authority. Instead of directing action, they are facilitating the smooth accomplishment of work processes. Coaching and cheerleading are more valued today than in the past because the manager coaxes along a team rather than directing a collection of individuals.

☑ *If you are a manager, expect a wider span of control*. With fewer middle managers, the average number of direct reports is increasing substantially. Oft-quoted consultant Tom Peters, among others, has predicted that spans of control will soon approach 75 to 100 people. Obviously the traditional approach to management does not allow for such a wide range. Imagine conducting 100 performance appraisals once or twice a year! To make such wide spans of control feasible, considerable self-management will be necessary. For example, teams within the span will contribute heavily to their own evaluations.

☑ *Master the new technologies that help measure and control performance*. Several companies, including Cypress Semiconductor, use an information system that tracks performance on weekly goals for each employee. If necessary, hire a computer expert to teach you how to access the company information system with the personal computer on your desk.

☑ *Acquire extensive knowledge about information technology and computer science.* Read computer manuals and books. Take an evening or weekend course. Go beyond the minimum knowledge required to perform your job. Most of the new workplace changes incorporate extensive use of information technology.

☑ *Acquire information that computers cannot supply, the so-called thick information.* High-performing managers and professionals have a natural or acquired facility for taking in subjectively and intuitively this kind of information, which is rich in color and detail. You can acquire such information best by interacting face-to-face with team leaders and trusted team members. The company information system can take you only so far. You need to get into the trenches to learn about morale problems, stress levels, or the subjective reactions customers have to your products or services.

2

Personality, Skills, and the Reengineered Work Force

*F*ew businesses have ever succeeded without a competent work force. Competent workers are also needed in the revamped workplace. The difference, however, is that the level of competency has been elevated. A reengineered workplace, for example, requires mentally nimble and flexible people. In contrast, a person of modest problem-solving ability can often perform quite well in a repetitive, stripped-down assignment.

A team of consultants from McKinsey & Company observed that many reengineering projects fail because only average performers are assigned to them. Companies that make this mistake often figure that top talent cannot be spared to work on the redesign project and instead staff it with undistinguished performers from headquarters or the field. One company assigned a mediocre sales manager to direct its reengineering project, reasoning that he would not be missed in the field. Unfortunately, because this manager lacked credibility he could not successfully lead the reengineering project.[1]

Understanding the personal qualities and characteristics required for success in the reconstituted workplace is fundamental, yet this issue is often overlooked. Many leaders in the quality movement speak glibly about every employee performing error-free work. It is assumed that, given the right training, encouragement, and slogans, any worker who chooses to can accomplish work that is 99.9 percent error-free. In reality, of course, people's innate and acquired talents vary so enormously and many are incapable of performing work without making numerous errors. With the right people in the right slots, however, the promises of the revamped workplace can come true.

The purpose of this chapter is to describe the personal characteristics and attributes that are essential for success in the new workplace. In the jargon of human resource management, these human requirements are called *specifications* or *position specifications*. A common theme in the new workplace modifications is that they rely heavily on teams. Teams are the building blocks of reengineering, the horizontal structure, total quality management, and the virtual corporation. The chapter continues, therefore, with a description of the personal characteristics necessary to be an outstanding team performer.

INDIVIDUAL DIFFERENCES

People's characteristics vary considerably, and these individual differences may be inbred or learned. Some people are smarter, or warmer, or more rigid, or slower-paced, or more energetic, or more creative than others. Place the right people on your strategic alliance team, and your company will benefit from its venture into becoming a virtual corporation. Assign people with limited imagination and foresight to the same team, and your strategic alliance will be a losing proposition. Here we look at some of the most relevant sources of individual differences in terms of how successful people may be in the revamped workplace.

People Differ in Productivity

A rigorous analysis of individual differences in work output illustrates the magnitude of human variation in job performance. Three researchers synthesized studies that involved more than

10,000 workers. They found that as jobs become more complex, individual differences have a bigger impact on work output.[2]

The fact that individuals differ in productivity, especially in complex jobs, has important implications for the redesigned workplace. Assume that your company has assembled quality-improvement teams as part of a shift to total quality management. A major task of the teams is to search for quality improvements that will make a difference to customers. The best people to assign to the teams would be those who have been productive in previous assignments.

Workers with a track record of high productivity will rise to the surface again when asked to contribute to a team. Workers with a poor record of productivity are unlikely to be transmuted into high producers just because they are now team members. You might even find that the hitherto unproductive workers look upon team membership as an opportunity to slack off. They are quite willing to let teammates do the heavy thinking required in searching for quality improvements.

People Differ in Ability and Talent

Factors such as ambition, desire, self-confidence, a favorable appearance, and the ability to play office politics are not sufficient for getting the job done. People also need the right abilities and talents to perform a job well. A relevant example comes from process redesign, another name for reengineering. A commercial construction firm decided to make an initial effort at process redesign. The owners believed that the current process of responding to inquiries and finally making a bid was too time-consuming and expensive. One of them attended a three-day seminar on process redesign, and returned to her firm excited about the prospect of reengineering the inquiry-to-bid process.

The nuts and bolts of redesign involved the completion of process maps. A sample map is on pages 300–301 of the Appendix. Although the task looks relatively straightforward, there was considerable variation in quality among the 10 process maps that staff members completed. All the members of the firm had received the same amount of instruction and coaching from the owner. Yet, most staffers produced a process map that provided no insights into how to improve the inquiry-to-bid process. One construction estimator, however, a 23-year-old with an associate's degree in architectural technology, performed a winning analysis. His process map revealed that considerable time was consumed in getting bids on materials from various suppliers. He suggested an electronic hook-up with suppliers who were willing to participate.

The technician reasoned that communication by computers would shorten the time taken getting estimates from suppliers by 10 days. It took several of the suppliers a long time to commit their estimates to a written report, have it word processed, and mailed. In contrast, preparing estimates on electronic mail hastened the process by as much as two weeks. Getting accurate bids completed 10 days earlier could mean winning many more contracts.

People Differ in the Importance They Attach to Interesting Work

People with a passion for work are looking for stimulating, exciting, or enriching jobs. Not every member of the work force is seeking that kind of work. Many people actually prefer jobs that require a minimum of mental involvement and responsibility. In contrast to those who like routine, people who seek variety and responsibility in their work are well satisfied in the revamped workplace.

Teamwork, with its emphasis on multiskills, is an excellent opportunity for the person seeking fulfillment on the job. The benchmarking specialist assigned to a total quality management team will find ample excitement as he or she visits various companies in search of ideas to emulate. Similarly, members of the virtual corporation will have access to the latest information technology as they interact with other organizations.

People Differ in the Style of Leadership They Prefer and Need

Many workers prefer as much freedom as possible on the job and can function well within a loose leadership style. Other individuals want to be supervised and monitored more closely by their manager. People also vary in the amount of attention they require. In general, less competent, less motivated, and less experienced workers require more supervision.

The revamped workplace generally calls for a leader who coaches and facilitates, but does not closely supervise and monitor workers. In a downsized firm the manager may have so many direct reports that he or she lacks time to closely supervise team members. Workers who have problems with self-reliance—and therefore need a lot of monitoring—are a poor fit for today's workplace innovations. Such workers are better suited for employment in a more traditional organizational unit where they can receive closer supervision.

People Differ in Their Need for Contact with Others

Individual personality traits and occupational interests greatly affect the amount of contact with others that workers need to keep them satisfied on the job. Some people can work alone all day and remain highly productive; others become restless unless they are engaged in business or social conversation with another employee. Many managers and professionals schedule business luncheons more out of a need for social contact than because they need to discuss job problems.

THE REVAMPED WORKPLACE GENERALLY CALLS FOR A LEADER WHO COACHES AND FACILITATES, BUT DOES NOT CLOSELY SUPERVISOR AND MONITOR WORKERS.

People with a strong need for people contact enjoy the new workplace. Almost all the workplace innovations emphasize teamwork that includes group problem solving. Team members are required to meet regularly with other members to resolve problems that they might previously have worked on in isolation. This is not always welcome. To quote a staff specialist in a firm being managed under a system of total quality management:

> I worry about losing my ability to really concentrate on problem solving. We do so much group work that I don't have time to let a problem jell. I might be thinking through alternatives to a problem, then bang! Somebody blurts out a solution. The group accepts the person's solution. We then move on to another topic. If a person had the time to develop his or her thinking, we sometimes might reach a superior solution.

This person thinks better alone than when interacting with co-workers. It would be better for him to do his heaviest creative thinking outside the group. A preference for independent work does not preclude someone's being a team player. It just means that the person has to plan to set aside time to think independently.

People Differ in Their Degree of Commitment and Loyalty to the Firm

Many workers are so committed to their employers that they act as if they were part-owners of the firm. As a consequence, committed and loyal employees are concerned about producing quality goods and services. They also maintain superior records of attendance and punctuality, which helps reduce the cost of doing business. At the other extreme, some employees feel little commitment or loyalty toward their employer. Botching a customer request or missing work for trivial reasons causes them no pangs of guilt.

The revamped workplace requires workers who are both loyal and highly committed. The fact that they are given more responsibility makes it vital that they take any mistakes personally. A worker at any level should feel, "If I mess up this project, I am letting myself and my customer down." Under ideal conditions, empowered team members would regard their work as seriously as if they were producing parachutes or automobile brakes. In reality, of course, a mistake in processing an insurance claim might not be as serious as producing a defective parachute. Yet the exceptionally committed and loyal worker will always feel that a wronged customer is a potential lost customer. Furthermore, the same customer might bad-mouth the firm, thus jeopardizing future business.

Workers Vary in How Much They Want to Be Empowered

Not everybody wants more responsible work, nor does everyone want to be empowered. Empowerment takes place when managers share power with group members, and as a result the members feel more effective. To be empowered means having more responsibility and authority. An extreme form of empowerment is for workers to decide how to divide up a pool of merit increases among fellow group members.

A service firm empowered teams to assign merit increases among their members. One team composed of five members was allotted $10,000 to distribute among themselves. At the meeting called to accomplish this task, one member said, "I feel very uncomfortable voting on who should get how much money. If management doesn't want to do its job, I say let's just take $2,000 each and be done with it." After 40 minutes of discussion, the rest of the team agreed. Dividing up money among themselves was more empowerment than they wanted. As another team member put it, "Why create enemies just to get a few hundred dollars more than somebody else?" In contrast, another team accepted the challenge of allocating members' pay increases based on the amount each contributed to the project. This team welcomed extreme empowerment.

PROBLEM-SOLVING ABILITY AND THINKING STYLE

The intellectual demands of the revamped workplace are considerable. Managers and workers have to challenge what currently exists and search for problems that have not already surfaced. Workers are under constant pressure to think of ways to accomplish the same amount of work in less time with fewer resources. They also must have the insight (and courage) to analyze whether the work they are presently doing adds value for the customer or their employer. New hires must often demonstrate that they have *learned how to learn*, not merely to have acquired a portfolio of valuable skills.

As a prelude to pinpointing the intellectual requirements for effective members of the reconfigured workplace, scrutinize the accomplishments of one process redesign team. The case history of process redesign (or reengineering) at an Italian bank has an important message.[3] It illustrates the breadth and depth of intellect required to create a high-impact process redesign.

Problem-Solving Ability

An obvious requirement for playing a key role in the revamped workplace is to possess good problem-solving ability or intelligence. People of ordinary intelligence would rarely be able to conduct the elaborate diagnoses required for such activities as the process redesign at the Italian bank. Intelligence, however, is not a pure characteristic. The preponderance of evidence suggests that intelligence consists of a general factor along with specific factors. The general (or "g" factor) helps explain why some people seem to perform so well in so many different tasks.[4] People with a strong "g" factor will tend to score well on mental ability tests and achieve good grades in school. Although the specific components of intelligence are debatable, at a minimum it is composed of verbal and numerical abilities.

Symbolic reasoning is another component of intelligence that is important for some of the demands placed upon workers in

CASE STUDY

Process Redesign

Picture this: a customer walks into a branch of a midsize Italian bank. In front of her is a small airy office where the securities officer sits ready to assist her in making investment decisions. There are not other offices or "back-stage" spaces. Instead, a single line feeds to the three tellers, the manager sitting at an open desk directly facing the line.

The customer fills out a deposit slip with her name, account number, total sum of the five checks she is depositing, and the amount to be withdrawn. No one is standing in line, so she steps up to the closest teller. The teller types in the account number and total amount of the deposit and then feeds the checks through a scanner. While he's waiting the two or three seconds for the checks to be recorded in the system and for the correspondent bank to be notified electronically, he calls up the customer's profile and sees that she looks like an excellent candidate for a certificate of deposit. As a receipt containing detailed information about the five checks prints out, the teller asks the customer if she's interested in a CD. Meanwhile, a help screen on his terminal provides him with detailed information about CDs: their benefits and common customer objections and responses. After the discussion, he hands her the deposit receipt and some promotional material on CDs. The transaction has taken 30 seconds. Meanwhile, the checks have already been debited and credited to the appropriate parties. The teller will handle the checks only once more: when he counts the total number at the end of the day and reconciles that total to the one on his computer. And because of the new process, the teller doesn't need any back-office support.

As futuristic as this may sound, this is the Banca di America e di Italia today. Owned by Deutsche Bank, BAI has undergone a radical transformation. The CEO recalls, "We had very few strategic strength, a very dispersed network, and a very high operating-cost structure. We had to find a way to grow rapidly, while reducing the cost-per-branch and improving customer service."

BAI's transformation started with the CEO's obsession to strengthen the bank's strategic position by creating a "paperless" bank based on just-in-

continued

CASE STUDY *continued*

Process Redesign

---

time manufacturing principles. The CEO immediately signed on Andrea Giochetta—currently BAI's chief information officer—who shared the CEO's drive and had the technological know-how to create a paperless bank.

The two set out to redesign the branches, focusing on improving customer-service levels as well as front-office efficiency and effectiveness. In this way, they could reduce the number of people per branch and open new branches. To reach this goal, they had to redesign all retail-branch transactions from scratch. With 80 to 85 percent of BAI's revenue and costs coming from retail banking, the widespread branch redesign ensured that the project would be broad enough to produce bottom-line results.

At BAI, two teams systematically diagnosed processes and then redesigned them without considering the constraints of the current organization. As a result, the teams came up with innovative new approaches to retail banking. First, the organization team, whose members came from all over the organization, broke down all transactions into ten "families": payments, deposits, withdrawals, money orders, bills, consumer credit, foreign exchange, credit cards (merchant and credit-card holder), sourcing, and end-of-the-day branch processes (the stocks, bonds, and securities process was included later). The team carefully documented the flow of a specific process within one of the families: for instance, depositing a check drawn from a correspondent bank into a customer's account. The analysis was painstakingly extensive, covering accounting flow, all relevant forms used by both customers and the bank, and controls for maintaining financial security and integrity.

With a detailed picture of a transaction, the team could effectively redesign it from scratch. The check-deposit transaction, for example, previously required 64 activities, 9 forms, and 14 accounts. After redesign, it needed only 25 activities, 2 forms, and 2 accounts. The redesigned process then became the prototype for restructuring all transactions within that family. Finally, the organization team handed off the prototype to the technology team, charged with thinking through the IT implications.

continued

the revamped workplace. Symbolic reasoning refers to the ability to manipulate abstract symbols mentally and to make judgments and decisions that are sound. To imagine how a bank could eliminate many of its usual routines would require a high degree of symbolic reasoning.

Symbolic reasoning also involves the ability to evaluate whether adequate information is available to make definite decisions. A team leader on a quality-improvement team might have to decide whether the team really knows for sure the root of a quality problem. In one situation, customers complained about the quality of a shipping container. When the produce was shipped more promptly, yet with no improvement in the defects, complaints about the container declined dramatically.

Another approach to understanding intelligence also helps explain which workers can make important contributions to workplace innovations. The concept of *practical intelligence* suggests that intelligence should not be evaluated only in the traditional sense. Instead, intelligence is said to consist of three components.[5] One subtype of intelligence is *componential*: the traditional type of intelligence we have just described.

The second subtype is *experiential*: the type of intelligence required for imagination and combining different ideas and objects in creative ways. Experiential intelligence is a fundamental requirement for thinking of new ways to conduct a work process or modify it significantly. Creative thinking is so important for the revamped workplace that it receives separate attention in the next chapter.

The third subtype of intelligence is *contextual*: the type of intelligence required for adaptation to one's environment or for changing the environment to suit one's needs. Contextual intelligence is needed to be street-smart. A street-smart quality specialist might be good at sizing up which competitive products are the best ones to benchmark. The same person might possess an intuitive sense about which competitors might be willing to be benchmarked. The last point is significant because not every company welcomes would-be benchmarkers visiting their operations and borrowing ideas for their own company's use.

Thinking Style

As carefully articulated by authors and consultants Michael Hammer and James Champy, reengineering requires inductive thinking.[6] Unfortunately, most managers and professionals have more skill and experience in *deductive* thinking. The difference between the two is important and requires explanation. Induction is basically the process of discovery. The inductive thinker discovers something of interest perhaps through analyzing a situation. He or she then generalizes to other situations where this fact might apply. The logic is that if something works once, there must be other useful applications. Inductive thinking

> A MANIFESTATION OF INDUCTIVE THINKING IS FIRST TO RECOGNIZE A SOLUTION TO A PROBLEM AND THEN FIND PROBLEMS THAT BENEFIT FROM SUCH A SOLUTION.

Six Basic Skill Requirements for Every Workplace

1. Ability to communicate
2. Ability to calculate mathematically, prepare budgets, analyze data, and use statistical techniques
3. Ability to use information technology
4. Ability to sell: to persuade others, negotiate, and promote
5. Ability to maneuver politically
6. Thorough knowledge of some functional area, such as sales, production, accounting, or information systems

moves from the particular to the general, and is an important part of creativity.

To think inductively, according to Hammer and Champy, managers should ask, "How can we use technology to allow us to do things we are *not* already doing?" The incredible growth of the photocopying industry has been attributed to the ability of photocopying to perform services that go far beyond the use of carbon paper, mimeograph machines, and the like. Before the advent of photocopying, sharing of information was much more restricted. Automatic teller machines (ATMs) enable people to do things they never thought of doing before—such as withdrawing money while grocery shopping at midnight.

Law offices are also undergoing a productivity-enhancing transformation. The traditional method of finding legal precedent for a case is for the attorney to painstakingly search through volumes of cases. Case research has been one of the most laborious and time-consuming aspects of practicing law.

Many law offices have been reengineered to solve this problem. Lawyers now use personal computers that can access thousands of cases stored on CD-ROMS in several minutes. Abstracts appear on the screen, and the most appropriate cases can be retrieved and printed. The case-research process is now less time-consuming, which means that attorneys can handle more cases. Law firms can therefore generate more revenue with the same number of attorneys. Inductive thinking about databases and CD-ROM made this radical transformation of legal case research possible. In the near future lawyers will be photographed standing in front of a pack of CD-ROM instead of leather-bound law books!

Deductive reasoning proceeds by making observations about a number of situations, and then reaching a conclusion. If six different customers say that they would like to receive shipments more promptly, the manager would conclude that late shipments are a problem. The shipping system could then be revamped to make faster delivery possible. Deductive reasoning also takes the form of defining a problem and then evaluating alternative solutions to it. Managers and professionals will always need to think deductively. Yet for most complex organizational problems, a solution cannot be found merely by pulling together available evidence.

The revamped workplace often calls for inductive thinking. Corporate downsizing provides another example. After downsizing many firms are short-handed. A deductive approach to this problem is to look for alternative solutions to make work more efficient. An inductive approach leads one to ask, "Why not just eliminate some of the work we do?"

SKILL AND ABILITY REQUIREMENTS

To succeed in the modern workplace managers and professionals need a combination of skills both old and new. Whether the

Two New Skills Requirements for the Revamped Workplace

1. Ability to work rapidly
2. Ability to think and work across functional lines

workplace is revamped or traditional, managers and professionals must possess basic skills and abilities, such as being able to communicate effectively, analyze data, and work with computers. Inductive reasoning is important because it facilitates problem-solving skills.

A major reason that skills are discussed here is that new work processes inevitably require new skills. Process redesign often leads to more worker empowerment and a broader set of tasks. The new skills required involve a greater depth of job knowledge.[7] More breadth will be required also because team members perform a variety of tasks. There are six basic skills required in the revamped workplace, and two skill requirements that are new.

Communication Skills

The importance of communication skills has increased because structures such as process teams require considerable give and take and negotiation among their members. Work team members must also communicate well with people from other departments. The use of electronic mail to communicate with both company insiders and outsiders has grown explosively. In the past, office assistants used to edit and correct letters written by their bosses. With electronic mail, messages are sent unedited.

Managers need effective message-writing skills both to communicate effectively and to avoid embarrassment.

The give and take in a team setting requires excellent listening skills. Understanding customer requirements also requires listening acuity. A member of a quality-improvement team who worked for a consumer electronics firm visited a nonprofit training and development firm. She asked what the trainers liked and disliked about her firm's line of professional camcorders. (Her company had gained considerable market share by offering reasonable quality at a low price.) By listening carefully, the improvement-team member discovered that the low price was not in fact a selling feature.

What trainers feared most was the embarrassment that stemmed from equipment failure during a training session. The woman brought this information back to the company. A decision was then make to build sturdier components into the camcorders even though this would necessitate raising their selling price. Despite this, market share increased after the firm's advertising brochures emphasized the enhanced reliability of the camcorders.

Foreign language skills have gained in importance because of the globalization of business. The advances in information technology are bringing businesses around the world closer together. If you were a key player in a virtual corporation, it would be to your advantage to specialize in one language and culture in addition to your own. Facility in a second language would establish extra support with some companies in your network. Benchmarking is another workplace innovation that is going global. It would facilitate benchmarking to be able to speak the language of key people in the company whose product or process you wanted to emulate. Americans often ask, "Isn't English the universal language of business? Why is it important to speak another language?" The answer is that rapport builds rapidly when you speak another person's native language—even if that person wants to take the opportunity to speak English.

Mathematical and Statistical Skills

Being able to calculate mathematically, prepare budgets, analyze data, and use a variety of statistical techniques are all skills that contribute to your effectiveness in the reconfigured workplace. Quality professionals as well as production workers need to be able to prepare statistical charts, perform cause-and-effect analyses, and prepare Pareto diagrams. These diagrams illustrate a method of diagnosing which activities are responsible for most of the results in a given situation. Because 80 percent of the results are often attributed to 20 percent of the activities, the Pareto diagram is also referred to as an 80–20 diagram.

The role of the benchmarking professional illustrates the importance of mathematical and statistical skills in the revamped workplace. Benchmarkers proliferate because they are central players in total quality management. Up to this point we have not explicitly stated the nature of benchmarking. This is how a benchmarking professional describes the process:

> A systematic and rigorous examination of your organization's product, service, or work processes measured against those organizations recognized as the best. The purpose is to produce changes and improvements in your enterprise. The most effective benchmarking is continuous, as your organization consistently seeks out feasible new areas to benchmark, eventually integrating benchmarking into strategic planning and corporate vision.[8]

Benchmarkers need information technology skills because they rely on databases to help identify which firms might be able to share information with them. After a visit has been set up, the benchmarker may be presented with a mass of data that require good statistical skills to interpret. For example, the company being benchmarked might graciously show the benchmarker charts and statistical information describing how customer inquiries are handled. To make the information useful, the benchmarker will have to interpret the data. Sometimes there is a limit to how much assistance the benchmarked firm is willing to provide.

Information Technology Skills

Workplace innovations such as reengineering, process innovation, and process redesign have been made possible because of advances in information technology. Even if a manager did not make extensive personal use of the technology, it would still be important to understand how others on the team are using it.

Sales Skills

The revamped workplace requires no more selling to external customers than a traditional one does. Yet if sales skills are defined more broadly as persuading others, negotiating, and promoting, their relevance increases. (Although negotiation was listed as a communication skill earlier, it can also be considered an important part of selling.) Sales skills are of heightened importance because in many situations people will have little formal authority over the workers they need to rely on. Even a team leader has relatively limited formal authority over team members. When placed on a task force in a downsized firm, you may not have formal authority over the people whose cooperation and input you need. A marketing specialist assigned to a task force expressed it this way:

> Here I was an entry-level marketing specialist. My analysis showed that the company would benefit from using the manufacturer's representatives for several of our product lines. One of the people on my task force was the sales manager. It took a lot of fancy footwork to convince him that it was uneconomical to keep sales representatives in certain territories for certain lines. He had a big personal stake in maintaining as large a sales staff as possible.

Political Skills

Political maneuvering can escalate to fever pitch in a revamped workplace. Imagine the scenario when the CEO announces that a reengineering program will begin on the first of the year.
For many managers the term reengineering connotes downsizing and erosion of power. For some managers, however, the term reengineering represents a new corporate thrust. It is therefore a personal opportunity to look good in the eyes of top management.

Many managers eager to hold on to their firmly entrenched functional departments will conduct political campaigns to convince top management of the importance of their function. At the other extreme, some managers will quickly volunteer for reengineering. Some of them will have a legitimate concern for revolutionizing work; others will be more concerned about appearing to be a good corporate citizen.

Political behavior may also increase as various managers attempt to prevent the downsizing that usually accompanies process redesign. They will look for ways to convince upper management that they and their staffs are vitally needed to carry out the company's mission. One example: An accounts receivable department at a food processor was targeted for process redesign. A process redesign consultant and the company president visited the department to explain the purposes of process redesign. To the manager and her staff, process redesign translated into "Get the work done with fewer people."

The manager of accounts receivable decided to take the offense against downsizing. She put together a package that described the important contributions she and the staff were making. It included statements of how large a return on investment the department was contributing to the company, and also presented summary data on the above-average performance appraisals her staff had received in the last few years.

The manager's political initiative proved beneficial. Three positions were eliminated from the department, but all three people were placed elsewhere in the company in worthwhile positions. And the manager herself became the company's first *process owner.*

To cope with these political thrusts it is important to question the motives behind people's actions during workplace revamping. Is another manager manipulating you into fighting his or her campaign against top management? If you think so, confront that person. In one company, an advocate of total quality management was trying to sell the system upward. He wanted to get top management interested in applying for a Malcolm Baldrige National Quality Award (a U.S. Government quality award for business and industry).

The TQM proponent realized that the president of the company was ambivalent because of the time, expense, and paperwork associated with applying for the Baldrige Award. As part of his political ploy, the manager took a series of key people to lunch. During lunch he attempted to get a commitment from his luncheon guest to telephone the president and pitch the Baldrige application. His thrust was, "Here is an opportunity to bring national attention to our company. If we can only convince Jim (the CEO)."

If you were in this situation, it might be true that you could help your company by championing the Baldrige application.

> **WORKERS ARE UNDER CONSTANT PRESSURE TO THINK OF WAYS TO ACCOMPLISH THE SAME AMOUNT OF WORK IN LESS TIME WITH FEWER RESOURCES.**

The downside risk, however, is that you would alienate yourself from the president.

Functional Skills

An unfortunate perception of the revamped workplace is that functional skills are less important than before. The misperception comes about because many people in a revamped workplace perform their work in multidisciplinary groups. Although you work with people from other disciplines, a thorough knowledge of your own discipline remains important. Finance people will be asked finance questions, marketing people will be asked marketing questions, purchasing people will be asked purchasing questions, and so on. Without functional skills you lack expertise.

Functional skills also provide an important hedge in case you are reassigned to a traditional department or choose to join another firm that has not revamped its workplace. Many people in the modern workplace have abandoned their original functional expertise to become quality specialists. For most of these people it would be better to keep their functional skills honed, as a supplement to their expertise in quality. As quality becomes incorporated into every organizational function, there will be less need for stand-alone quality professionals. Again, retaining functional skills is a vitally important career hedge.

Ability to Work Rapidly

Speed is an asset in the modern workplace. Product cycle times have shortened for many products, and customers demand prompt service. Because fewer people may be around to perform the work survivors have to work more rapidly to achieve targets. Lethargic, plodding people are at a distinct disadvantage in a competitive company.

A new contributor to the importance of working rapidly is *time-based competition*. Time is equated with money, as it has been or many years. Time-based competition, however, extends this thinking further. It contends that time is also the equivalent of productivity, quality, and innovation. Proponents of time-based competition explain that time, like costs, is manageable. It can also be a source of competitive advantage throughout every process in the organization. George Stalk, the consultant who popularized the concept of time-based competition, was impressed with how rapidly Japanese companies brought their products to market. He concluded that getting products to market rapidly was giving many of these firms a competitive advantage.[9]

Speed of delivery is perceived by customers as an important dimension of service. A cornerstone of Domino Pizza's marketing strategy is speed of delivery. (Domino's later soft-pedaled speed as a primary service factor after losing a traffic accident lawsuit.) Getting software to market on time provides an important competitive advantage. This is especially true because even the best-known players in the field are notoriously late in delivering new software. The ubiquity of late software has led to the term "phantom-ware," meaning software that is promised but never fully developed or delivered.

Working rapidly is thus an important skill for the modern workplace. To work rapidly, people need to have high energy levels and good concentration. Daydreaming is a major cause of working slowly. Despite the emphasis on speed, rapidly performed sloppy work is not an asset. As a successful literary agent in New York tells her authors, "Better late than lousy."

Cross-Functional Skills

In addition to preserving your functional skills, it is also important to be able to work comfortably with people from other functions. An essential component of cross-functional skills is the ability to look at problems from a broad (multidisciplinary) perspective. Imagine the following scenario: You are asked to investigate customer complaints that your product is too expensive. The functional viewpoints on the problem are:

- Finance must find a way to lower the cost. Costs are obviously out of line.
- Manufacturing must squeeze some more cost out of the product. (Maybe we can buy lower-priced components and cut down on overtime.)
- Marketing must find a way to explain why this product is a bargain at its present price.

A person with cross-functional skills will encourage the group to look at several perspectives in resolving the problem. From the cross-functional perspective, the horizontal organization has a *business* problem—not a finance, marketing, or manufacturing problem.

Another component of cross-functional skills is the ability to relate comfortably to people from different disciplines. To be able to do so, a person must overcome many stereotypes about other functions. Stereotypes may have some validity, but they can often block communication of the potential contribution of other members of the cross-functional team. Here are a few of these stereotypes:

- Marketing people care much more about sales volume and market share than earning a profit.
- Finance people just don't understand that you have to spend money to make money.
- Human resources people are much more concerned about job satisfaction than profits.
- Manufacturing people care mostly about achieving an orderly flow of work. Customer needs are of much less concern.
- Engineers are into gadgetry, bells and whistles, and quality at any price. They are much less concerned about delivering products of interest to customers.

> # EVERYTHING YOU
> # MAKE IS
> # A SELF-PORTRAIT.

The person with effective cross-functional skills would understand the perspectives of the various disciplines. He or she would use this empathy to help find common interests and build bridges across disciplines. A marketing specialist made this comment to a group dealing with a sticky customer problem: "I don't care whose ox gets gored. Let's satisfy the customer and make some money at the same time."

THE QUALITY ATTITUDE

Quality improvement, and therefore total quality management, is only possible if workers have positive attitudes toward quality. Quality problem-solving tools (such as cause-and-effect diagrams) will achieve small gains unless workers have a sincere desire to improve quality. One important contributor to a positive attitude toward quality is conscientiousness. A variety of meanings have been attached to this personality trait, but it generally means being dependable. Equally important, a conscientious person feels morally obligated to meet his or her responsibilities. A conscientious garment worker will not knowingly ship a suit with a dangling button. And a software developer will not knowingly ship a program with incorrect instructions.

As implied from the two examples just cited, conscientiousness also involves paying careful attention to details. Many quality problems stem from glossing over details. An automobile might have to be recalled because a wire was placed too close to the engine. Under prolonged exposure to heat, that wire might catch fire. For total quality management to succeed, employees have to be coached on the importance of paying attention to details. A caption under one of Norman Rockwell's paintings put it memorably: "Everything you make is a self-portrait."

ONE COMPANY'S PORTRAIT OF AN EFFECTIVE TEAM MEMBER

Teams are an integral part of the revamped workplace. Unfortunately, not every worker is suited by a temperament or talent to work effectively as part of a team. An organization needs a relative high-quality work force for the team concept to succeed. To serve effectively as team members, employees have to be mentally flexible, alert, and possess at least average interpersonal skills. Team members must take pride in their work and enjoy working cooperatively. Employers must select team members carefully.

Selection devices such as interviews and personnel tests are used to find a good match between job candidates and job requirements. Although candidates for a team are usually current employees, they are always carefully screened.

The Rohm & Haas chemical plant in LaPorte, Texas, provides a representative example of how the selection process works. All workers in the area where a job opening exists are involved in the interview. Candidates for team assignments are questioned about the characteristics presented below.[10]

Responsibility and Work Ethic. A team member must maintain a high standard of work performance and dedication to quality. Team members are expected to work hard, making a strong work ethic important.

Interest Match. On successful teams, the assignment activates the personal interests of workers. For example, team members should enjoy developing multiple skills.

Versatility. On a team, the ability to handle multiple tasks, interruptions, and diverse assignments is important. Note that interest alone is not sufficient; it must be combined with ability.

Honesty. A team member must maintain ethical standards related to the job and admit mistakes.

Self-Starting Ability. Successful team members tackle assignments without having to be prodded by a team leader or supervisor.

Cooperativeness and Teamwork. A team worker is more concerned about achieving team goals than individual accomplishment. Everybody may look out for number one to some extent, yet a team player also shows a genuine concern for group welfare.

Openness. Productive team members are genuine in dealing with each other, and are willing to relate openly. Instead of ignoring or suppressing conflict, they bring it out on the table.

Tact and Sensitivity. A team member must be responsive to the impact of his or her behavior on the feelings, dignity, and performance of others.

Though these characteristics are related to success as a team member, not every team member can score high in all the categories. Perhaps not even the CEO of a revamped firm would score at the top on all these characteristics.

SELECTING PEOPLE FOR POSITIONS IN THE REVAMPED WORKPLACE

Workers have to be carefully selected for team member positions in the revamped workplace. Similarly, members have to be selected for other positions such as process team member, reengineering team member, and case manager. Selecting people for these positions does not require new methods of screening employees. Traditional methods of personnel selection are sufficient. Whether external or internal candidates are chosen for the new positions, standard procedures should be followed. Human resources professionals should provide the technical expertise for choosing effective and fair selection techniques.

Measurements should be made of the personal characteristics mentioned throughout this chapter. The measurement methods will ordinarily include interviews, results of past performance appraisals (for present employees), and personnel and psychological tests. Following the Rohm & Haas approach, group interviews with team members can be illuminating. Results of past performance appraisals are useful to search for evidence of the candidate's being a good team player and thinking imaginatively. Psychological testing can provide useful clues about such factors as problem-solving ability. Traits such as conscientiousness and attention to detail are also amenable to psychological testing.

Closely related to psychological tests are situational tests. The candidates are placed in a problem-solving situation in which they have to interact with other workers. Trained observers then rate the candidates on such factors as problem-solving ability and interpersonal skills.

CHECKLIST OF THE SKILLS AND TALENTS NEEDED IN THE REVAMPED WORKPLACE

The summary checklist below will help integrate the information presented in this chapter. Not everyone assigned to a revamped workplace will be ideally or equally qualified. The greater the number of the following traits and skills you possess, the more qualified and sought after you will be as a team member.

☑ Superior performance in general: Mediocrity is a negative factor, especially for complex activities such as process redesign.

☑ Desire to be part of a team having total responsibility for a task, including a desire to be empowered.

☑ Desire for autonomy in conducting work, within the limits of wanting to be part of a team.

☑ Ability to think inductively as well as deductively. Ability to recognize solutions to problems people did not know they had.

☑ Solid communication skills, including speaking, writing, and listening.

☑ Mathematical and statistical skills, combined with information technology skills.

☑ Cross-functional skills, with an emphasis on working smoothly with people from other disciplines.

☑ Positive attitude toward quality, including conscientiousness and concern for detail.

3

Shaking Loose
Creative Thinking

Creative thinking is necessary to accomplish the type of workplace changes we have been describing. A significant change in a work process, a surge in quality, or an effective downsizing will rarely happen without imaginative and creative problem solving. The terms *innovation* and *creativity* are often used interchangeably in this chapter. In a work environment, however, innovation often refers to a creative idea that has actually been put to use. Whichever term you prefer, the message is the same. To achieve significant improvements in productivity and quality, managers and individual contributors have to solve problems and search for opportunities in bold and imaginative ways.

Creative thinking is acutely necessary for radical work redesigns that achieve leaps in productivity. An example is a redesign that allows 10 people to accomplish the same job that required 80 people previously. Smaller breakthroughs that enhance customer service without eliminating many jobs also require creative thinking. Remember those long checkout lines in hotels, particularly toward the end of a convention? Observing this chaos month after month, a hotel official at the Milford Plaza in New York City challenged the system. She said to herself and her workmates, "There must be a better way to check people out of our hotels."

The better way has been to give guests more than one option. If guests want to pay in cash or by check, or want to dispute any charge, they still have the option of waiting in line. Another group of guests prefer to wait in line because they prefer the traditional checkout method. For those guests who want to leave the hotel without waiting in line, several other options now exist. All were made possible by information technology involving the use of bank credit cards.

One option is to have a statement slipped under your door the morning of checkout. If a new charge accrues, your credit card is billed. Another option is to reconcile your bill before departure, using interactive television in your room. A receipt arrives at your home several days later. Another option is for a statement to be mailed to your home without your having seen the bill while at the hotel. In addition, a few hotels have machines in the lobby that generate a bill after the guest inserts a credit card.

This innovative approach to checking out guests has spread rapidly among hotels. Time-conscious travelers so strongly prefer to bypass checkout lines that a hotel using only the traditional checkout system would be at a competitive disadvantage.

In this chapter we describe approaches that managers can use to foster the type of innovative thinking necessary to revamp the workplace. Keep in mind, however, that not every employee is capable of generating useful ideas. It may be true that traditional management practices have sometimes discouraged innovative thinking. Yet it is naive to believe that a brilliant imagination lurks in the mind of every worker, and that with the right prodding by a manager the worker's creative spirit will break loose.

OVERCOME TRADITIONAL THINKING

The major challenge in becoming more creative is to overcome the habit of looking at problems in traditional or conventional ways. In the new workplace, overcoming a traditional mental set often means challenging old assumptions. The hotel official just mentioned challenged the assumption that the only way for guests to check out is to wait in line at the cashier's desk.

Consultant and author Michael Hammer explains that *discontinuous thinking* is at the heart of reengineering. This type of thinking is characterized by the ability to recognize and break away from outdated rules and fundamental assumptions that underlie operations. He adds that managers must challenge old assumptions and discard old rules that created business problems in the first place. Some examples: "Local warehouses are necessary for good service," and "Merchandising decisions are made at headquarters." In response to the first point, advances in information technology allow warehouses to be centralized. In response to the second, many division personnel are sufficiently creative to make their own merchandising decisions.[1]

Creative problem-solving in general requires an ability to overcome traditional thinking. The creative person looks at problems in a new light and transcends conventional ways of thinking about them. For many years, banks were unable to solve the problem of how to decrease the cost of customer withdrawals. Then an inventor from outside the banking industry, John Diebold, asked, "Why not find a way to allow customers to deposit *and* withdraw money automatically?" This seminal thought led to the automatic teller machine (ATM).

The central task in becoming innovative is to break down rigid thinking that blocks new ideas.[2] A conventional-thinking manager might accept the long-standing policy that spending more than $5,000 requires three levels of approval. An innovative manager might ask, "Why do we need three levels of approval for spending $5,000? If we trust people enough to make them managers, why can't they have budget authorization to spend at least $10,000?" Elevating the minimum expenditure that requires multiple approvals eliminates delay and paperwork. Most large organizations would benefit from eliminating more delay and paperwork.

The message here is that you have to question traditional assumptions in every phase of your work. Practice the same questioning attitude off the job, too. An effective questioner of standard practice might ask, "Why am I raking grass clippings and putting them in plastic bags? Maybe I should use a mulching mower. I would save time by not raking up clippings an not bagging them. Also, I would cut my expenses by not purchasing plastic bags. Because the mulched clippings are natural fertilizer, I would also save a lot of money buying much less fertilizer." (If you feel guilty about an income loss for your local gardening store, invest your savings in lawn furniture.)

The other message here for managers is to confront team members when they are thinking in traditional ways that could block problem resolution. A team member might say, "I guess we are going to have to live with poor service. The teenagers we hire for these close-to-minimum-wage positions don't stick around long enough to learn to do their jobs well." You might respond, "Then why are you hiring teenagers?"

The team member might retort, "Because teenagers are the only people available for these low-paying customer service jobs." You might reply with, "Hold on. You're making an assumption that might not be true. Could it be that plenty of seniors and early-retirees would welcome these customer service jobs?"

The concept of overcoming traditional thinking is critical in the development of innovative problem solving. I will therefore approach it from several other angles. All five of the ideas that

THE MAJOR CHALLENGE IN BECOMING MORE INNOVATIVE OR CREATIVE IS TO OVERCOME LOOKING AT PROBLEMS IN TRADITIONAL OR CONVENTIONAL WAYS.

> # FIVE WAYS TO FREE YOURSELF FROM TRADITIONAL THINKING
>
> 1. Think outside the box.
> 2. Avoid hardening of the categories.
> 3. Develop new paradigms.
> 4. Overcome traditional mental sets.
> 5. Overcome traditional wisdom.

follow point to the importance of shaking loose from the usual way of thinking about problems.

A Creative Person Thinks Outside the Box

A box in this sense is a category that confines and restricts thinking. Many executives save millions of company dollars by thinking outside the box that headquarters must be located in a major city. A box in reference to corporate downsizings is that the swiftest way to increase profits is to reduce head count, thereby saving payroll costs. Top management is often faced with no other apparent alternatives. Yet the top managers from some companies are finding alternatives to layoffs as a way of increasing profits. Employees are sometimes asked to take small pay cuts, preserving some jobs.

In France, the federal government has encouraged state-subsidized companies to reduce the 40-hour work week to 32 hours in order to preserve jobs. One job is preserved when five employees each reduce their work week by one-fifth, or eight hours. You may or may not believe that the proper role of government is to mandate the length of work weeks to preserve jobs, but the reduction demonstrates thinking outside the box.

A vice president of operations showed the same type of thinking outside the box during a staff meeting. The president had just announced that a tenth of the company work force would have to be laid off. The vice president responded, "Hold on, Jerry, you're framing this problem in terms of a solution. The problem you define is that our costs are too high for our revenues. Why not explore solutions to the problem other than laying off workers? How about selling one of our buildings to consolidate our work space? Or how about an average 10 percent reduction in pay for everyone?"

The vice president's thinking outside the box in the end preserved half the jobs scheduled for elimination. The president asked for only a 5 percent reduction in payroll and he also sold one building, which gave the company sufficient operating cash while it sought to improve sales.

Thinking outside the box is applied today to the shipping of products, both literally and figuratively. The result has been greatly to the advantage of both vendors and their customers. A bothersome problem for many buyers is the disassembling and disposal of the packaging that large products have been shipped in. Some companies give the used packaging to recyclers in exchange for the recycler removing the packaging from the premises. A shortcoming of this method for the original vendor is the high expense of the initial packaging. And the customer has some costs involved in disassembling the packaging and gathering it for the recycler.

Several companies have attacked the problem of expensive packaging by questioning why industrial products have to be shipped in disposable packaging. The alternative solution is to ship goods in permanent, reusable packaging. The reusable packaging is much like a polyurethane shell that forms a snug-fitting mold. After the goods are unpacked, the vendor arranges to pick up the reusable shell. For regular customers, retrieving the shells can be timed with a shipment of new goods.

This modern redesign of the shipping process has a historical precedent in the distribution of milk to end users. Milk was delivered by truck in reusable glass bottles. When the milkman re-turned with another delivery, he picked up the old bottles. Fur-thermore, at one time people need to bring buckets to the local bar for their takeout beer. The beer distributor made the end consumer responsible for the containerization of beer consumed in the home. Although these last two examples may appear friv-olous, they illustrate an important point about innovative thinking. Old basic concepts can be recycled for use in the re-vamped workplace.

People Who Are not Creative Suffer from Hardening of the Categories

A noncreative person thinks categorically: "Only men can climb telephone poles," or "Only women are successful in customer service positions."

An example of categorical thinking that has backfired for many companies is the habit of classifying people they interact with as either employees or customers. In reality, many em-ployees are also external customers. In addition, they may be customers of a company's customers. When employees who are customers are laid off, they quickly become former customers, creating a reverberation throughout the economy. If your cus-tomers lose as their customers those people you laid off, your customers might well cut back their purchasing from you.

To quote an official of the Amalgamated Clothing Workers Union: "A lot of the textile workers who lost their jobs said they would never again buy clothing carrying the [label of the company that laid them off]. Many of them told family mem-bers and friends to do likewise. Little by little these laid-off workers are getting revenge."

To Be Creative, One Must Develop New Paradigms

A paradigm, one of the business buzzwords of the 1990s, is a model or framework. An example of a quality-inhibiting para-digm is that suppliers can be treated shabbily because they need the company more than the company needs them. In reality, firms noted for their high-quality products form partnerships of mutual respect with their suppliers. Long before others made this paradigm shift, several divisions of Burlington Industries regularly held supplier-appreciation days. Representatives from key suppliers, such as DuPont, would be feted in the way most companies treat customers.

Creativity Requires Overcoming Traditional Mental Sets

A traditional mental set is a conventional way of looking at things and placing them in familiar categories. One example of such a set is that a company pays a supplier after the company receives the invoice. The people involved in the pioneering work in reengineering at Ford Motor Company looked at the payment process differently. From now on, they decided, Ford would pay for goods when they were received. As a result the accounts payable operation was dramatically streamlined.

If you are a manager, you can help people overcome traditional mental sets by asking probing questions such as "Why are you doing your work that way?"

The new office manager in a large legal firm noticed that the billing department was so busy at the end of the month that several employees worked overtime. "Why are you so busy at the end of the month?" he asked the head bookkeeper. "We send out the bills at the end of the month. It is our policy to have all the bills mailed the last working day of the month," the head bookkeeper replied.

The office manager dug further. "Why is that our policy?" To which the head bookkeeper responded in an exasperated tone, "Because anybody who has ever worked in a law office knows that bills are sent out at the end of the month." The office manager pointed out that tradition is not inevitably a good reason for choosing the best way of organizing an activity as important as managing cash. Based on the office manager's willingness to challenge tradition, the billing department has modified its

> **A MANAGER CAN HELP PEOPLE OVERCOME TRADITIONAL MENTAL SETS BY ASKING PROBING QUESTIONS SUCH AS, WHY ARE YOU PERFORMING YOUR WORK THAT WAY?**

billing process. Bills are now sent out weekly. As a consequence, the law firm has a much improved cash flow and overtime costs in the billing department have been virtually eliminated.

Creative People Overcome Conventional Wisdom

A final perspective on traditional mental sets is that they are often regarded as conventional wisdom. In recent years many unionized manufacturing firms have been able to revamp work processes by forming team structures. The conventional wisdom overcome here is that labor unions would never accept the flexible job classifications required in a team structure. To form a work team in manufacturing, team members must work outside tight job classifications and descriptions. In exchange for some guarantees of job security, the firms found that labor unions—such as the United Auto Workers Union—were willing to accept flexible job classifications.

Helping yourself or team members overcome traditional thinking requires mental flexibility. Challenging your own assumptions regularly, along with those of your workmates, can help you enhance your mental flexibility. Another approach is to engage periodically in exercises that demand mental flexibility.

One classic exercise is the unusual uses test. The only material required for this is a word processor, typewriter, or a piece of paper and a writing instrument. Working alone, or with your team members, develop as many uses as possible for each object described below. Allow 15 minutes to generate uses for each one.

- A standard red brick
- A newspaper
- A plastic bucket
- A wooden cooking spoon

Do not be discouraged if you are not prolific in your first attempt at the unusual uses test. Try again next month with a fresh set of everyday objects.

ENCOURAGE YOUR STAFF TO CHALLENGE THE STATUS QUO

Innovation, by definition, is a departure from the status quo. To bring about the creative change required in the revamped workplace, managers and professionals must continually challenge current practice. Consultants and authors James M. Kouzes and Barry Z. Posner surveyed more than 2,000 business leaders to find out when they were performing at their personal best. A consistent finding about these moments of high performance was that they occurred when the leaders brought their operations into new territory.

Leaders in different functional areas and from different organizations explained how they had turned around losing operations, initiated untested procedures, or greatly improved business results. Their personal best moments resulted in far more than incremental improvements. The magnitude of change was often several hundred percent. In the words of Kouzes and Posner:

> The personal best leadership cases were about firsts, about radical departures from the past, about doing things that had never been done before, about going to places no one else yet had discovered.[3]

Challenging the status quo makes it possible to bring about process redesign as well as the incremental improvements that are so vital to total quality management. To challenge the status quo, Kouzes and Posner recommend that you make a list of organizational practices that reflect the thinking, "That's the way we have always done it around here." Challenge each one of these practices by asking two questions, "Is this useful for becoming the best we can become?" and "Is this for stimulating creativity and innovation?" If your answer to each is a resounding yes, keep that procedure or practice. Review every policy and procedure you might have the authority to change. Ask yourself the same questions for each one and take the same action. Make a commitment to eliminate all rules and routine that do not enhance productivity, profits, or quality.

Another way to challenge the status quo is to tell people to ignore the maxim "If it isn't broken, don't fix it." Assume that virtually any process or procedure can be improved. Challenge team members to take a fresh look at the way your organizational unit is run.[4] Ask what-if questions such as:

- What if we eliminate outside selling and instead use telemarketing?
- What if we eliminate one-third of our meetings and devote that time to dealing directly with customers?
- What if we simplify our expense account procedures by giving each manager and sales representative a fixed entertainment budget for each quarter, and per-diem travel allowances?

A unique way to challenge the status quo is to critically examine what features of your operation internal and external customers might not like. In other words, use your own resources to evaluate what you might do differently. One approach to this self-examination method is called the pet-peeve technique. Through brainstorming, team members develop a list of complaints. Sources of complaints include inside customers, outside customers, competitors, and suppliers.

During the brainstorming session, the group throws in some imaginary and some humorous complaints. No holds are barred. Group members sometimes prepare for the meeting by soliciting feedback from the various target groups. The feedback should be conducted informally, in keeping with the informal, breezy style of the pet-peeve group. Rather than approaching target groups with a survey, the inquirers might tell people about the upcoming pet-peeve session, then ask, "What complaints can you contribute?"

The humorous complaints are especially important. Humor requires creative thinking, thus sharpening the creative problem-solving approach of the pet-peeve technique. After all the complaints have been aired, action plans are drawn to remedy the most serious problems.[5] The pet-peeve technique challenges the status quo by questioning whether an organizational unit is providing the best service. For instance, a sales promotion department within an office supply company identified the following six peeves:

Peeve 1: "A lot of people think our job consists of thinking up low-priced plastic novelties to send to customers."

Peeve 2: "People think we dream up ways to discount our merchandise to the point that all the profit is squeezed out."

Peeve 3: "Our promotions are so trivial that we could hire elementary-school students to replace us."

Peeve 4: "Suppliers say we undercut the commissions our outside sales reps could make by giving merchandise away."

Peeve 5: "Many people think we should change our name to 'inventory clearance department.'"

Peeve 6: "Customers think the only merchandise we discount is the chipped, the dented, and the obsolete."

As a result of these penetrating, albeit exaggerated, self-criticisms, the sales promotion department developed an effective action plan. The department's director arranged brief meetings with units throughout the organization to discuss the sales promotion department's role. She also answered questions. During these discussions, the director of sales promotion was able to explain how sales promotion supports marketing strategy. She also encouraged her various constituents (sales group, customers, and so forth) to blow the whistle when any promotion was perceived as inappropriate or ineffective.

The linking of the pet-peeve technique to revamping the workplace always centers on quality of service. After the sales promotion department had examined its possible weak points as perceived by others, it made a few constructive changes. Those changes, in turn, led to higher internal customer satisfaction. There was also promise of enhancing external customer satisfaction, too, by dealing with the issue of which merchandise received the most promotion.

SEVEN KEY MANAGERIAL ACTIONS TO ENHANCE INNOVATION

Success in the revamped workplace is heavily dependent on innovation. Managers must engage in activities daily that foster innovation. A worker's talent for creative thinking, combined with a desire to accomplish, is the biggest driver of innovation. The manager makes a major contribution by creating an atmosphere that encourages such creative expression.

The most basic approach to enhancing innovation would be for you, as manager, to establish innovation goals for the team. In essence, you tell the team, "Our mandate is to be innovative." You then explain in detail what you mean by innovation. In addition, you give examples of innovative process redesigns that have been achieved in another part of the company. Simply telling people to be innovative and establishing goals that require innovation is likely to foster at least some innovation. Yet your approach can be faulted for being too mechanistic and too shallow.

Leaders who achieve genuine innovations engage in a variety of practices that stimulate creativity. Not every leader who is successful at fostering innovation engages consistently in all of the activities we describe below. Yet the more of these activities and attitudes you incorporate into your repertoire, the greater the chance that you will encourage innovation among your team members.

The most influential step a manager can take to bring about creative problem solving is to develop a permissive atmosphere. A permissive atmosphere contributes to innovation because it encourages people to think freely and take intellectual risks. At the same time, team members must feel that they will not be penalized for making honest mistakes.

For example, one group member suggested that a work process (preparing bids on interior designs of office buildings) could be streamlined by eliminating spot-checks for quality. The manager and the other group members agreed that removing spot-checks would speed the bid-preparation process in this competitive business. Omitting the quality checks, however, resulted in several mispriced bids and several others with design flaws. After the errors became apparent, the manager explained the problem to the team member who had suggested that the quality checks be eliminated. The team member was also told that process redesign often results in a few glitches. The manager explained that successful innovators make their share of mistakes.

Permissiveness is also fostered when the manager makes a statement such as "Give me a few wild ideas on how we can squeeze a few more steps out of our proposal process. In this preliminary stage of our thinking no idea is too off-the-wall." A statement of this nature subtly communicates the idea that no idea will be ridiculed. One reason many people do not make their potentially innovative ideas public is that they fear ridicule.

Research supports the importance of permissiveness for fostering innovation. Teresa M. Amabile and S. S. Gryskiewicz interviewed 120 research and development scientists in order to gather critical incidents. One incident was to illustrate high creativity, and one low creativity. In describing incidents of high creativity, about 74 percent of the scientists mentioned the following conditions:

- freedom to decide what to do and how to do one's work
- freedom from constraints such as tight financial controls
- an open atmosphere.[6]

Collectively, these findings suggest that a permissive atmosphere is appropriate for nurturing innovation. The same conclusions apply outside a research and development environment. For example, to foster innovation the leader of a quality-improvement team should grant members as much freedom as organizational policy permits. "Freedom" might mean such things as discretion to switch budget lines or to bring another member onto the team who might add a creative spark.

A maverick manager, as proposed by author Donald W. Blohwiak, is the type of permissive leader who fosters innovation. Such a manager actively encourages team members to "color outside the lines" (the same as thinking outside the box). Maverick managers also seek ways to do new things and new ways to do old things.[7] At Westinghouse Corporation, many customers were receiving multiple bills from the company each month. A leader who qualifies as a maverick manager challenged his team to simplify the company's billing system; the manager welcomed all suggestions. As a result, the accounts receivable group agreed upon procedures that simplified enormously the paperwork for customers.

> **A MAVERICK MANAGER ACTIVELY ENCOURAGES TEAM MEMBERS TO "COLOR OUTSIDE THE LINES."**

Another tactic for creating a permissive atmosphere is for the manager to accept partially developed ideas.[8] Managers of productive research laboratories listen to and support half-formed proposals and encourage team members to develop their ideas. Managers in other disciplines also should avoid nipping innovation in the bud by discouraging the flow of ideas. During one corporate downsizing a staff member suggested that the company reduce costs by eliminating all customer-service centers in the field. Several of the other staff members laughed, but the president said, "You might be on to something. Why not play with your idea further?"

Playing with the suggestion for closing customer-service centers eventually led to the closing of 10 low-traffic centers. The company maintained a local telephone listing in the cities where the offices were closed. Local calls were automatically routed by telephone equipment to a central location. An attempt was made to fix problems by giving instructions over the telephone. When this was not possible, the company dispatched a customer-service technician within 72 hours to visit the customer's site. The half-developed idea led to a valuable cost-saving suggestion.

A leader can also enhance innovation by giving positive feedback when an innovation succeeds. Innovation is its own reward to some extent. Nevertheless, innovators still enjoy knowing the specifics about how their idea made a contribution. A sales representative for a clothing manufacturer said she had a quality-improvement suggestion that would give the company's line of overcoats and raincoats a competitive edge. The sales director said, "I'll listen, but I'll keep my fingers crossed that we can afford your brainstorm."

The sales representative explained that her low-cost suggestion would be an excellent investment for the company. A major problem with competitor companies' coats was that buttons fell off regularly with normal use. She recommended that all buttons on all overcoats be reinforced with a durable, yet lightweight thread. The thread-reinforcing suggestion was incorporated into a marketing campaign to attract retailers, which proved successful. The retailers, in turn, found that reinforced buttons were a good selling point for customers. Feedback was given to the sales representative by sharing with her information about the success of the marketing campaign.

Feedback about innovative suggestion should be supplemented with financial rewards. Innovators, like most workers, appreciate financial rewards. The financial reward is important in itself and also reflects recognition of outstanding performance. Many large firms have systematic programs for rewarding innovative suggestions with cash payments. Many suggestions programs carry cash awards. Several high-tech firms reward innovators with a small percentage of the profits stemming from their innovations.

Many research and development specialists at 3M, for example, have profited handsomely from their market innovations. Salaries and promotions at 3M are linked to the successful spearheading of new products from the idea phase to market implementation. Closely related to financial rewards is the opportunity 3M offers a person who champions a successful new product. The new-product champion manages the new product as if it were his or her own business.

A willingness to stretch organizational policy is another way to foster innovation. Managers must know when to stretch company policy in order to launch an idea. One example would be spending unused travel budget money to help purchase equipment needed to develop a prototype for a new product. In many instances process redesign can only be accomplished by investing in information technology, such as new software, to replace a manual system.

An ability and willingness to make quick decisions contributes to an atmosphere in which innovations can flower. Managers who foster creativity can spot a good idea and decide quickly whether to use organizational resources to develop it.

The willingness to respond quickly to good ideas is important because creative people are eager to see their ideas translated into action.

If you are a manager who wants to encourage innovation, it is helpful to broaden your outlook and that of your staff, too. Innovative thinking is often hampered because people are thinking only about the job at hand. Your horizons can be broadened by bringing in outsiders to talk with you and your staff. The most important requirement is that the outsider be a person who can generate a fresh perspective. Many retired senior executives are eager to talk with a new generation of employees. Drawing on their past successes, they can sometimes inspire employees to think in fresh ways.

Another approach is to bring in someone who is an expert on a topic of interest to your staff, whether or not it is directly job-related. For example, a specialist in virtual reality might inspire you and your staff to think in new ways. Experts in direct mail might provide fresh perspectives on thinking about customers, thus giving your staff new ideas about reaching a target market.[9]

A broadened or fresh perspective is important for another reason. Lack of innovation often stems from a narrow outlook, such as thinking that expenses and receivables must always be tightly controlled. (The foregoing may be generally true, but to think that any standard practice is *always* the most appropriate is a narrow outlook.)

A robust method of creating an innovation-friendly environment is for the leader to encourage a hunger for ideas. Creative people characteristically seek out new ideas constantly, both on and off the job. They scan vast amounts of printed and electronic information to come away with a few nuggets that might lead to the commercialization of an idea.

John Dessauer, one of the creative forces behind the rise of xerography, said that diligence brought the Xerox Corporation into existence. He came upon the prospects of xerography through unremitting vigilance. Dessauer read every document and every publication that might hint at a new product idea for the Haloid Corporation (the predecessor of Xerox). Finally, he came across Chester Carlson's xerography invention and recognized its hidden promise.

The manager can contribute to the development of an idea-hungry group by asking such questions as "What idea have your read, seen, or heard lately that could help us?" Similarly, the manager might periodically commit an entire staff meeting to sharing new and potentially useful ideas.

Yet another perspective on what a manager can do to enhance innovation is to avoid actions that are likely to inhibit creativity. Creativity dampeners, such as telling people not to upset the status quo, discourage people from introducing innovative ideas. Here is a list of creativity dampeners.[10]

1. Frequently saying "Don't rock the boat."
2. Frequently saying "Don't make waves."
3. Using the expression "If it isn't broke, don't fix it."
4. Saying yes to new ideas but then doing nothing about them.
5. Being the exclusive spokesperson for everything in one's area of responsibility.
6. Putting every idea through formal channels.
7. After hearing a suggestion for change, quickly responding that it would cost *money* to implement.
8. Rejecting ideas that are "not invented here."

CREATIVITY TRAINING

One direct action to enhance innovation is to sponsor creativity training for people who are required to think creatively. Under total quality management and process innovation all workers are supposed to think creatively about work-process improvements. Our purposes will be met here by describing some examples of creativity training. They have the common intent of encouraging people to think more flexibly. The pet-peeve technique for operational problems described on pages 68–69 is one way of developing flexible thinking. Three additional ways follow.

You Are the Product

A role-playing exercise well suited to new product development is called "You are the product." The core of the technique is for participants to pretend that they are a product, and discuss how being that product makes them act, feel, or perceive.[11]

Creativity consultant Jim Ferry had executives at Pitney-Bowes invent new product ideas for a postage meter. The team accomplished this by forming a human postage meter, with each executive playing a different part of the machine. One "part" of the machine said, "I'm just glad I wasn't the envelope sealer."

At Rich Products Company the task was to name a new healthy dessert topping for sale to restaurant owners. One person played the role of the dessert, one played the topping, and a third the dessert eater. The dessert said he "didn't want something too heavy to lift." The topping said he wanted to befriend the dessert so that he could "get along with him well." The dessert eater explained, "I don't want anything too messy." Top Life was the winning name, particularly because it implied a dessert topping for a healthy lifestyle.

Consultant Perry also had a successful new product development session at the Polymer Technologies Division of Bausch & Lomb. Executives were paired off in teams, with one playing the eyeball and other playing Bausch & Lomb's rigid gas-permeable contact lens. One eyeball-person persistently requested a pillow to cushion the hard and "insensitive" contact lens. The result was a new research initiative by the polymer division to bond a special space-age cushioning material directly onto the contact lens. The more eye-friendly contact lens has been a commercial success.

"You are the product" can be readily applied to reengineering. Several people pretend they are part of the process to be reengineered, thus aiming for simplification. To develop the right mental set for this exercise, imagine that you are a contract that is supposed to be issued to a customer. Think about how you would feel being routed from one department to another, waiting for approvals from seven different people. Imagine how lonely it would be lying in the corporate attorney's in-box for five days. Your goal is to be sent to your true home, the customer's office. Think of how you would fight and squirm to avoid having so many people decide on your fate.

The Forced-Association Technique

A widely used method of releasing creativity is to make forced associations between the properties of two objects to solve a problem. The method is applied by people working independently or within a group. Either alone or in a group, the essential process is as follows: The individual selects a word at random from a dictionary. Next, the person lists all the properties and attributes of this word. Assume you randomly choose the word, *rock*. Among its attributes are "durable," "low-priced," "abundant in supply," "decorative," and "expensive to ship."

You then force-fit these properties and attributes to the problem you are facing. The force-fit is supposed to help solve the problem. A link is found between the properties of the random object to the properties of the problem object. Your team might be attempting to improve the quality of an office desk chair. Reviewing the properties of the rock might give you the idea to make the seat covering more durable because this is a quality hot point.

An additional example will help clarify the random-word technique. A new way of delivering medicine was supposedly developed by listing the properties of a time bomb. One key property of the bomb was "slow release." The slow release led to creating a medicine that goes to work several hours after it is taken—a time capsule.

The Excursion Method

The forced association technique has a spinoff that should prove valuable for enhancing your and your teammates' mental flexibility. Using the excursion method, the problem solver makes word associations that relate to the problem. The association can be to another word or object. The leader of a company process-improvement team wanted to increase the visibility of the group. During a problem-solving meeting, team members were asked to take an excursion with (or free associate to) the word *visibility*.

Among the word associations made to *visibility* were "big," "tall," "bright-colored," "shining light," "no fog," "sunny day," "media coverage," and "television." an indirect but powerful link between the work *television* and the problem flashed in the team leader's mind. Television related to video. What about becoming more visible by making a videotape showcasing the group? Copies of the videotape could be sent to executives around the company who would watch it at their leisure. Perhaps they would encourage their staff members to watch the video.

The group ultimately prepared a videotape that explained the process redesign team's mission and some of its accomplishments in streamlining work. The video, in turn, led to more exposure such as coverage in the company newsletter.

A CHECKLIST FOR SHAKING LOOSE INNOVATIVE THINKING

A summary checklist of what you and the organization can do to foster innovative thinking will integrate the information presented in this chapter. Not even the most wildly innovative firms would score high in each characteristic. Use this checklist as a thought piece for a staff meeting about innovation. Rate yourself, your total firm, your organizational unit, or your process team on each one of the points below. If an item appears relevant to you or your firm, yet a deficiency is noted, develop action plans for change.

☑ Recognize that a wide range of workers are capable of contributing innovative ideas but that not *everybody* is likely to be innovative.

☑ Overcome looking at problems in traditional or conventional ways. Break down rigid thinking that blocks new ideas.

☑ Recall that discontinuous thinking fosters reengineering. Recognize and break away from outdated rules and fundamental assumptions that underlie operations.

☑ Develop new paradigms, or models, of how you conceptualize business problems and situations. (For example, is it really true that your suppliers need you more than you need them?)

☑ Use the pet-peeve technique to determine what changes team members may have to make to satisfy internal and external customers.

☑ Provide feedback and financial rewards for innovative suggestions.

☑ Champion creativity training.

☑ Have fun because humor triggers creative thinking.

Implementing
Radical Change

4

Workplace transformations such as reengineering translate into radical change for the people involved. The managers involved in implementing the change must first explain to those affected that these changes will be far-reaching and challenging. Using the word *program* can do psychological damage to the change effort. A program connotes a set of activities that have a beginning and ending. A workplace initiative such as reengineering, total quality management, or a focused factory transcends a program. Such an initiative becomes a way of life, to the delight of those who are properly oriented and to the chagrin of those who resist change.

A reengineering initiative at a large business unit within AT&T was assisted by a team of McKinsey & Company consultants.[1] (See Case Study on page 82.)

A major interpretation of the Global Business Communications System experience with redesign is that it led to profound changes. Jobs and reporting relationships were changed, and an autonomous sales force was acquired for the business unit. The dedication and top-management attention paid to the redesign effort paid off in improved business results. An important implication for managers spearheading reengineering efforts is to explain in advance that changes will be radical—and painful—at times. Knowing in advance about changes can help a person pre-

CASE STUDY

Reengineering Initiative

Since the mid-1980s, AT&T's executive committee had been trying to improve the lackluster performance of Global Business Communications Systems (GBCS), the $4 billion unit that sells business telephone systems (PBXs). By early 1989, frustration had set in. Despite credible progress, the business unit seemed to have hit a wall. According to GBCS President Jack Bucter, while each year the business unit met higher performance targets for individual functions, its overall performance did not improve.

Believing that only radical change would invigorate performance, Bucter decided to assemble teams to redesign the business's core processes. Glenn Hazard, an 11-year veteran of AT&T known for building a top-performing sales branch from scratch, was enlisted as a team leader to reengineer the process for selling and installing PBXs. Bucter also assigned full-time team members from a wide range of functions: sales, services, product management, Bell Labs, manufacturing, materials management, information systems, and training. Bucter was candid about the stakes of the project. If performance continued to stagnate, the PBX business would be sold or liquidated.

Diagnostic: June 1989–February 1990. The team took a wide-lens approach, surveying process steps from initial customer contact through to the collection of funds, including a range of system sizes, geographic areas, and customers. By interviewing employees and customers and following paper trails, the team reconstructed 24 cases, which became the basis for the diagnostic. The team then pored over the cases, identifying every person involved, their activities, and now their time was spent.

The team found several areas for improvement. First was the problem of rework. Too many handoffs between functions and a lack of clearly defined roles and responsibilities resulted in significant inefficiencies. An account executive negotiated the sale; a system consultant determined the specifications for the system; and a system technician installed the hardware. In all, 16 handoffs were required to complete a system, and no one took responsibility for the entire transaction. The manufacturing and delivery cycle also generated excessive rework. Final installation came months or even years

continued

after the customer and account executive negotiated a deal. In the meantime, if the customer's needs changed dramatically, the system that had been agreed to earlier frequently came up short. The price of this delay was heavy: dissatisfied customers and substantial write-offs.

In addition, the team found that the front-line employees were insensitive to profitability, largely because they lacked information. Marketing was often focusing on the least profitable customers, while sales concentrated on maximizing revenues, often to the detriment of the profitability of the deals they negotiated.

Finally, indirect expenses were excessive. The case studies revealed that headquarters and centralized support groups were not critical to selling and installing most of the systems, but the services of both were employed on virtually every system.

But a still thornier issue hid beneath these problems. Critical line functions—namely, sales and manufacturing—did not report to the head of GBCS. At the time, AT&T had a single sales force that sold PBXs, long-distance communication services, and other products to larger businesses. Given the size and demands of the long-distance they sold so many complex products, they often had only superficial familiarity with the products they were selling. But customers expected salespeople to have a depth of technical knowledge about these products, and AT&T's competitors, whose sales forces specialized in a single product, could provide their customers with that high level of expertise.

Bucter was certain that creating a dedicated PBX sales force was essential for success. Only then would the redesign be broad enough to include all the functions critical to selling and installing PBXs. This task, however, went far beyond the original scope of the project and could not be undertaken without the input of AT&T's executive committee. Fortunately, the other business units sharing the sales force were coming to the same conclusion.

Clean-Slate Redesign: March 1990–March 1991. The executive committee agreed to the autonomous sales force and turned to Pat Russo, a nine-year veteran of AT&T in a variety of sales and service roles, to build

continued

and run the new PBX sales force. With Russo on board, Hazard's redesign team set to work in earnest. One key target was minimizing the time between sale and final installation. The team cut the number of project hand-offs from 12 to 3 and created a new position, project manager, to oversee sales transactions from inception to completion. Sales and installation activities were integrated at the local branch level, and centralized sales support was greatly reduced. Finally, the team ran computer simulations of the effects of the redesigns on cost, cycle times, and error rates. The predictions were heartening: for a typical small system, cycle time would drop from three months to three weeks; total costs would drop by about one-third; and errors would approach zero.

The team then turned its attention to the organizational ramifications of the redesign. The radically different job responsibilities and skill redesigns posed an immense human-resource challenge. The staff would need training and job support to understand their new roles and the new emphasis on customers and profits. For example, before redesign, account executives focused on relationships rather than on technical expertise to sell their product. The redesign team created a program that taught account executives the required new skills, while at the same time convincing them that increased technical know-how would only make them better salespeople.

The team also began to modify technical systems to support the redesign. Using PCs and off-the-shelf software, existing systems were simplified, and new systems were designed to reduce cycle times and provide accurate profit estimating and tracking on each job. In September, Hazard and the team tested their work in a pilot program and got results strikingly similar to those they had forecasted.

To direct additional senior management attention to the new design, Bucter asked Barry Karafin, then head of R & D, to oversee the project on a full-time basis. Karafin turned his immediate attention to ensuring that all conditions necessary for successful implementation were in place.

continued

CASE STUDY *continued*

Reengineering Initiative

Rollout: April 1991–April 1992. As the pilot neared completion, Russo, Karafin, and Hazard faced another complication. Bucter, who had started and continuously supported the redesign effort, was transferred, and a new president, Jerre Stead, was brought in. What could have been a devastating setback became instead a vindication of the team's efforts. In fact, Stead was so impressed by the redesign project that he made it central to his program for the business. And with good cause: admittedly, as the business accumulates experience, some job descriptions have been changed and some hastily assembled IT systems refined, but all in all, the results of the redesign have been dramatic and extensive. Customer willingness to re-purchase has climbed from 53 percent to 82 percent; adjustments have dropped from 4 percent to 0.6 percent of revenues; bills paid within 30 days of installation increased from 31 percent to 71 percent; and 88 per-cent of customers rate the project management of their system sale and in-stallation as "excellent." Russo has also noted a new profit and customer focus. The process changes at GBCS are successfully producing an analo-gous change in corporate culture.

Reprinted by permission of Harvard Business Review. "How to Make Reengineering Really Work" by Gene Hall, Jim Rosenthal, and Judy Wade, November–December 1993. Copyright ©1993 by the President and Fellows of Harvard College. All rights reserved.

pare, thus lowering the shock. Managers must also recognize that many people will find a way to resist change.

WHY PEOPLE RESIST MAJOR WORKPLACE CHANGES

Attempts to implement such major workplace changes as reengi-neering, total quality management, and the shift to focused fac-

tories often meet with resistance. The customer service department in a telecommunications company was undergoing process
redesign. When asked by a consultant how the redesign would
affect her job, the representative replied: "I don't care what the
company does. I know my job and what I have to do. One week
after the redesign project starts, I'll be back dealing with customers the way I've always done."

Understanding the major reasons why people resist change
can help you formulate effective tactics for overcoming resistance. When people resist change, it is usually because they
think the change will do them more harm than good. Deliber-
ately or automatically, people formulate subjective hunches
about the effects of a particular change. If their subjective probability is high that the change will be beneficial, they are positively inclined toward the change. Conversely, if they calculate
that the odds of the change helping them are not in their favor,
they resist change.

The customer service representative mentioned above probably regarded process redesign as a grand inconvenience. In her
perception, she would now have to change her usual pattern of
processing customer service complaints. She doubted that her
customers would like her any better and thought it unlikely that
her pay would increase.

Here we look at seven key factors that account for most of
the reasons employees resist (or even obstruct) change. All have
relevance for the revamped workplace because such changes are
so far-reaching that they trigger anxiety in the people affected.

Financial Concerns

Money enters into the decision-making process of workers at all
levels. If the organization introduces a change that employees
think will provide them with more money, change is welcome.
If employees think that a work-related change will cost them
money, they are likely to resist that change. Many workers resist
process redesign because it poses the threat of an enormous fi-

nancial loss known as unemployment. Some managers resist a shift to total quality management because they have heard stories about TQM's being a substantial drain on profits. The pressure on profits can stem from investing so much time and money into conforming to quality standards and applying for a quality award.

Fear of the Unknown

People sometimes resist change simply because the outcome of the change is not entirely predictable. A manufacturing engineer informed that the company is shifting to the focused factory concept might ruminate: "What's going to happen to me and my job? If the company operates with smaller, lower-technology subfactories, where does that leave me? Will high-level manufacturing professionals still be in demand around here? Will my expertise be in demand, or will I be regarded as superfluous?"

Threats to Power and Influence

A potent reason why middle- and higher-level workers resist change is that they perceive it as a threat to their power and influence. All of the major innovations shift power toward teams and team leaders and away from middle managers. Middle manager positions are frequently consolidated, and in consequence some middle manager must scramble for another position within or outside the firm.

A related threat to power and influence is that workplace innovation can lead to less respect for hierarchy. Under process redesign, the people carrying the most prestige are often the information technology experts rather than managers. Another subtle shift in power is that the process manager becomes the new corporate superhero or superheroine. The executive back at headquarters is seen by some workers as less relevant to the new challenges facing the organization.

Difficulty in Breaking a Habit

Workplace innovations require people to change their established routines or habits. A habit is difficult to break because a series of responses are programmed in our brain. Recently, I was painfully reminded of the power of habits. I have been driving the same minivan for years for purposes such as supermarket shopping, hauling goods, and ski trips. The rear-end door originally lifted hydraulically to a height three inches above my head. As the minivan aged, the back door gradually shifted to a lower height when fully opened.

One evening, while loading the van in a supermarket parking lot, I crashed my forehead into the edge of the van. Sprawled on the ground, I wondered at first if I had been shot or hit with a rock. When my head cleared, I diagnosed the problem. My conditioned reflex (a simple habit) was to move my head forward at a height of approximately 71 inches while loading the van. But, unfortunately, the van door had sunk to a height of approximately 70 inches. My habit had conflicted with the change of a door height to one inch lower than I was used to. Habits, unfortunately, sometimes remain in place with no respect for logic.

When workplace innovations are introduced, many workers are forced to change entrenched habits. The longer the habit has been in place, the more people will resist changing their behavior. After downsizing in her company, the vice president of sales requested that sales representatives no longer return to the office on Friday afternoon to handle paperwork. With fewer

> **WHEN PEOPLE RESIST CHANGE,
> IT IS USUALLY BECAUSE THEY
> THINK THE CHANGE WILL DO
> THEM MORE HARM THAN GOOD.**

SEVEN KEY REASONS WHY WE RESIST MAJOR CHANGE

1. Financial concerns
2. Fear of the unknown
3. Erosion of power and influence
4. Old habits are hard to break
5. Inconvenience
6. Prior negative experience
7. Legitimate concerns about the change

---

salespeople, the vice president believed that the remaining sales force should spend more time in the field. She even eliminated the procedure that sales representatives complete a weekly call report summarizing all contacts with customers and prospects.

Four weeks after the Friday-afternoon-in-the-field edict had been invoked, the vice president found a sales rep in the office on a Friday afternoon. Asked what he was doing in the office, the sales representative replied, "I'm filling out my weekly call report. Friday afternoon is when we've always done it."

Personal Inconveniences

Most workplace innovations result in personal inconvenience of some kind for affected employees. A major inconvenience for many employees is to leave a functional department to become a member of an interdisciplinary team. Membership in a functional department can be a cozy arrangement. People of the same discipline are likely to respect the importance of your work and not challenge the value of your contribution.

Placed on an interdisciplinary team (such as a process team), it can be inconvenient to have to sell the worth of your contribution to other team members. Instead of warm acceptance, you may encounter blank stares. Even worse, other members of the team may have the audacity to sniff at your ideas.

A credit analyst assigned to a process team was attempting to explain that the interest rates on loans might be a bigger factor in making a decision to buy than the absence of defects. The other members of the team basically ignored his comments. Rather than submit to such cavalier rejection of his ideas, the analyst prepared carefully for the next meeting. He went to the inconvenience of searching a library database for a study supporting his contention that interest rates on loans have a major impact on purchasing decisions. Despite the empirical support he found for his ideas, the credit analyst still faced a lukewarm reception.

Negative Experience with Change

A person who had a negative experience with change in the past will resist change in the future. The previous experience can even trace back into childhood. For example, parents about to move to another town may have told a child that the geographic relocation would be a wonderful experience. In reality, the child felt lonely and friendless in the new location. Later in life, an executive tells that same person that she will enjoy relocation to another company division. Childhood memories predispose her to balk at being relocated.

Many employees resist the changes brought about by reengineering because of recent negative experiences. Process innovation consultant Thomas H. Davenport discovered that many employees at a major telecommunications firm viewed reengineering as another buzzword meaning job loss. The company had gone through four major change initiatives in seven years that led to major reductions in the work force. One manager observed, "Whenever our people hear the word 'reengineering,' they run for cover."[2]

Legitimate Concerns About Proposed Changes

Workers sometimes resist workplace innovations for meritorious reasons. They are aware of weaknesses in the proposed changes that may have been overlooked or disregarded by management.[3] An industrial products company was going through a redesign of its marketing process. The sales manager resisted the company's proposal to shift a key product to dealer distribution. She explained that dealers would give so little attention to the product that sales would plunge. Despite her protests, the firm shifted to dealer distribution. Sales of the product did indeed plummet and the company subsequently returned to direct selling.

Now that we have analyzed many of the reasons why people resist major workplace changes, it is time to describe strategies and tactics for overcoming this resistance. Without the cooperation of the people involved, change efforts have a dim chance of success.

METHODS OF GAINING COMMITMENT TO CHANGE

All successful workplace innovations, including downsizing the organization and setting up focused factories, require that workers—including managers—commit themselves to the necessary changes. The phrase *commitment to change* is stronger than *acceptance of change*. Management researcher Gary Yukl was the first to make this important distinction. According to his analysis, the success of an influence attempt can be defined by three anchor points on a continuum. Commitment indicates the highest degree of success, when the target of the influence attempt is enthusiastic about carrying out the request and makes a full effort. An example would be a person who responded to the process owner, "Yes, I'll do everything in my power to eliminate useless paperwork in our inventory control system."

Compliance, the midpoint on the continuum, means that the influence attempt is partially successful. Compliance is akin to acceptance. The target person is apathetic about carrying out the request and makes only a modest effort. In the example at hand, the person might record one or two glaring examples of useless paperwork. Resistance, the third point, is an unsuccessful influence attempt. The target is opposed to carrying out the request and either finds ways not to comply at all or does a poor job.[4]

We caution managers against naively assuming that because top management sponsors a major workplace innovation, the new system will take hold automatically. Any workplace innovation requires considerable influence attempts in the trenches before it takes hold. As a middle manager responded when asked how well total quality management was proceeding in her bank: "Oh, it was nice for awhile. We had a flurry of activity which maybe improved the quality of our service. But bit by bit we dropped the whole idea. It was too much of a bother."

Three process redesign consultants, Gene Hall, Jim Rosenthal, and Judy Wade, maintain that executives must overcome resistance and convince employees of the need for change. If ignored or improperly handled, political forces can wreck an otherwise successful redesign project. Several political problems can surround reengineering. The executive committee may not have fully accepted the new work design. Employees do not see the need for change at an emotional level, although intellectually they can point to deficiencies in the present system. Organizational rumors create stress, thus lowering productivity. Employees may feel powerless and confused about how their jobs will be modified. And, perhaps worst of all, valuable people, anticipating that they might be downsized, begin a job search.[5]

Here we describe seven methods for gaining commitment. Usually, several of them will have to be used simultaneously to facilitate the workplace innovation taking hold. To design a new system, such as reengineering, without overcoming resistance to change is to waste time and money.

Gain Political Support for Change

In practice, few workplace innovations get through firms without the change agent forming alliances with people who will support his or her proposals. Top management must buy into, and preferably sponsor, the program. Gaining political support often means selling the proposed changes to senior executives before proceeding down the hierarchy. It is much more difficult to create change from the bottom up.

Maintain Continuous Dialogue Between Top Management and the Innovation Teams

A robust method of gaining commitment to change is to establish regular communication between top management and the teams charged with designing and implementing the changes. Other workers who will be affected by the change should also be brought into the communications loop.

Sensitive issues, such as the number and type of reductions in staff that might result from the redesign, should be confronted. A reasonably honest evaluation of how many people may be let go in a redesign effort is helpful. A description of plans to soften the impact of the reductions through redeployment is particularly helpful.

The implementation of a total quality management system or focused factory may not pose major threats to job security. Nevertheless, any workplace innovation carries with it some con-

> **WORKERS SOMETIMES RESIST WORKPLACE INNOVATIONS FOR MERITORIOUS REASONS.**

cerns about job security. During a communication session between top management and operation workers about process redesign, one worker asked, "What happens to the people who
don't have the right skills to make up one of these new teams?
Will there be any old-fashioned jobs left for them in our company?"

Process innovation expert Davenport suggests that communication to the organization as a whole should start well in advance of implementation. After the business unit head has built
commitment among executives, he or she should communicate
with business unit members. The sponsor should make speeches
and hold meetings to prepare and rally workers for the upcoming changes.[6] Employees need reassurance that the new
system will benefit the organization.

Point Out the Financial Benefits

Because so many employees are concerned about the financial
consequences of work changes, it is helpful to discuss these
matters openly. Suppose, for example, that the firm was moving
toward becoming a virtual corporation for introducing new
products. Employees would welcome learning how these
strategic alliances might translate into higher employee earnings. If employees will earn more money as a result of the
change, this fact can be used as a selling point. Employees might
be shown data, in the example at hand, of how other companies who have entered into strategic alliances increased their
profits substantially. It would also be important to explain
how increases in company profits could add to worker compensation.

Place Adaptable People in Key Spots

An important action for the effective introduction of change is
to place the right people in jobs directly associated with the
change. The "right people" in this instance are those with a rep-

utation for being adaptable and flexible. People assigned to the process redesign teams are required to assume a clean-slate mentality. In the past, when an inside sales representative received an order, he or she would call the warehouse to see if the desired merchandise was in stock.

The sales rep must be flexible enough to think, "For the present, after receiving an order, I check with the warehouse. But tomorrow, the whole system might change. I might check product availability from a database. Or the customers might use their own PCs to check our inventories. I cannot assume that today's system is the only way to fill an order."

Allow for Participation

The best documented way of obtaining commitment to change is to allow people to participate in the changes that will affect them. Workplace innovations rely heavily on shared decision making and widespread participation, which is a force for gaining commitment. A good example is process mapping. The workers who handle basic tasks daily are given the opportunity to analyze how their output interacts with the work of others. Typically, workers are given the opportunity to make suggestions for simplifying procedures. A level of involvement of this type is far removed from having an outside consultant present a set of tight procedures for workers to follow.

Allow for Discussion and Negotiation

Resistance to change can be reduced by discussing and negotiating the more sensitive aspects of change. The fact that discussion is a form of participation contributes to its effectiveness. Discussion also often leads to negotiation, which further involves employees in the change process.

Assume that, as part of workplace innovation, the company is going to disband several departments in favor of forming process teams. Some of the functional specialists might be con-

SEVEN METHODS FOR GAINING COMMITMENT TO RADICAL CHANGE

1. Gain political support for change.
2. Maintain continuous dialogue between top management and the innovation teams.
3. Point out the financial benefits.
4. Place adaptable people in key spots.
5. Allow for participation.
6. Allow for discussion and negotiation.
7. Avoid change overload.

cerned about losing expertise because they will be forced to work as generalists. These highly skilled professionals might be reassured by being told that they will still have the chance to rotate through assignments that call for their professional expertise. Such an assurance is not a shallow promise because few organizations will abandon professional expertise as a consequence of reengineering. Sacrificing all professional expertise because functional departments have been dissolved is not desirable. Would you want to be a passenger on an airplane that was designed and manufactured by a group of multiskilled generalists?

Avoid Change Overload

Too much change in too short a time leads to negative stress. So it is helpful to avoid overloading employees with too many sweeping changes in a brief period of time. (This suggestion would appear to run counter to the sentiment expressed as "Let's make all our layoffs at once. This way we

won't have people sitting around worrying about who is next."
In this case, however, the stress from ambiguity is greater than
the stress from the change of having co-workers laid off.
Therefore, the sentiment is probably correct, and so is the suggestion.)

Too much simultaneous change also causes confusion, leading
to foot-dragging about the workplace innovation. The more far-
reaching the workplace innovation, the greater the reason for
not attempting other innovations at the same time. Assume that
an organization is just getting started with total quality management. Top management should wait until the new system has
been in place for about a year before announcing a program of
reengineering. After a year, reengineering can be introduced as
an extension of the process improvements that are part of total
quality management. Phasing in reengineering in this manner
will help to reduce the threat of major change. Shifting from one
major change effort to another can foster the attitude that top
management is pursuing fads.

FACILITATING CHANGE WITH VISION AND MISSION STATEMENTS

A strategic way of gaining acceptance for change is to inspire
people with uplifting statements about the firm's future and its
present purposes. As with most business buzzwords, *vision* and
mission carry several meanings.

> **FEW WORKPLACE INNOVATIONS GET THROUGH FIRMS WITHOUT THE CHANGE AGENT FORMING ALLIANCES WITH PEOPLE WHO WILL SUPPORT HIS OR HER PROPOSALS.**

A practical way of understanding a vision is to regard it as an exciting image of where the organization is headed and how to get there. A vision in relation to workplace innovations might describe a world-class process for handling customers' orders in which costs are at a minimum and customer satisfaction is at a maximum. The leader of the workplace innovation might talk in exalted terms about extraordinary cooperation among disciplines, a minimum of paperwork, and a streamlined organizational unit.

A mission is usually more precise than a vision because it defines the general field in which a firm or organizational unit will operate. The mission is also the unique purpose that sets a business, or organizational unit, apart from others of its type. A mission statement reflects the firm's or unit's character, and the contribution it intends to make. A process team, for example, might have the mission of developing new products that will gain substantial market shares of untapped markets.

In practice, vision statements and mission statements generally include similar information. Both statements provide a framework for directing activities and an indication of purpose. One consulting firm might help clients develop mission statements for process redesign, while another firm might work on vision statements. The output from both exercises is likely to read similarly. For example, the following statement might be regarded as a mission by some and a vision by others: "We will delight our customers with the highest quality, lowest cost fiber optic products and services in the world."

A problem with many vision and mission statements is that they are lofty, idealistic, and pontifical. As such, they fail to inspire or produce change. Another problem is that most mission and vision statements sound so much alike that they could have been bought off the shelf with only minor modification for a specific organization. Many vision and mission statements fail to inspire people to change because the statements are too all-encompassing. It is difficult for individuals and teams to identify with statements that are overly comprehensive. To illustrate, here is an excerpt from the mission statement of Shell Oil Company: "Our mission is to excel in three principal businesses— exploration and production, refining and marketing, and chemical."

Perhaps a few senior executives from Shell might be inspired by this lofty mission statement. Yet members of a process re-design team 18 levels down from the corporate office might perceive no direct link between what they are attempting to accomplish and the mission statement. In contrast, a clear and specific mission statement can function as a compass to guide people through problems that threaten to throw them off course.[7]

The mission statement of the team or teams involved in the workplace innovation should contain a specific goal, purpose, and philosophical tone. A quality-improvement team's mission might read: "To plan and implement new total quality approaches to enhance our quality image and bolster our competitive edge." A process redesign team's mission might read: "To radically redesign the customer order process so that customers will be delighted and our costs of serving them will be the lowest in the industry."

It is best to specify the mission when a team is first formed. Nevertheless, a mission can be formulated after the workplace innovation team has already undertaken its task. Developing a mission for an already-operating team breathes new life into its activities. Being committed to a mission improves teamwork, as

---

SHIFTING FROM ONE MAJOR CHANGE EFFORT TO ANOTHER CAN FOSTER THE ATTITUDE THAT TOP MANAGEMENT IS PURSUING FADS.

does the process of formulating a vision. The dialogue necessary for developing a clearly articulated mission establishes a climate in which team members can express feelings, ideas, and opinions. Participative leadership is required in developing a mission because all team members should feel they have an active role in structuring the team.

Revamping the workplace often involves formulating a process or reengineering vision. (Note that this is not the same as the corporate vision.) An important guideline is to make the process vision easy to communicate to the organization. The vision should be nonthreatening to those who must implement, or are affected by, the process changes. Creating a nonthreatening process vision is a challenge because process redesign is inherently upsetting. Process redesign can result in the disruption of comfortable working relationships among employees, and in job losses. Because employees work more efficiently after job redesign, there may also be less need for overtime. Less need for overtime translates into less total compensation for many employees.

A process vision should not include a statement such as "maximizing output with a minimum number of people." Nor should it refer to "eliminating functional silos, " or "ending departmental handoffs." Despite the era of reengineering, organizational functions still serve many useful purposes such as performing creative and highly specialized work.

The process vision should also be as inspirational as measurable targets allow. A quantifiable target such as "world-class producer in the industry" would be inspirational because so many people are rank-conscious. Another measurable target included in a process vision or mission statement might be "Achieve a 100 percent return on investment for the corporation."

The criteria just specified for a process vision make a headcount reduction objective unsatisfactory. The term *headcount reduction* has a sonorous ring to an outside stock analyst. Most stock analysts believe that a profit increase is almost guaranteed after a layoff, and that profits will continue to increase in direct proportion to further headcount reductions. A term such as *operating efficiencies* in a vision or mission statement is preferable to the more threatening *headcount reduction*.

When cost reduction is the ultimate objective, it should be included with other intermediate objectives such as reduction in cycle time and quality improvement. These intermediate objectives might also generate cost improvements. Thomas Davenport has observed that when cost reduction is the stated rationale for a process innovation program, many workers are reluctant to participate in or cooperate with the program.[8]

Firms that include such objectives as improving quality, better work life, more employee learning, and time reduction often achieve cost reduction as well. Process redesigns that establish cost-reduction targets almost exclusively may fail to reduce costs. A blatant statement about cost reduction may lead some employees to resist the redesign program for fear of job loss or reductions in compensation.

A confusion point is that often both the larger organization and the team responsible for a workplace innovation have individual visions and missions. Adding to the confusion, the organizational and subunit statements might have elements in common. Although organizational and team vision and mission statements may overlap, those established for the team are more likely to precipitate change. Many workers feel too far removed from corporate vision statements for these to serve as motivating forces for change.

BUILDING A TEAM MISSION STATEMENT

The guidelines for designing team mission statements as developed by the OSD Consulting Group, specialists in reengineering, are described next. The clarity of this approach to formulating mission statements has contributed to its success. Here we emphasize developing a mission statement for a process redesign team. The same approach, however, can also be used to design an organizational mission statement.

Step 1

Clarify customer requirements. Among the requirements would be shorter delivery times, lower cost, higher quality, and customized features. Customer requirements are sometimes surprising. A commercial printer was going through process redesign for the preparation of gift catalogs. The process team assumed that customers wanted higher quality in terms of more opulent-looking color tones and sharper photographs.

In-depth discussions with two major customers revealed that the perceived quality of the catalogs was fine. The ultimate users never complained about color tones or the sharpness of photographs. A major quality-related issue for the catalog sales companies was minimizing errors in price and ordering information. Even more important was getting the catalog shipped in time for whichever season it was intended.

Step 2

List the team's distinctive competencies. For example, "Our team has the best record in the company for bringing back customers who have not done business with us for five or more years." The comparison groups on which to base such competencies can be the company, a division of the company, the

> THE MISSION STATEMENT OF THE TEAM INVOLVED IN THE WORKPLACE INNOVATIONS SHOULD CONTAIN A SPECIFIC GOAL, PURPOSE, AND PHILOSOPHICAL TONE.

industry, the city, the state or province, or the country. If the team leader makes the category small enough, any team can compare favorably to others, thus identifying a distinctive competency.

A 30-minute brainstorming session will usually suffice to identify the team's comparative advantage. Such internal analysis can be supplemented by asking a few internal and external customers what they think are the team's distinctive competencies.

The team leader is instrumental in convincing the group that it performs some function better than others doing comparable work. If the group is truly a world-class player in performing its process or function, pride follows naturally. Being a world-class player, however, is usually an unrealistically high standard to attain. A more realistic tactic is to identify a specific activity that the team does better than other groups.[9] Among these comparative advantages are higher output per worker, lower turnover, more creative ideas per year, lower operating costs, or stronger ethics.

A process team in a package-delivery company, for example, identified these distinctive competencies:

- Almost never mislabel a package.
- Specialists in transporting scientific instruments and medical products where delicate handling is required.
- Extraordinary reliability in never damaging a package.
- Superb tracking system for locating the status of a package.
- Virtually never receive complaints about billing mistakes.

Step 3

Have each individual write a mission statement that meets the criteria for a good mission statement. According to the OSD Consulting Group, an effective mission statement meets the following criteria: (a) it provides energy, excitement, and attraction, (b) it is simple; (c) it is concise; and (d) it is easily remembered. A mortgage lending group within First National Bank developed this mission statement: "We will completely process a mortgage application within 21 working days, including notifying the mortgage applicant of our decision. We will give each rejected applicant a thorough explanation of why we decided not to lend him or her the money."

Step 4

Underline the key words in each mission statement. When mission statements are brief, almost all words except for prepositions and conjunctions are key words.

Step 5

Create and reach consensus on a mission statement. The various mission statements submitted by team members can be placed on flip charts. If the process is done electronically, the statements are entered into computers and can be observed simultaneously by team members.

Steps 3 and 5 can be combined by the team working collectively to hammer out a mission statement. The quality of these group-prepared mission statements tends to be high when the assignment is tightly structured. Contrary to widespread practice, the preparation of mission statements does not require several lengthy retreats. Three hours is ample time complete the mission statement after data about customer requirements have been collected. Some groups can produce a mission statement within 30 minutes that compare favorably to the mission statements that some executive work on for a year. (Could it be that the process of developing mission statements in many organizations is a prime candidate for process redesign?)

If team members identify with the mission statement they have developed, it will become a motivating force for keeping them moving toward constructive change. The assumption is that freshly prepared mission statements have an uplifting quality and point toward a new standard of excellence. A case in point is the mission statement prepared by the customer service manager at an educational foundation. The foundation has a typical lofty mission: "To increase and diffuse knowledge." The customer service staff had a difficult time seeing how that broad mission statement applied to their activities of fielding calls from customers who wanted to receive or return a product.

The customer service manager developed a mission statement with her staff: "Our division helps customers get what they deserve from the foundation." In the manager's opinion, this mission helps them get through the day: "Whenever we find ourself wondering 'what does this customer want from us?' we read the mission statement. The statement serves a reminder as to why we are here. It encourages us to take a proactive role with customers. We cannot diffuse knowledge for telephone callers, but we are able to help them get what they deserve."[10]

THE TEAM LEADER AS CHANGE AGENT

The major innovations of today rely heavily on team leaders to facilitate change. Team leaders are expected to encourage team members when progress toward an improvement goal gets bogged down. The team leader has to remind other members frequently that theirs is an important mission; that without the team's contribution, the organization cannot move to a higher plane.

Process teams, quality-improvement teams, and other teams in the revamped workplace are organized so that expertise is diffused among their members. Team members share skills and perform multiple tasks. Because of this arrangement, there is less need for a leader whose technical competence far exceeds that of team members. Nevertheless, a role still exists for the team leader to precipitate change by presenting information to the group that points to the necessity for change.

The leader of a process redesign team in a pharmaceutical firm brought information into a meeting that dramatized the importance of speed-to-market. A major purpose of process re-design in this instance was to shorten the cycle time for getting drugs to market. The team leader presented facts about the success of the pharmaceutical firm Schering-Plough in introducing an anti-yeast infection drug to market. The firm was able to dominate a new $400 million over-the-counter market by narrowly beating a competitive drug to the market place. As the team mulled over the details of Schering-Plough's success they experienced a new sense of urgency about the importance of reducing cycle time for getting a drug to market. The team leader's message had hit home.

The team leader plays an important liaison and spokesperson role throughout the organization in championing the cause of the team. People from outside the team may ask, directly or indirectly, "What are you folks really up to?" This is especially true when the team is involved with process redesign. Another question frequently asked is "Is your assignment really to eliminate as many jobs as possible?"

The change effort will gain greater support throughout the organization if the team leader can paint a positive, but honest, picture of what the team is doing. An effective response to questions about job reduction might be "We're trying to help the company get work accomplished in a radically easier way. At times a few people will be redeployed to other jobs where they are more urgently needed. But it's not the team's job to make decisions about headcount. We are trying to streamline and simplify work. By so doing we want to improve productivity and quality."

THE BIGGEST CHALLENGE OF ALL: BRINGING ABOUT CULTURAL CHANGE

To many executives, researchers, and management consultants the biggest challenge in implementing workplace innovations is to bring about cultural change. Establishing flashy new systems and structures can start an organization moving in a positive direction. But for changes to be sustained, the organizational culture must change. Workers' attitudes and values have to alter if the spirit of innovation is to keep smoldering.

The major attitude shift required by process innovation is that standard approaches to work should be challenged. Furthermore, people must believe that new and better ways can be found to accomplish work. The cultural climate for reengineer-ing and quality improvement should focus strongly on the improvement of business operations.[11] An even more penetrating shift in attitude is that people must learn to question whether the work they are performing really makes a contribution.

Cultural shifts are also important for total quality management to enhance organizational effectiveness. No matter how thorough the TQM training may be in areas such as problem solving and statistical process control, quality improvement demands changes in attitude. CEOs and human resources professionals at Fortune 500 companies were surveyed on their perceptions of service quality in American service businesses. The authors of the survey concluded that employees and management must change their thinking before service can improve. A lack of concern among workers and inattention of managers were perceived by company officials to be the biggest obstacles to improving service quality.

Almost half of the executives surveyed believed that worker attitudes and managerial attention to quality must be changed to make substantial improvements in service quality. One of the CEOs said: "Too much lip service has been given to quality from all levels within companies. Inspired leadership and commitment from management must be coupled with a well-adjusted work force that is trained and empowered to deliver quality service."[12]

What kind of cultural values create the right environment for workplace innovations to take hold? Most of these values are

VISION AND MISSION STATEMENTS FOR REENGINEERING TEAMS

Vision Statements
1. To become a team that achieves a 100 percent return on investment to the corporation.
2. To become a world-class core process team in terms of developing new products in consumer electronics.
3. To develop an order fulfillment process that requires 90 percent fewer staff members than the industry standard.

Mission Statements
1. To plan and implement new total quality approaches to enhance our quality image and bolster our competitive edge.
2. To radically redesign the customer order process so that customers will be delighted and our costs of serving them will be the lowest in the industry.
3. We will completely process a mortgage application within 21 working days, including notifying the mortgage applicant of our decision. We will give each rejected applicant a thorough explanation of why we decided not to lend him or her the money.
4. Our division helps customers get what they deserve from the foundation.

similar to those that have always contributed to organizational effectiveness and greatness. Workers involved in the changes must place a high value on speed, simplicity, quality, and innovation. A belief in continuous improvement is synonymous with total quality management. For the virtual corporation to be able to work effectively, key people must develop the values that sharing resources is good and that other companies can be trusted.

How organizational cultures can be changed is a key aspect of a field of study called *organization development*. It is worth describing here several features from a practical road map for developing an organization's culture.[13] Development can also be regarded as change because the culture moves from one type to another. The road map or framework is referred to as HOME, an acronym derived from the initial letters of *history*, *oneness*, *membership*, and *exchange*.

History

Growing a new culture begins with the development of a sense of history. The history of innovation can be communicated by stories about extraordinary feats of improvement in methods, such as how the processing time for credit applications at IBM was reduced from weeks to days. Core values such as a belief in superior customer service and values can be communicated and institutionalized through recruitment brochures. Orientation programs and courses for people already on the payroll can disseminate a sense of history.

Trainers can be supplied with entertaining anecdotes about the origins of a workplace innovation. A story might be presented about how a strategic alliance began over a business luncheon with the two partners drawing sketches on restaurant napkins. When John Scully was at Apple Computer Corporation, several of his strategic alliances with international companies began in precisely this way.

Organizational heroes and heroines can be identified and requested to present their sense of history to other workers through newsletters, electronic mail, and videotapes. Personal sonal testimonies about workplace innovations create good legends.

> # THE BIGGEST CHALLENGE IN IMPLEMENTING WORKPLACE INNOVATIONS IS TO BRING ABOUT CULTURAL CHANGE.

A manager might tell a story about how work streamlining began in her division when 10 people quit simultaneously. the company was unable to replace so many people in a hurry. So the staff members who remained quickly analyzed which work activities could be spared without sacrificing useful output. To the department's delight, 20 people were not performing the work that 30 people did in the past. Work streamlining was so successful that the group was not working longer hours.

Oneness

Leadership plays a key role in creating a sense of oneness or belonging. Workers notice the practices, attitudes, philosophies, and example-setting of top management, and gear their behaviors to be compatible. If top management can get by with a trimmed-down support staff, lower-ranking managers are less likely to attempt to pad their own staffs. In contract, when senior managers each have two personal assistants, lower-ranking managers become less concerned about reducing support staff to a minimum. Conducting oneself in a similar manner to top management expresses feelings of belonging to the organization.

A powerful method for changing the organizational culture is for top management to serve as role models for the desired attitudes and behavior. Leaders must behave in ways that are consistent with the values and practices they wish to see imitated throughout the organization. Few people would argue with the axiom just stated. Yet being an appropriate role model for workplace innovations is not always easy. The leader has to be alert to opportunities for being a role model. It is especially important for word and deed to correspond. Assume that you are spearheading a redesign effort that involves minimizing the flow of paperwork. Given a choice, you should communicate electronically rather than through paper memos.

Membership

A sense of membership in the organization is promoted through many human resources management systems. These systems help develop a new culture by reinforcing the values that are appropriate to it. A prime example is that of setting up reward systems within an organization. Properly designed and administered, reward systems provide unequivocal guidelines to organizational values and norms. A firm determined to reengineer might give generous salary increases and more responsibility to people who display knowledge of process management. Similarly, process managers might be given as much public recognition as vice presidents.

Career management is another system that promotes membership. Workers whose behavior reflects a commitment to the new culture can receive the higher, more visible positions. At an office products company, one financial manager promoted total quality management in accounting and finance. He took the initiative to read articles and books and attend seminars about how TQM could be applied to financial services. Another financial manager shrugged off the potential application of total quality management to finance and accounting. Fortunately for the first manager, and unfortunately for the second, the CEO was obsessed with total quality management. The first manager received a promotion to chief financial officer.

Recruiting and staffing of new organizational members can also be done to help change the culture in a direction that supports workplace innovations. Should top management want to shape a lean and mean culture, they are best advised to hire newcomers with a track record of creating a trimmed-down organization. Executive recruiters are typically asked to find new executives whose values and behaviors fit the culture the firm is attempting to promote.

A headhunter based in New York City was given this job specification for a human resources vice president to work at a consumer products company: "Make sure the man or woman you find has proven ability to show us how to run with a skeleton staff."

Training and development programs are gaining acceptance as a vehicle for helping to change organizational culture. One example is the popularity of executive lead-ins. An executive helps kick off the training program by affirming its value and explaining how the program supports the new culture. At a training program about the focused factory an executive might explain how these new structures fit the company's new flexibility and responsiveness.

Exchange

When organizational members exchange ideas, the opportunity increases for cohesiveness and shared values. Formal arrangements such as regularly scheduled staff meetings facilitate exchanging ideas, reflecting on values, and learning what behavior is in versus out. Encouraging informal meetings can often achieve the same purpose with a higher degree of effectiveness. If staffers talk in the halls and in lounges about how the company is deemphasizing departments and functions, a process culture can really take hold.

Participatory decision making is a natural vehicle for promoting the exchange of ideas and information. Each instance of shared decision making promotes an integration of cultural values. Assume that team members get into a huddle about process redesign. They are much more likely to incorporate values about process redesign than if their only role is to implement a program handed down from higher management.

A Checklist for Implementing Radical Change

The checklist that follows summarizes key ideas for shifting smoothly from a traditional to a substantially revamped work system. Regard each item on the checklist as a call for action.

☑ Implementing change is likely to be a continuous process because major workplace innovations often take five years for completion.

☑ Major workplace changes are likely to encounter resistance, and you must be prepared to deal with this resistance. Workers generally resist changes that seem to have more negative than positive consequences.

☑ A strategic way of gaining acceptance for change is to inspire people with uplifting statements about the firm's future and its present purposes.

☑ A robust method of gaining commitment to change is to establish regular communication between top management and the team charged with designing and implementing the changes.

☑ The best documented way of obtaining commitment to change is to allow people to participate in the changes that will affect them.

☑ Workers involved in major workplace changes must place a value on speed, simplicity, quality, and innovation.

☑ A powerful method for changing the organizational culture is for top management to serve as role models for the appropriate attitudes and behavior.

5

The New Leadership and Managerial Roles

*A*n oft-repeated concern among first- and middle-level managers whose organizations are being revamped is "Where do I fit in? What happens to my job as we empower people, create team leaders, and thin out the hierarchy? In what ways will my role change?"

The answers to these questions are complex. Managers who are part of a revamped workplace often shift jobs. Some middle managers become first-level managers with more authority than the traditional supervisor. Other first-level managers become team leaders. Some first-level and middle-level managers shift into individual contributor positions. Other middle managers become process managers or case managers. Many managers who are squeezed out of larger firms join smaller firms; other become self-employed. Some managers return to school to upgrade their skills to meet the demands of today's job market.

A more complicated issue than job changes, however, is understanding the shift in the roles of managers and leaders in the revamped workplace. First, we must differentiate between the terms *leader* and *manager*. A clue is provided from the standard view of the concepts of management functions: planning, organizing, directing (or leading), and controlling. Leading is a major part of a manager's job, yet a manager must also plan, organize, and control.

Leadership deals with the interpersonal aspects of a manager's job. Planning, organizing, and controlling deal with the administrative aspects. Current thinking reflects the idea that leadership deals with change, inspiration, motivation, and influence. In contrast, management deals more with maintaining equilibrium and the status quo.

Leadership is of paramount importance in the revamped workplace. But so is management. If they are not backed by careful organizing, planning, and controlling, such initiatives as reengineering, total quality management, and the focus factory will fail. Managers must be leaders, but leaders must also be good managers. Employees need to be inspired and persuaded, but they also need assistance in developing a smoothly functioning workplace. A lot of managing, for example, is required to help process teams carry out their varied tasks. The person in charge must create visions *and* help implement them.

The broadest change in the revamped workplace is that the new leaders and managers are changing their emphasis. In the past many managers emphasized control over people and work processes. Today, support and facilitation receive more emphasis. The new manager and leader, particularly at the first two levels of management, emphasize coaching and facilitation.

The shift in managerial and leadership emphasis has been less pronounced for executives. Although they may sponsor such workplace initiatives as process redesign and quality management, most executives are removed from implementation. For example, the marketing executive may champion a redesign of the order-fulfillment process. Yet she does not have to work directly with customer-service representatives to help empower them to solve problems. The CEO of a company going through reengineering is more likely to be found making a presentation to stock analysts than encouraging a process team to overcome a work-flow problem. An exception is when a senior executive becomes a process champion.

The new leadership and managerial roles described here give cause for optimism. They are part of a shift in the nature of leadership and management that has been taking place for at least a decade. Managers and leaders are making better use of their talent and interpersonal skills than of formal authority to help teams accomplish their goals. Yet hierarchical organizations are unlikely to disappear any time soon despite many predictions of this nature. Furthermore, a workplace can be revamped within the framework of a well-managed bureaucracy.

FOUR DESIRABLE LEADERSHIP STYLES

A participative and coaching style of leadership is best suited to help manage team-based workplace innovations. A more autocratic leader is generally less well suited to bringing out the best in teams. Yet there are times when an autocratic leadership style is effective because the leader's expertise in decision making is essential. In addition, a decisive leader may be required when a short cycle time is at a premium. The autocratic leader's chances of fitting well into a team increase when he or she is a good coach.

Four styles of leadership—I describe them as transformational, coaching, "SuperLeadership," and entrepreneurial—are especially relevant in the revamped workplace. Transformational leaders are required to help bring about major changes. Coaches are needed to bring out the best in team members. SuperLeaders can help team members become self-reliant. To add to the mix, the leader who fits the revamped workplace should have an entrepreneurial mentality.

> **THE AUTOCRATIC LEADER'S CHANCES OF FITTING WELL INTO A TEAM INCREASE WHEN HE OR SHE IS A GOOD COACH.**

Transformational Leadership Style

Major workplace innovations such as reengineering, total quality management, and virtual corporations encompass sweeping changes. A high-ranking leader has to point the way toward changes that will benefit the organization's members in the long run. The transformational leader establishes a vision of how great the firm will be once the changes are complete. The leader paving the path toward reengineering might explain how powerful and efficient the firm will become after its work processes are overhauled. Transformational leaders typically possess charisma which helps them attract people who want to participate in their vision. A transformational leader offers an exciting vision of where the organization is headed and how the workplace innovation will get them there.

When George Fisher was the CEO at Motorola, he inspired many people to identify with his vision of Motorola's becoming a world-class manufacturer of high-quality electronic products. Other members of the three-person Motorola executive team were also regarded as highly charismatic.

To inspire people, the transformational or charismatic leader uses colorful language and exciting metaphors and analogies. To describe the virtual corporation, a leader might talk about a "boundary-less" firm in which our capabilities will multiply geometrically as we pool resources with an ever-increasing supply of talented people." Language that points to job loss is uninspiring. When an executive who was spearheading a reengineering pilot project in the purchasing division of an automotive supplier said, "Imagine a purchasing organization being twice as productive with one-tenth the personnel," we suspect that he did not excite people in purchasing who thought they might lose their jobs.

A transformational leader must also inspire trust. A past record of honesty, a convincing plan, or a sincere facial expression (or a combination of all three) lead to trust. Workers throughout the organization believe so strongly in the integrity of charismatic leaders that they will risk their careers to pursue the chief's vision. An unethical charismatic leader can abuse this trust by misleading people. Many people trusted Frank Lorenzo to transform the several airlines over which he gained control. He made optimistic promises of improved financial performances. Lorenzo did bring about downsizing, but, unfortunately, downsizing included selling off valuable assets and declaring bankruptcy. Lorenzo walked away from the bankrupt Eastern Airlines with $30 million in compensation. Eastern Airline's employees lost their jobs, and many of Eastern's creditors were left with worthless accounts receivables.

An important skill in a transformational leader is to help group members feel capable and self-confident. A way of putting this aspect of transformational leadership into effect is by enabling people to succeed in relatively easy tasks. You then praise them for their accomplishments and move them to a more difficult project. If you were initiating a reengineering project, you might ask people to begin by identifying the most useless, time-consuming activity in their department. With encouragement, most people can identify at lease one wasted activity in their work area. After success on this task, they might move on to process mapping. The initial success makes the next task seem less formidable.

Another distinguishing feature of the transformational leadership style is an energy and action orientation. Like entrepreneurs, transformational leaders are energetic and serve as models for getting things done on time. A sense of urgency facilitates transformations because they usually require getting more work accomplished in less time. An important component of quality management, for example, is to reduce cycle times. Process redesign also emphasizes speed in task accomplishment. A bank department that ordinarily requires 15 days to process a business loan might be asked to reduce the time to 2 days.

> **WORKERS THROUGHOUT THE
> ORGANIZATION BELIEVE SO STRONGLY IN
> THE INTEGRITY OF CHARISMATIC LEADERS
> THAT THEY WILL RISK THEIR CAREERS TO
> PURSUE THE CHIEF'S VISION.**

Reengineering is designed to be a smooth and efficient process. Beating down cycle times, however, can leave team members feeling as if they are being rushed.

A human touch contributes to effective transformational leadership. A key characteristic of transformational leaders who are also charismatic is their ability to express feelings openly. A bank vice president claims that much of the charisma people attribute to her can be explained simply: "I'm up front about expressing positive feelings. I praise people. I hug them, and I cheer if necessary. I also express my negative feelings, but to a lesser degree." Nonverbal emotional expressiveness, such as warm gestures and frequent handshaking of group members, is also characteristic of charismatic leaders.

Transformational leaders are typically risk takers, and risk taking adds to their appeal. The willingness to undertake a profound workplace transformation is a very big risk. Creating a horizontal organization is a prime example of such a risk because it changes the whole way people think about their work.

Imagine that your firm has been successfully manufacturing executive planners for 30 years. As a newly hired manager, your job is to revamp the production of these planners to create more models in a shorter period of time. You decide that the way to achieve your goals is by creating a horizontal organization. You now propose several substantial changes. You must yank people out of their comfortable functional departments, reconfigure the manufacturing area, and teach people to become multiskilled generalists.

If any one of the major changes you make creates confusion and chaos, the horizontal organization will backfire. Because you spearheaded those changes, you become the newly hired corporate goat. You may have to start packing. Despite the possibility of such a gloomy scenario, the transformational leader is willing to take the risk. No transformations, no breakthroughs, no heroics are possible without taking risks.

Coaching Leadership Style

The team structure of the new workplace elevates the importance of coaching. As a coach, the manager and leader makes on-the-spot suggestions for performance improvement and encourages team members frequently. The coach also blows the whistle when a team member makes a bad move, and offers suggestions for improvement. Coaching is valuable because it provides a human touch to workplace innovations. Downsizing and reengineering in particular are often perceived as mechanistic and unfeeling. Here we look at some straightforward suggestions to improve your coaching skills.

An effective coach *provides specific feedback*. To coach a team member toward higher levels of performance, pinpoint what behavior, attitude, or skill requires improvement. A good coach might say, "I read the product-line expansion proposal you submitted. It's OK, but it falls short of your usual level of creativity. Each product you mention is already carried by competitors. Have you thought about . . . ?"

Active listening is an essential ingredient in any coaching session. An active listener tries to grasp both the facts of what is said and the feelings behind the words. Observing the group member's nonverbal communication is another part of active lis-

> THE TEAM STRUCTURE OF
> THE NEW WORKPLACE ELEVATES THE
> IMPORTANCE OF COACHING.

tening. The manager must also be patient and not poised for a rebuttal to any difference of opinion between him or her and the team member.

Part of being a good listener is encouraging the person being coached to talk about his or her performance. Asking open-ended questions facilitates a flow of conversation. For example, ask: "How did you feel about the thoroughness of your analysis of the British company's financial stability?" A close-ended question covering the same issue would be: "Do you think you could have done a better job of analyzing the British company's financial stability?" Notice that the team member can readily respond Yes or No to the second question, which allows little room for talking about performance improvement.

Giving emotional support is the linchpin of a coach's job. By being helpful and constructive, the leader provides much-needed emotional support to a team member who is not performing at his or her best. A coaching session should not be an interrogation. An effective way of giving emotional support is to use positive rather than negative motivators. For example, the leader might say, "I liked some things you did yesterday. Yet I have a few suggestions that might bring you closer to peak performance."

Emotional support can be instrumental in helping team members cope with some of the demands placed on them in striving to meet stringent quality targets. A materials-handling specialist might say, "We are trying to reduce damaged shipments down to one box in 10,000. That goal seems impossible. We pack the boxes the best we can. I don't know how we can do any better." A coaching-style manager might respond: "I know you've made great strides. But with a little more investigation of the nature of the breakage, I think you can do even better. As soon as you are ready, let's talk about your investigation of packing defect."

Downsizing is another workplace change that can generate the need for coaching. As a consequence of reductions in force, many workers feel overworked and overwhelmed in addition to worrying about further job cuts. A team member might say to the team leader, "I just don't know how I can keep up with this workload. It's like the company dumps a large wastebasket of new work for me to process every morning. I never get my backlog down to zero. I fall further behind every day."

To bolster the overwhelmed worker emotionally, the coaching-style manager might respond: "You're right, the work is really piling up. And I appreciate how hard you are working. Keep slashing away and you'll soon see a light at the end of the tunnel. Maybe we can look for work you are doing that could be eliminated. That would help to make your load more manageable."

As several of the examples have shown, a good coach is adept at *reflecting feelings*. Reflection-of-feeling responses typically begin with "You feel . . ." Suppose the manager asks an inventory-control technician why a report is late. She answers: "Those clods in manufacturing held me up again." The manager responds: "Your feel angry with manufacturing."

The inventory control technician, now feeling encouraged, might vent her anger about manufacturing. The manager's reflection of feelings communicates the fact that he or she understands the real problem. Because the technician feels understood, she might be better motivated to improve.

A related coaching technique is to *reflect content or meaning*. Reflecting feelings deals with the emotional aspects of someone's personality. Reflecting content or meaning deals with the intellectual or cognitive aspects of a personality. An effective way of reflecting meaning is to rephrase and summarize concisely what the group member is saying. A substandard performer might say: "The reason that I've fallen so far behind is that our company has turned into a bureaucratic nightmare. We're being hit left and right with forms to complete for quality improvement. My electronic mail has 25 messages waiting to be read."

You might respond: "You're falling so far behind because you have so many forms and messages that require attention." The team member might then respond: "That's exactly what I mean. I'm glad you understand my problem."

An effective coach *gives some constructive advice.* Too much advice-giving interferes with two-way communication, yet some advice can elevate performance. The manager should assist the group member to answer the question, "What can I do about this problem?"[1] Advice in the form of a question or suppositional statement is often effective. One example is "Could the root of your problem be insufficient planning?" A direct statement such as "Obviously, the root of your problem is insufficient planning" is likely to make people resentful and defensive. By responding to a question, the person being coached is likely to feel more involved in making improvements.

Another effective coaching technique is to *show the group member by example what constitutes the desired behavior.* Assume that a customer service representative has been making statements to customers that stretch the truth. One of his truth-stretchers is that the product meets a zero defects standard. In coaching him the manager might allow the service representative to observe how she handles a similar situation with a customer. The manager might telephone a customer and say, "You have been inquiring about whether we have a zero defects standard for our laser printers. Right now we are doing our best to produce error-free products, yet so far we do not have a formal zero defects program. But we stand by our printers and will fix any defect at no cost to you."

Gaining a commitment to change is also an important part of coaching. Unless the manager receives a commitment from the team member to carry through with the proposed solution to a problem, the member may not improve performance. An experienced manager-coach develops an intuitive "feel" for when employees are serious about improving their performance. One clue that commitment to change is lacking is overagreeing about the need for change. Another is agreeing to change without a display of emotion.

Suppose that as part of a process redesign the team agrees to stop writing confirmation letters about orders. (The new procedure saves time by electronically transmitting confirmation orders on standard forms stored in the computer.) Yet one of the inside sales representatives continues to slow down the process by mailing out confirmation letters. You coach the representative about the problem. At the end of the session she says, "Oh yeah, sure," with a disinterested expression. You will probably have to monitor her performance closely because she is not yet committed to the change.

Do the exercise presented in Figure 5-1 to evaluate your own facility in coaching group members. The exercise also gives you an opportunity to plan your personal development as a coach.

SuperLeadership Style

In a team-based organization self-sufficiency and self-management are emphasized and direct supervision is de-emphasized. Although inspirational leadership may still be in order, the ideal situation is that team members manage their own work. A new way of viewing the leader's role in promoting self-sufficiency is called SuperLeadership.

In a nutshell, a SuperLeader is a manager who leads others to lead themselves.[2] When people are self-directing they require a minimum of external control. A SuperLeader prompts others to lead themselves by acting as a teacher and a coach, not a director. The SuperLeader inspires others to motivate themselves. A charismatic leader, in contrast, maintains a high profile indefinitely.

The key aspect of SuperLeadership deals with teaching the right thought patterns. Charles C. Manz and Henry P. Sims, Jr., the formulators of the SuperLeadership theory, explain that the leader must teach team members how to think constructively.[3]

FIGURE 5-1

Characteristics of an Effective Coach[4]

DIRECTIONS: Below is a list of traits, attitudes, and behaviors characteristic of effective coaches. Indicate next to each trait, attitude, or behavior whether you need to improve (such as the need to become more patient). Then prepare an action plan for improving each trait, attitude, or behavior that you need to develop.

TRAIT, ATTITUDE, OR BEHAVIOR	ACTION PLAN FOR IMPROVEMENT
1. Empathy (putting self in other person's shoes)	*Sample:* Will listen until I understand person's point of view. *Your own:*
2. Listening skill	*Sample:* Will concentrate extra-hard on listening. *Your own:*
3. Insight into people (ability to size them up)	*Sample:* Will jot down observations about people upon first meeting, then verify in the future. *Your own:*
4. Diplomacy and tact	*Sample:* Will study book of etiquette. *Your own:*
5. Patience toward people	*Sample:* Will practice staying calm when someone makes a mistake. *Your own:*
6. Concern for welfare of people	*Sample:* When interacting with another person, will ask myself, "How can this person's interests best be served?" *Your own:*
7. Minimum hostility toward people	*Sample:* Will often ask myself, "Why am I angry at this person?" *Your own:*
8. Self-confidence and emotional	*Sample:* Will attempt to have at least one personal success each week. *Your own:*
9. Noncompetitiveness with team members	*Sample:* Will keep reminding myself that all boats rise with the same tide. *Your own:*
10. Enthusiasm for people	*Sample:* Will search for the good in each person. *Your own:*

Adapted with permission from Leadership Systems Corporation. Copyright ©1985. All rights reserved.

The purpose of constructive (or productive) thinking is to enable workers to gain control over their behavior. The SuperLeader serves as a model of constructive thought patterns. For example, the leader should minimize expressing pessimistic, self-critical thoughts to team members. Instead, he or she should reward employees when they think constructively.

Several methods of establishing and altering thought patterns have been developed and are discussed here. These methods are well worth your consideration both for purposes of self-development and for developing a high-performing team.

The first step is to identify destructive beliefs and assumptions. After identifying these negative thoughts, replace them with more accurate and constructive ones. For example, a team member might regard the manager's criticisms as an indicator of personal dislike. A more productive thought is that the manager is just trying to help him or her perform at a higher level. Another destructive belief and assumption is that if a worker discovers how to make a work process more efficient, his or her job will be eliminated. More efficient work methods admittedly can lead to layoffs. Yet a worker who has problem-solving ability keen enough to simplify work is likely to be perceived as extremely valuable. A more constructive thought for the worker is therefore to imagine that being able to make a work process more efficient will lead to career advancement.

Another important tenet of self-leadership is to talk to oneself positively and constructively. Convert negative thoughts into positive ones. Avoid statements such as "My communication skills are too poor to make a presentation to higher management." Instead say, "To make an impressive presentation to management, I will have to improve my oral communication skills. I'll get started tonight." Another negative thought might be "I'll never be able to do a good job of managing 20 direct reports." Instead say "I've never managed more than 10 direct reports before. I will have to acquire new managerial skills to perform well. I will schedule time tomorrow to investigate helpful resources for becoming a more efficient manager."

It is also important to visualize methods for effective performance. Imagine yourself moving effortlessly through a challenging assignment, using methods that have worked in the past. Visualize making a hard-hitting presentation to management, on the lines of a presentation of lesser importance that you have made in the past. You might also use visualization to enhance your performance on a longer-term assignment. Imagine yourself as the leader of a high-performance team that becomes the envy of your company.

In short, the SuperLeader helps create conditions whereby team members require very little leadership. Achieving such a goal is important because the revamped workplace has fewer managers. Furthermore, organizational structures such as work teams and horizontal structures require a high degree of self-management.

Entrepreneurial Leadership Style

In the revamped workplace managers must think and act as if they were self-employed. The attitude shift toward self-employment and away from playing a small role in a large corporation is significant. Losing a customer, or making another mistake, can be dismissed from the mind when one has the attitude: "In the corporation scheme of things, one small mistake is infinitesimal. We have thousands of other customer to compensate for one problem." In contrast, the process manager or team leader

A SUPERLEADER IS A MANAGER WHO LEADS OTHERS TO LEAD THEMSELVES.

with a self-employed mentality worries about the financial consequences of every mistake.

The manager with a self-employed outlook manages with the same sense of urgency as an entrepreneur does. A team leader of a customer service unit at Ameritech, one of the regional Bell companies, explains her leadership approach in these terms: "I tell my team to act as if we will have to file our own profit-and-loss statement at the end of the year. We must prove that our 50-person customer service operation is a good return on investment for Ameritech. If we can't give the company a good return, it has the right to shut us down. I expect our group to serve our customers well and to have fun. At the same time, we have to be a profitable investment. I keep reminding our team of this fact."

The four leadership styles described here are not mutually exclusive. A perceptive leader can blend the various styles to suit the needs of the occasion. For example, in starting a new enterprise for your firm, you might be a SuperLeader and an entrepreneurial leader simultaneously.

PERSONAL ATTRIBUTES OF THE NEW LEADERS AND MANAGERS

Not every person has the right stuff to carry out the new leadership and managerial roles. Certain personal attributes are required. Many of the traits described in Chapter 2 as important for members of the revamped work force also apply to leaders and managers. Among them are good problem-solving ability, a combination of inductive and deductive thinking, cross-functional skills, and a quality attitude. Imagination, creativity, and the willingness to communicate openly that we described in Chapter 3 are also essential. Attributes of a good coach were specified in Figure 5-1 of this chapter. Here we describe several other attributes that contribute to the success of leaders and managers in the new workplace.

Honesty, Integrity, and Credibility

A strikingly consistent finding from leadership research is that group members believe their leaders must display honesty, integrity, and credibility. Leaders themselves believe that honesty makes a difference in their effectiveness. Several studies surveyed a total of 7,500 manager from private and public organizations about what they looked for or admired in their organizational leaders. In each survey, honesty was the most frequently chosen characteristic. Eighty-seven percent of the respondents selected honesty of their leaders by their behaviors. The researchers noted:

> Leaders are considered honest by their constituents when the leaders do what they say they are going to do. Agreements not followed through, cover-ups, inconsistency between word and deed are all indicators of lack of honesty. yet if a leader behaves in ways consistent with his or her stated values and beliefs, then we believe we can entrust to the person our careers, our security, even our lives.[5]

Honesty is always important, but in planning the revamped workplace the opportunity for deception is so great that honesty becomes even more vital. Leaders and managers have to guard against making glib statements about the positive consequences of change that prove to be false. Here are two such glib statements:

> "After we trim down the organization this once, no further cuts will be necessary. We will have eliminated all waste and costs will be in line." (In reality, downsizing can weaken a firm's ability to satisfy customers, thus leading to profit decreases. Profits consequently shrink further and more payroll cuts are made.)

> "After our total quality management system takes hold our products will be so superior that profits will spike dramati-

cally. The profit increases should result in substantially improved compensation." (In reality, total quality management quite often improves product quality but not the demand for a product. Customers may have been quite content with the quality of products before a system of total quality management was initiated. Xerox Corporation, for example, has planned to eliminate 10,000 jobs to help boost profits. Yet the same company is acknowledged as a world leader in the quality movement.

Enthusiasm

In almost all situations it is desirable for the leader to be enthusiastic. Group members tend to respond positively to enthusiasm, partly because it may be perceived as a reward for doing the right thing. Enthusiasm is also a desirable leadership trait because it helps build good relationships with team members. Enthusiasm can be expressed verbally by such statements as "Great job," "I love it," or "Way to go." Enthusiasm can be expressed nonverbally through gestures and smiles. It is important because if the leader is not excited about a program or policy, team members will hold back. Holding back can prevent a workplace innovation from achieving a successful launch.

Initiative

Being a self-starter is a key leadership trait that has considerable relevance for the revamped work force. Initiative is also related to problem-finding ability. The interorganizational alliances that form the heart of the virtual corporation require problem finding or opportunity finding. The leader must always be vigilant for potential fits with other organizations.

Another activity that requires considerable initiative is spearheading process redesign. An opportunity-finding orientation facilitates figuring out what process might profit from redesign, particularly when a process is not broken. Some processes are in obvious need of fixing, such as a job transfer within a company that requires 60 days and 10 approval signatures. Excessive customer complaints shrilly signal that process redesign would be helpful.

An example of how an opportunity-finding orientation identified a candidate for process redesign took place in a health maintenance organization (HMO). The chief administrator was looking for ways to improve operating efficiencies and increase revenues. A driving factor was that medical insurance payments were not increasing as rapidly as the organization's costs. The administrator began listing the major work processes of the HMO. After 15 minutes of deep thought he asked, "What is the process by which patients visit our office? How do people decide when they need professional medical attention?"

An analysis of the intake process revealed that quite often it was the telephone receptionist who either encouraged or discouraged a person from making an office visit. The basis for the receptionist's decision was the patients' descriptions of their symptoms. One implication of this process was that a person without formal medical training was advising patients to buy or not buy medical services.

A new process was designed whereby a physician's assistant, nurse practitioner, or registered nurse would speak to patients who were vacillating about a visit to the HMO. The revised intake process resulted in more patient visits and more revenue to the health maintenance organization.

Self-Directing

People who are self-directing believe that they are the primary cause of events happening to them. Being self-directing (or having an "internal locus of control") helps a leader to be a take-charge person. An important link exists between being self-directing and success as a leader in the revamped workplace. The new team structures are the most effective when team members believe they are in control of their own destinies. Under ideal circumstances, team members come to believe that they are the primary contributors to profit and loss. Instead of blaming or crediting senior management, members blame or credit themselves because they control both their fate and the company's fate.

A self-directing leader facilitates team members becoming self-directing by the attitudes he or she projects. A purchasing manager with an internal locus of control might say to the team, "We take too long to get our work done. We drown other departments in the paperwork we generate for them. We have got to change what we are doing wrong if we are to become a high-performing unit." In contrast, a purchasing manager with an external locus of control would project blame onto other departments. He or she might say, "Other departments are very impatient. They resist important documentation. We have got to meet other people's schedules if we are to become a high-performing unit."

The problem with external locus of control thinking is that it serves as an easy rationalization for the low performance of the purchasing department. An effective technique for team leaders is to give take-charge, internal locus of control-oriented pep talks like the one given by the first purchasing manager.

Tenacity

Typically, effective leaders are tenacious. Leaders are better at overcoming obstacles than nonleaders. Tenacity multiplies in importance for leaders in the new workplace because it can take so long to implement a new program. Many executives who have been responsible for upgrading quality have discovered that such change proceeds slowly. As one manager placed in charge of an error-free work program said:

> I thought we would make quantum leaps in quality improvement immediately. Employees completed the training programs all charged up and ready to become disciples of total quality management. Shortly thereafter, when progress was slow, I knew I had to fight to improve quality every day. Many workers leaped back into their usual way of doing things. We are making progress, but it consumes a lot of my energy.

A leader must be tenacious to sell other key managers on the need for a workplace innovation. And to the chagrin of many leaders, the need for tenacity does not diminish after the sale or the start-up of the program.

An organizational design consultant from Atlanta was hired to help a Charlotte, North Carolina, company trim down its work force by eliminating unproductive work. He spent five days per week for six weeks on company premises. The consultant's major activity was to help the company identify and eliminate unproductive work. After a follow-up visit six months later, he reported:

> Bit by bit, managers were slipping back into doing some of the unproductive work they did in the past. Memos were written that people never read. Unnecessary meetings were called. Many managers still spent much of their day reviewing work performed by others. Managers were once again conducting lengthy business lunches that served no focused purpose.

NEW ROLES FOR MIDDLE MANAGERS

A pressing issue to which we keep returning from different perspectives is "Where do middle managers fit into the revamped workplace?" At the outset of the chapter we listed a few possibilities such as middle managers becoming team leaders or individual contributors. Here we examine more closely several optimistic possibilities for middle managers that are taking place now or are likely to occur in the future.

Reengineering Visionary and Czar

As the shift to teams becomes more commonplace many managers will shift toward such leadership activities as being visionaries. The middle manager as leader must answer such questions as "What will the new business process look like" "What will a high-performance team do that our teams are not already doing?" "How will becoming a network organization change the way we do business?" In the past, creating visions was primarily reserved for top-management leaders.

An exciting new role as a reengineering czar is envisioned for selected middle managers by authors Hammer and Champy.[6] According to their analysis, process owners and their teams focus on specific process redesign projects. The reengineering effort will be strengthened when one manager provides leadership to all the various redesign projects taking place throughout the corporation. The czar functions as the CEO's corporate vice president for reengineering. Such a position could be referred to as the functional vice president for reengineering. A concern, however, is that the term *functional* would be paradoxical. Reengineering and process innovation both downplay the importance of organizational functions, so use of the word "functional" is therefore discouraged.

The reengineering czar has two main purposes. One is to enable and support the process owner (equivalent to team leader) and reengineering team. Enabling and support could take such forms as providing the necessary financial, material, and human resources. The czar's second purpose is to coordinate all reengineering activities.

To carry out these two purposes efficiently, the czar should be the resident expert and internal consultant on reengineering and process redesign. He or she should maintain an extensive network of others engaged in similar work. Developing a library of printed and electronic information about process redesign is also important. At one insurance company the reengineering czar gives all managers and professionals engaged in reengineering a loose-leaf binder containing relevant articles about process redesign. He periodically sends these personnel updated information for insertion in the binder.

The emergence of a reengineering czar underscores an important fact about reengineering, process redesign, and the horizontal organization. Proponents of these innovations lionize multifunctional structures and multiskilled teams. Nevertheless, highly skilled specialists are important. The presence of a reengineering czar can be justified because the person is a subject-matter expert—in effect, a functional specialist.

Planners and Coordinators

The shift to work teams has a major impact on the traditional activities of first-level supervisors. Team leaders now take over such activities as on-the-job training, assigning people to jobs, and technical troubleshooting. Middle managers also become further removed from basic supervisory activities as they deal with the supervisors and individual contributors who report to them. In business firms, managers who supervise professionals are typically classified as middle managers. (In governmental firms, however, the managers who supervise professional-level workers are referred to as supervisors.) Professionals are sometimes organized into self-managing teams, and these groups take over some traditional middle-management functions.

Figure 5-2 presents information about the shifts in responsibility that have taken place in several companies as a consequence of team structures. Note that middle managers have a reduced set of responsibilities. Middle managers can therefore

FIGURE 5-2

Transfer of Responsibility Matrix

	TEAM NOW (1)	TEAM LATER (2)	MANAGE-MENT (3)
Sign work orders		✔	
Schedule vacations	✔		
Determine and plan for needed overtime	✔		
Call for maintenance help	✔		
Complete production and waste reports	✔		
Troubleshoot equipment	✔		
Schedule and carry out changeover		✔	
Maintain area records and documentation			✔
Assign workers to jobs	✔		
Train new employees		✔	
Plan and lead work unit meetings		✔	
Handle disciplinary problems			✔
Coordinate work flow		✔	
Call Engineering when needed	✔		
Attend managers' meeting			✔
Solve problems when they arise	✔		
Monitor safety	✔		
Ensure that work standards are met	✔		
Provide and prepare annual budget			✔
Respond to intra-company complaints			✔
Conduct performance appraisals		✔	

(1) Responsibility given to team now.

(2) Responsibility transferred to team within one year.

(3) Responsibility retained by management.

Reprinted with permission from Richard S. Wellins, William C. Byham, and Jeanne M. Wilson, Empowered Teams: Creating Self-Directed Work Groups That Improve Quality, Productivity, and Participation *(San Francisco: Jossey-Bass, 1991), p. 135.*

coordinate the activities of several teams, and devote more time to planning. Fewer middle managers would be needed under the transformation to work teams. The surplus middle managers would therefore have to be redeployed inside or outside the firm.

Group Executives, Enterprise Unit Managers, Business Process Managers, and Team Leaders

In recent years organizations have paid serious attention to developing more efficient organization structures. Many large and medium-sized firms have followed the advice of organization theorists and moved toward flatter structures. A much heralded example is Asea Brown Boveri, Ltd. (ABB). An international leader in electrical equipment manufacturing, the company has annual sales of about $25 billion. By design, the company never has more than five layers of management between the chief executive and first-level supervision. In contrast, many firms the size of ABB have 15 layers of management.

The five-layer management structure at Asea Brown Boveri is responsible for about 250,000 people. The company is divided into 4,000 individual enterprise units, each with an average of 62 employees. With such lean supervisory structures, the firm emphasizes the horizontal organization.[7]

Organization structure specialist Elliot Jacques has proposed a flat management structure similar to the one used at ABB. A major contribution of the structure is that it emphasizes the time spans of primary concern to managers at each of the five levels. As shown in Figure 5-3, the top management team has a 10-year perspective. Group executives have a 5-year perspective, "enterprise unit" managers a 2- to 3-year perspective, business process managers a 1-year perspective, and team leaders and reinforced job holders a 3-month perspective. Considerably more management skill is required at each successive level of management.[8]

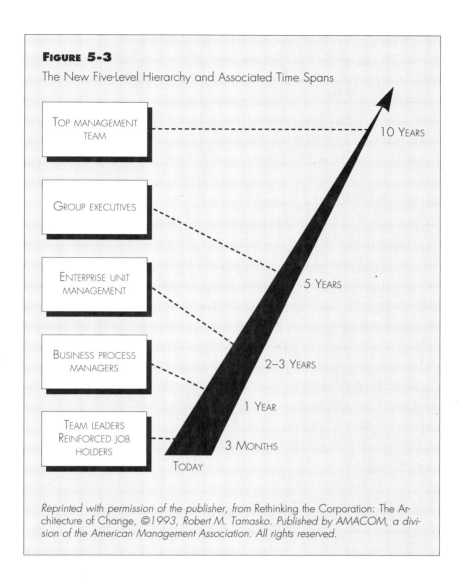

FIGURE 5-3

The New Five-Level Hierarchy and Associated Time Spans

TOP MANAGEMENT TEAM — — — — — — — — — — — — 10 YEARS

GROUP EXECUTIVES

ENTERPRISE UNIT MANAGEMENT — — — — — — 5 YEARS

BUSINESS PROCESS MANAGERS — — — — 2–3 YEARS

1 YEAR

TEAM LEADERS REINFORCED JOB HOLDERS — — — 3 MONTHS

TODAY

Where might middle managers fit into this new five-layered structure? A select number of middle managers will become group executives, akin to vice presidents in the traditional organization. A larger number of middle managers will become enterprise unit managers, while a still larger number will become business process managers. Many other former middle managers might become team leaders. An encouraging aspect of these assignments for middle managers is that the group executives, enterprise unit managers, and business process managers all hold exciting, far-reaching positions. The team leader positions might also be exciting, but most middle managers aspire to a higher organizational level.

Servant Leader

Another new role for middle managers is a reinforcement of what many managers are already doing. The middle manager in the revamped workplace is required to devote less energy to pleasing the boss and more energy into helping his or her own team succeed. According to the concept of servant leadership, strong leadership is provided when the manager is concerned about taking care of group members. The manager also elicits from the members what needs to be done.[9]

The servant leader may not have the right answers but does ask the right questions. She or he asks the right questions of people who are in close contact with work processes and customers. The servant-leader model is thus a good fit for the horizontal organization with its customer focus.

By definition, the servant leader works to support the best interests of team members. The leader makes sure that the team is getting an equitable share of resources and rewards. A servant leader will approach the next level of management as an advocate for the group. During a downsizing, a leader in a consumer products company, acting in the servant role, scheduled a meeting with his vice president. He explained to the vice president:

> The company has ordered an across-the-board cut of 10 percent of employees. I cannot quibble with top management's decision to reduce payroll in order to stay profitable. I am alarmed, however, that our group is being

asked to make cuts. We have several of the most profitable products in the entire company. We are already under-staffed and losing some money because of lost opportunities. If we cut staff, the net effect will be to lose money for the company.

The middle manager backed up his presentation with carefully prepared data. He was so convincing that the vice president brought the request for an exemption from the cuts to the president. The middle manager was ultimately given a favorable compromise: His group was asked to reduce just one position, and that position could be collapsed by not replacing the next person in the group who left through attrition.

A middle manager who acts as the group servant leader helps to keep the group focused on serving customers and building products or services instead of preparing information for higher management. The middle manager takes care of all requests from the hierarchy. He or she might even challenge upper management as to why certain information is needed.

Consultant Robert M. Tomasko illustrates servant leadership in practice. If you ask a Fedex employee how many group members report to his or her manager, the employee will probably say something to the effect: "Sorry, you seem to have it backwards. My manager works for the twelve of us to help us succeed at our jobs."[10] In 1992, H. Ross Perot campaigned for the presidency of the United States, using a servant leadership model. Perot may not have won the election but his assertion

---

THE SERVANT LEADER WORKS TO SUPPORT THE BEST INTERESTS OF TEAM MEMBERS.

that he would be the servant of the people attracted a large number of supporters.

The servant-leader role is also important because it dovetails with the general role of the middle manager in the modern workplace. First, the manager sets direction, which includes helping prepare a vision and mission statement at the department or business-process level. Second, the manager provides support, such as negotiating for the resources necessary to accomplish the group's goals. Third, the manager measures results and dispenses rewards and punishments accordingly. (Punishments might include a low performance evaluation, recommendation for no raise, or a demotion. In a team-oriented culture, a sizeable portion of the rewards and punishments might be based on team performance.)

ELIMINATING LOW-VALUE WORK

For managers, the revamped workplace often means managing more people. As a result of eliminating some management positions, the managers who remain are often responsible for two or three consolidated departments. The span of control, or number of people reporting directly to a manager, can increase substantially.

After consolidation, managers are often expected to accomplish volumes of work that were previously done by two or three people. Instead of conducting 10 annual performance appraisals, the manager must now conduct 30. As part of total quality management, a state university eliminated department head positions; self-managing teams replaced departments. The academic deans were now responsible for about 75 performance appraisals each. Asked how she accomplished this feat, one dean replied: "That's easy. Faculty members in their first or second year are reviewed once a year. More experienced faculty members receive a review every three years." Observe carefully that the dean simply eliminated some work that nobody complained about having been eliminated.

Managers in a downsized organization frequently complain that their workload is excessive. Total quality management can also increase workload because the system often results in many more meetings and much more paperwork. For example, internal groups keep sending each other surveys asking how they are doing. The total quality gurus did not intend TQM to create busywork. Nevertheless, busywork is often created because people placed in charge of total quality management efforts are so overly concerned that no detail be neglected.

To handle post-downsizing (and sometimes post-total quality management) responsibilities, managers regularly need to work at night and on weekends. The remedy for the problem has a reengineering spin. Managers must eliminate as much low-value work as possible. They should justify whether every work procedure, meeting, or ceremonial activity is contributing value to the firm. For example, the number of group luncheon meetings away from the office might be cut in half, giving staff members more time during the day to conduct urgent work.

A growing approach to streamlining work is to outsource activities to firms that can handle certain services at low cost and high quality. Among the candidates for outsourcing are payroll, benefit claims processing, printing, custodial services, and food services. The organization has to take care, however, that the costs of outsourcing do not exceed the salaries previously paid to full-time employees to deliver these services.

Related to work streamlining is the importance of sharpening your work habits and time management in order to perform well with a wider span of control. Update your To Do lists regularly, and make sure you take care of small items that can distract you if not accomplished. For example, you may have a few reference checks from other companies to process that you keep shuffling to the bottom of your in-box. Yet knowing that these tasks are undone distracts your attention.

Despite your attempts to streamline and become Robo-manager, remember to stay in touch with everybody under your span of control. When pressed for time, it can be convenient to neglect the steady performers in your group because they require so little attention. But to maintain contact, all that might be required is a two-minute conversation in their work areas or a quick "How are you doing?" telephone call. A backup approach is to leave messages of appreciation on voice mail or electronic mail after hours. The messages sent during nonstandard working hours reflect your strong work ethic and your interest in your group.

Another suggestion is to make sure that all your group members fully understand what they have to accomplish. Proper training is important because group members have less supervision. Strive to minimize time spent away from the office by such means as consolidating trips out of town. Keep in mind that many trips can be eliminated by making judicious use of phone calls and electronic mail.

A Checklist for Adapting to New Leadership and Managerial Roles

A checklist follows of the major changes in management and leadership roles within revamped organizations. Regard each item on the checklist as a possible action you should take to emerge victorious in today's business world.

☑ The new manager and leader, particularly at the first two levels of management, emphasizes coaching and facilitation rather than command and control.

☑ A transformational leader is required to set in motion major workplace innovations such as reengineering and total quality management. A transformational leader offers an exciting vision of where the organization is headed, and how the workplace innovations will get it there.

☑ The team structure of the new workplace elevates the importance of coaching. As a coach, the manager and leader makes on-the-spot suggestions for performance improvement and encourages team players frequently.

☑ In a team-based organization, employees are supposed to become self-sufficient and self-managing. Direct supervision of people is de-emphasized.

☑ A breakthrough shift in the thinking required for leadership excellence is more managers to think and act as if they are self-employed.

☑ One exciting new role for middle managers might be that of reengineering czar, or the corporation coordinator of reengineering program.

☑ A new five-layer organizational structure is on the horizon that could spell opportunities for middle managers. The three levels best fitting the needs of displaced middle managers are group executives, enterprise unit managers, and business process managers.

6

Building
Teamwork

A team goes one step beyond a work group. Like teams, members of a work group are involved in collaborative effort. Yet common commitment is stronger among team members, while members of a work group might be less focused on goals. More important than differentiating between a group and a team, however, is to recognize the importance of teamwork. Without good teamwork, a team remains a loose connection of individual contributors.

Teamwork means that there is understanding and commitment to group goals on the part of all team members.[1] Good teamwork enhances the chance of a team being successful. Notice the word *enhances*. Teamwork does not guarantee a successful team. Many small businesses go belly up despite a heavy commitment to group goals by the owners and employees. Perhaps they had the wrong product or service at the wrong time.

Given that teamwork is essential for success, you will enhance your effectiveness in the revamped workplace by contributing to teamwork. Many of the tactics and strategies for fostering teamwork described in this chapter are best accomplished by people with formal authority, such as team leaders. Yet any team member can still take many of the initiatives described. In a truly empowered workplace, all team members have sufficient authority to take leadership action.

FIGURE 6-1

R_x for Teamwork

The purpose of this checklist is to serve as an informal guide to diagnosing teamwork. Indicate whether your team has each of the following characteristics:

	MOSTLY YES	MOSTLY NO
1. Clearly defined goals and expectations	——	——
2. Clearly established roles and responsibilities	——	——
3. Well-documented guidelines of behavior and ground rules	——	——
4. Open communication in an atmosphere of trust and mutual respect	——	——
5. Continuous learning and training in appropriate skills	——	——
6. Patience and support by higher management	——	——
7. Rewards tied to individual as well as team results	——	——
8. Desire to continuously improve and innovate	——	——

SCORING AND INTERPRETATION: The larger the number of statements answered *Mostly Yes*, the more likely good teamwork is present, thus contributing to productivity. The answers will serve as discussion points for improving teamwork and group effectiveness. Negative responses to questions can be used as suggestions for taking action to improve teamwork in your group.

Source: Based on information in Mark Kelly, The Adventures of a Self-Managing Team (San Diego, CA: Pfeiffer & Company, 1991), p. 104.

As a starting point in sharpening your insights into building teamwork, do the exercise in Figure 6-1. Relate the questions to any present or past work group or team familiar to you.

SEVEN LEADER BEHAVIORS AND ATTITUDES THAT FOSTER TEAMWORK

Seven key leader behaviors and attitudes foster the teamwork vital for implementing today's workplace innovations. Described below, they are as follows:

1. Sense of urgency and demanding performance standards
2. Teamwork culture
3. Consensus leadership style
4. Fresh facts and information
5. Use of jargon
6. Encouraging honest criticism
7. Cross-functional thinking
8. Avoidance of micromanagement

Sense of Urgency and Demanding Performance Standards

As management consultants, Jon R. Katzenbach and Douglas K. Smith studied work teams in many organizations. At the top of the list of their findings was that team members need to believe that the team has urgent, constructive purposes. A demanding performance challenge helps create and sustain the team. Its members also want to know explicitly what is expected of them. The more urgent and relevant the rationale, the more likely it is that the team will achieve its potential.

The Saturn Corporation automobile manufacturing facility is organized by self-managing teams. Much of the high consumer demand for the Saturn is attributed to its high quality (despite more than one embarrassing recall). By 1994, the Saturn Corporation was still experiencing consumer demand well beyond forecast yet continuing to lose money. The problem lay in Saturn's start-up costs of over $3 billion—a problem unrelated to the teams. Work teams in the Spring Hill, Tennessee, factory faced substantial challenges. They were frequently asked to increase production without sacrificing quality. The challenge helped energize the teams to work together cohesively.

Teamwork Culture

A major strategy for teamwork is to promote the attitude that working together effectively is an expected standard of conduct. Developing a culture or norm of teamwork will be difficult when a strong culture of individualism exists within the firm.

Yet the leader can still make progress toward establishing a teamwork norm.

Some leaders encourage team members to treat each other as if they were external customers, thus encouraging cooperative behavior and politeness. The leader can also foster a culture of teamwork by explicitly stating its desirability. The manager of a group of credit analysts used the following comments, with good results, to promote teamwork:

> My manager is concerned that we are not pulling together as a cohesive team. We need to share ideas more frequently and to touch base with each other. From now on, performance appraisals in our group are going to have a different twist. When I evaluate performance, I'm going to give as much weight to group effort as I do to individual contribution.

The leader can also communicate the norm of teamwork by making frequent use of the words and phrases that support teamwork. Emphasizing the words *team members* or *teammates*, and de-emphasizing the words *subordinates* and *employees*, helps communicate the teamwork norm. To foster the culture of teamwork you can also devote portions of several staff meetings to a discussion about the meaning of being a team. During one such session an information systems specialist at Continental Insurance Company said, "To me a teamwork culture means that our work group is almost a family."

The leader can foster a teamwork culture indirectly by asking influential team members to support the importance of teamwork. A high-status team member might say to co-workers, "I'm glad this project is a joint effort. I know that's what earns us merit points around here." A small risk with this tactic is that the influential team member might appear to be shilling for the company, so you will be well advised to select someone to promote teamwork who can do so with great sincerity.

Consensus Leadership Style

Teamwork is enhanced when a leader practices consensus decision making. Contributing input to important decisions helps foster the feeling among team members that they are valuable. Consensus decision making also leads to an exchange of ideas with the group; including supporting and refining each other's suggestions. As a result, the feeling of working jointly on problems is enhanced.

The Japanese approach to human resources management is embedded in the philosophy of teamwork and group harmony. Advances in quality made by Japanese industry are partly attributed to strong teamwork. *Kaizen* groups, or quality-improvement teams, depend on workers cooperating with each other to make work improvements. To help achieve harmony, many Japanese managers use consensus decision making. When each person contributes important input, there is less likely to be conflict with other group members.

Consensus leadership helps build teamwork, but it is also time-consuming. To prevent consensus leadership from consuming inordinate amounts of time, the leader can make many small decisions individually without getting the group into a huddle. A three-minute conversation with a group member about a small decision is another way to avoid the pitfalls of consensus decision making.

A consensus decision-making style can also backfire when the leader obtains group consensus only on matters that are of little consequence. Roger, the CEO in a health-care firm, is a strong proponent of team-based management as part of quality management. He empowers teams to make such decisions as establishing flexible working hours in their units and purchasing supplies. Faced with a major decision, however, Roger forgets about consensus decision making. When he was conducting a search for a new vice president of administration, only two other executives were privy to the selection process. As a middle manager in the health-care firm expressed it, "When a big decision has to be made, Roger keeps his cards close to his chest."

Fresh Facts and Information

A sophisticated approach to enhancing teamwork is to feed team members valid facts and information that motivate them to work together. New information prompts the team to redefine and enrich its understanding of the challenge it is facing. As a result, it is likely to focus on a common purpose. The team will also set clearer goals and work together more smoothly.[2]

The fresh-fact approach is particularly suited to building teamwork within a process redesign team. Process redesign is an intellectual activity in which every shred of knowledge about simplifying a particular work process is potentially useful.

A catalog sales merchandiser was going through process redesign. The primary reason for it was that the cost of sales was getting too high in relation to sales revenues. One of the more laborious steps involved in the handling of merchandise was the development of distribution lists on electronic mail for internal purposes. The team leader brought to the attention of the redesign group a method of copying distribution lists by using a few simple commands.

The team worked together for part of an afternoon studying how this new fact about electronic mail could save time on internal communications. As the team engaged in joint problem solving, they found a new way to apply the distribution list sharing also to customer mailings. A surge of team spirit resulted from achieving another gain in task simplification.

Use of Jargon

A subtle yet potent method of building teamwork is for the team to use language that fosters cohesion and commitment. In-group jargon bonds a team and sets the group apart from outsiders. Jargon offers another psychological advantage. It reinforces unique values and beliefs, thus contributing to the corporation culture. Jargon can also enhance teamwork by enabling team members to communicate easily with few misunderstandings. Even the word *process* has become a piece of jargon that binds team members. Members of reengineering teams, process teams, and quality teams use the term in almost every paragraph. Listen to a modern workplace team and you are likely to hear such statements as:

- "Let's look at our process for deciding who should be the next team leader."
- "Have we clearly identified our process for determining if the price of a component is too high?"
- "What's our process for deciding how long a coffee break should be?"

Two management researchers analyzed reports contained in the best-seller *The Soul of a New Machine* by Tracy Kidder. A team named the Eagle Group outperformed all other Data General divisions to produce a new, state-of-the-art computer. Here is some of the jargon used by the highly cohesive Eagle Group:

- A "kludge" was something to be avoided, such as a machine with a loose wire held together with duct tape.
- A "canard" was anything false.
- "Give me a core dump" meant "Tell me your thoughts."
- A "stack overflow" meant that an engineer's memory compartments were suffering from communication overload.[3]

Microsoft Corporation workers, headed by the charismatic Bill Gates, are known for their cohesiveness and team spirit. Part of the organizational culture is to learn and use Microspeak, the firm's jargon. The following comments made by a software development team at Microsoft illustrate this teamwork-enhancing jargon:

Person A: "He's very bandwith." (*Bandwith* is a measure of intelligence, much like IQ.)

Person B: "Bill sent me some wicked flame mail." (*Flame mail* is hypercritical, emotional, and inflammatory electronic mail, often containing vulgarisms.)

Person C: "Your idea has not granularity." (*Granularity* is fineness of detail.)

Person D: "She's hardcore about spreadsheets." (*Hardcore* means serious about work.)

Person E: "He went nonlinear on me." (*Nonlinear* is out of control and angry."

Person F: "That's the most random thing I've ever heard." (*Random* means illogical.)[4]

Encouraging Honest Criticism

A superficial type of camaraderie develops when team members avoid criticizing each other honestly for the sake of group harmony. Avoiding criticism can result in groupthink—an extreme form of consensus in which the group fails to critically evaluate its own thinking. The team manager should explain that good team players offer honest feedback on mistakes and flawed ideas. the team benefits from mutual criticism. A stronger team spirit will develop because team members realize that they are helping each other through giving honest feedback.

Honest criticism and original thinking are success requirements of the revamped workplace. One of its potential problems is that some team members interpret being a good team player as being willing to go along with bad decisions for the sake of maintaining harmony. Others are afraid to express original ideas because they think the team leader would prefer them to conform to group thinking. Group members need to know that their opinions are important even when they are unpopular.[5]

An example of honest criticism took place in the shipping department of a manufacturer of small kitchen appliances. One member of a quality-improvement group had designed a satisfaction survey to mail to customers. The purpose of the survey was to investigate whether the packing materials were of satisfactory quality. Another member said, "Are you sure you want to do this? Will it annoy our customers? Why waste more paper? We've never had a complaint about packing materials."

The person whose idea was challenged was miffed at first, but then expressed appreciation. She said, "I guess I went a little overboard on trying to measure customer satisfaction. Maybe we should save our survey dollars for a more important issue."

Cross-Functional Thinking

One of the biggest challenges in reengineering and the development of horizontal structures is to get team members to think cross-functionally. As long as team members from multiple disciplines continue to view problems only from their own functional perspective, full cooperation will be lacking.

Assume that the marketing representative in a process team views all problems as marketing problems. Other team members are likely to feel that the marketing person is excluding their expertise and points of view. A marketing person with a cross-functional perspective would view problems as *business* or *organizational* problems. By so doing, the marketing representative's orientation is inclusive rather than exclusive.

The team leader can facilitate cross-functional thinking by helping members broaden their perspective. Frequent use of cross-functional statements by the team leader are important.

SOME TEAM MEMBERS INTERPRET BEING A GOOD TEAM PLAYER AS BEING WILLING TO GO ALONG WITH BAD DECISIONS FOR THE SAKE OF GROUP HARMONY.

The leader should confront the group with such statements and questions as:

- "What are the business implications of this new product?"
- "How can we integrate our knowledge to work out the best solution to this problem?"
- "Let's all put on five hats to tackle this customer request."
- "I know we can think more strategically than we have been doing so far today."

In each of these the leader is encouraging team members to look at the big picture rather than concentrate on one area of expertise.

Cross-functional teams are popular in new product development, and their use continues as many new product development efforts are reengineered. The Syntex Corporation came to rely on reengineering to develop new drugs more efficiently. Several years ago, the firm recognized that the pharmaceutical industry was undergoing substantial change. Developing a new drug was costing an average of $250 million and consuming five years. Leading-edge technology was then required to track and verify the multitude of clinical trials involved in introducing it.

Syntex's methods of coping with the mountains of data were stretched to their limits. The company looked to reengineering as a way of tackling new product development. Eva Davila, the vice president for quality and reengineering, said, "We realized that the systems had to be designed around the business processes. It became clear that we needed to make fundamental changes in the way we work. We needed to take a step back and reexamine every process associated with drug development before we could install the technology."

An examination of the organization structure and the processing of work indicated that scientists, clinical specialists, legal specialists, regulatory affairs personnel, and marketing specialists did not work smoothly across departmental lines. Many worked independently. Considerable time was lost as work shuffled between desks. In addition, many of the functional specialists had to keep track of several projects simultaneously, leading to errors and confusion.

Cross-functional teams of 8 to 12 people were created, each assigned to a particular project. Team members would still retain expertise in their fields, yet they would also acquire enough general knowledge to be able to answer internal and external inquiries about products. The cross-functional perspective reduced response time. Efficiency improved in part because voice mail and electronic mail messages were no longer left waiting for a response.

Syntex now has 12 more cross-functional product development teams, based on the success of the first ones. Product development costs and introduction times have been reduced by an estimated 20 percent.[6] Gains such as these from cross-functional teams are most likely to accrue when the members think cross-functionally. To encourage cross-functional thinking does not mean that functional thinking is never relevant. For example, in new product development the medical expert on the team would be asked about the worst-case scenario from a given drug's side-effects. It might also be important to ask the finance specialist to estimate the costs involved in following a particular direction.

Avoidance of Micromanagement

Before reading further, do the exercise in Figure 6-2 to examine your own tendencies toward micromanagement.

A popular pejorative term in the new workplace is to accuse a manager of *micromanaging*. Aside from being a general-purpose insult, the term refers to supervising group members too closely and second-guessing their decisions. Micromanagement and empowerment are polar opposites. Micromanagers give team members limited breathing room to manage activities. Furthermore, the micromanager is perceived as mistrusting team members.

FIGURE 6-2

Do You Have Micromanagement Tendencies?

Indicate how well you agree with each of the following statements by checking Mostly Agree or Mostly Disagree. If you are not currently performing managerial work, indicate how you probably would respond if you were working as a manager. If you have worked as a manager previously, think back to those times in answering the questions.

	MOSTLY AGREE	MOSTLY DISAGREE
1. I like to have a daily report on the progress of each group member.	____	____
2. It is important for me to tell workers what needs to be done and how to do it.	____	____
3. All reports that leave my department contain my signature, whether or not I have prepared them.	____	____
4. My instructions about tasks are quite detailed.	____	____
5. I carefully review each item on an expense account voucher that I approve.	____	____
6. My performance appraisals contain quite specific suggestions for work performance improvement.	____	____
7. I like to hold briefings with team members at the start of their workday.	____	____
8. The most important part of a manager's job is to control the work of subordinates.	____	____
9. All completed work in my organizational unit must pass my inspection.	____	____
10. When I am out of the office on a workday, I try to call the office at least twice.	____	____

SCORING AND INTERPRETATION: The greater the number of statements you checked Mostly Agree, the stronger your tendencies toward micromanaging. If you checked Mostly Agree to 8, 9, or 10 statements you might be supervising so closely that you are interfering with teamwork and a feeling of empowerment. On the other hand, if you checked each statement Mostly Disagree you might not be offering enough input as a manager or leader. Responding Mostly Agree to three or four statements probably suggests that you are achieving the right balance between micromanagement and macromanagement.

For greater accuracy in understanding your tendencies toward micromanagement, asked a trusted team member to respond to the questions above as they apply to you.

> # A POPULAR PEJORATIVE TERM IN THE NEW WORKPLACE IS TO ACCUSE A MANAGER OF MICROMANAGING.

Micromanagement can hamper a spirit of teamwork because team members do not feel in control of their own work. Much of what they do is designed to please the boss, as is often the case when people are closely supervised. Being micromanaged dampens morale because team members anticipate having considerable latitude. *Macromanagers*, on the other hand, grant considerable freedom to team members and allow them to make many important decisions. The macromanager also trusts team members' judgment.

SIX ORGANIZATIONAL ACTIONS THAT FOSTER TEAMWORK

The approaches for developing teamwork described so far can be implemented by the team leader acting alone without the support of an organizational program. Yet several tactics and strategies for fostering teamwork are part of a formal company program, such as offering pay incentives for teamwork. Few leaders have sufficient authority to implement a team incentive plan unless the plan is part of a company program. Recognize, however, that the leader must still play an active role to ensure that an organization program is implemented successfully. The discussion below concerns six actions for developing teamwork that are part of a formal company program:

1. Creating physical structures suited for teams.
2. Developing team incentives.

3. Creating team symbols.
4. Initiating peer evaluations.
5. Conveying a sense of team stability.
6. Supporting outdoor training.

1. Creating Physical Structures

Group cohesiveness, and therefore teamwork, is enhanced when team members are located close together and can interact frequently and easily. Frequent interaction often leads to camaraderie and a feeling of belonging. Much of the work performed by process redesign and reengineering teams is done in open areas. A reengineering consulting team typically works in a bullpen arrangement where they share data and rapidly exchange ideas. Furthermore, the horizontal organization usually requires that cross-functional teams interact with each other regularly in an open work area.

Many firms have difficulty finding space for interactive work because the existing work areas are designed for individuals. Managers and higher-level professionals, in particular, are accustomed to individual work areas for one-on-one conferences and to satisfy status needs.

A useful method for getting people to exchange ideas is to establish a shared physical facility, such as a conference room, research library, or beverage lounge. These areas should be decorated differently from others in the building and a few amenities added, such as a coffee maker, microwave oven, and refrigerator. Team members can use these areas for refreshments and group interaction.

Despite the value of open working areas for enhancing teamwork, some provision should be made for work privacy. Creative people need time to work alone away from the chatter of teammates. Report writing is an obvious example of work that is better done in an enclosed area. Provision for private work areas is also important because some types of creative thinking requires intense concentration.

One problem with abolishing individual work areas entirely concerns the boundaries between work and personal life. Managers and professionals employed by organizations invest an average of 55 hours per week in work. If there are no private work areas in the office, these people have to do almost all of their report writing and paperwork after hours. As many higher-level workers contend, "When I want to get any real work done, I have to do it at home." What they mean is that heavy thinking requires privacy.

2. Developing Team Incentives

A key strategy for encouraging teamwork is to reward the team as well as individual members. The most convincing team incentive is to calculate compensation partially on the basis of team results. The team as a whole must perform well for individuals to receive their share of the merit pay given.

Executives at a bank decided that every employee in its branch system needed to pay attention to the quality of customer service. Up to that point, bank employees had received incentives for the volume of new products sold and for cross-selling (referrals to other bank services). Customers complained that they were being oversold. Customers also perceived that bank employees were more interested in sales than service. A customer satisfaction survey indicated that the bank was losing more customers than it was gaining.

To stem the net outflow of customers, the bank implemented a series of initiatives to improve the quality of customer service. At the same time, it set up a team incentive plan, whereby results were measured in terms of customer satisfaction. Current payouts were received for current customer satisfaction scores and deferred payouts given for sustaining high customer satisfaction.

Although the team payouts siphoned off some profits, team incentives proved to be a good investment. The small decrease in profits was less than the previous costs of continually selling to new customers and closing out the accounts of parting customers.[7]

Team leaders can act on their own outside a formal program to use nonfinancial team incentives. Assume that a team leader receives a compliment from higher management that he or she has done an outstanding job. The team leader would share this praise with the group because most accomplishments reflect a team effort. Team celebrations for accomplishing milestones are another potentially effective form of team incentive.

3. Creating Team Symbols

Teamwork on the athletic field is enhanced by team symbols such as uniforms and nicknames. The term "Fighting Irish," for example, deserves some credit for contributing to the mystique of the Notre Dame football team. Symbols are also a potentially effective team builder in business. Trademarks, logos, mottos, and other indicators of products both advertise the company and signify a joint effort. Company jackets, caps, T-shirts, mugs, ballpoint pens, and business cards can be modified to symbolize a work unit.

Social symbols, such as group activities, also identify and build team unity. Many groups use ceremonies such as award banquets to recognize group effort. The shared laughter at such functions creates emotional closeness and teamwork. The manager can organize a ceremony announcing the successful completion of reengineering a process or the attainment of a difficult quality standard, each achieved by a team effort.

A KEY STRATEGY FOR ENCOURAGING
TEAMWORK IS TO REWARD THE
TEAM AS WELL AS INDIVIDUAL MEMBERS.

Eastman Kodak Company provides a dramatic example of how a symbol can help energize a team. The black-and-white film manufacturing group had lost its once-revered status because color film now dominates the amateur film market. Despite the increase in use of color film by amateurs, the black-and-white film business has annual sales of about $2 billion. Professional photographers use black-and-white film regularly, as evidenced by photographs in newspapers. Serious amateurs still shoot in black and white as well as color. Added to these applications of black-and-white film are 7,000 products used in printing, X-rays, and spy satellites.

Some 1,500 Kodak group employees work in a horizontal organization, called flow teams. These employees adopted the symbol Zebra, and the group is also referred to as Team Zebra. A 25-member leadership team watches the flow of work and regularly measures productivity. Zebras are divided into "streams" (manufacturing groups) that supply product to various Kodak business units. The business units are regarded as internal customers. These customers evaluate the streams against customer-satisfaction measures such as on-time delivery.

When the flow teams began in 1989, the black-and-white film group was 15 percent over budget. The group took up to 42 days to fill an order, and was frequently late. As measured by company surveys, the morale of the group had hit rock bottom. As the group shifted to a horizontal organization and took on the Zebra team symbol, productivity and morale began to climb. By 1992, the group was under budget by 15 percent, had reduced cycle time in half, and was late only 5 percent of the time.[8]

The team spirit that evolved as the concept of Team Zebra took hold is best understood in terms of a flow team, or stream, within the larger group. One day, Kodak managers were faced with a problem, so they asked Gordon Ackley and four other production workers how to solve it. The first think Ackley said was, "Will everybody leave the room? We'll let you know how we'll do it." In previous years, few workers would have been brazen enough to assume that they could solve problems without extensive involvement by management.

Ackley and his co-workers are members of a flow team at Kodak Park, the company's largest manufacturing facility. Workers are grouped by what product they make, not by what job they perform. Despite the various products they help make, all are united by their status as Zebras.

The problem facing the flow team was how to gear up quickly to make Ektamate paper, an ultrathin photographic paper used to print copies of microfilm slides. Kodak had stopped making Ektamate. Instead, the Kodak Business Imaging Systems unit had gone outside the company, to the 3M Company, for paper to be used with its microfilm machines. The Imaging Systems sales representatives, however, had found that some customers preferred the old Ektamate paper. The manufacturing division now had a chance to get Ektamate manufacturing back. The condition laid down, however, was that the group had to produce Ektamate quickly and at low cost.

The flow team of five Zebras swung into action and quickly grew to 15 members. The group established 12-hour shifts but did not cancel vacations. To accomplish their mission, the team retrieved old machines from storage. Many of these machines were found to have parts missing. The team figured out what help and supplies were needed. Other departments had to increase their output of paper and chemicals. Machinery was modified by maintenance workers who had volunteered for the project. Sometimes the project needed the help of key workers for as little as two hours at a time. This demand was met although company procedures allowed only week-long transfers outside departments.

Michael Graves, manager of development and manufacturing materials for Kodak Business Imaging Systems, expressed his positive opinion of the flow team: "I'm really impressed by how much they want to bring this business back within Kodak. The team spirit is enormous. They were absolutely determined, and they were up and running in 10 weeks. In an earlier day, workers might have taken many months to achieve this much."

Another Kodak executive compared flow teams to the past. His perception was that the old approach was a "Doberman system." As he put it, accounting "watchdogs" would go after manufacturing units that missed cost targets and productivity. Under the new system, each unit produces not only film and paper but a profit.[9]

The horizontal structure used by the manufacturing units for black-and-white film was a major factor in enhancing productivity. The Zebra experience also illustrates another important point about the new workplace. A combination of the right structure plus teamwork is required to achieve desired results. In this instance, the Zebra symbol served as an assist to fostering teamwork.

4. Initiating Peer Evaluations

In the traditional performance evaluation system, the manager evaluates team members at regular intervals. With peer evaluations, team members contribute by submitting evaluations of each other. Peer evaluations frequently contribute to teamwork because team members realize that helping each other becomes as important as helping the boss. Similarly, team members recognize that pleasing each other counts as much as pleasing the boss.

Peer evaluations, however, have a downside risk. Team members might hesitate to do anything that would interfere with their receiving a good evaluation, even if the action were productive. For example, for fear of receiving a negative evaluation, a team member might not confront another about an important mistake. Team members might also give high appraisals to team members they particularly like, and vice versa.

Favorable results with peer evaluations have been reported at Digital. Group input to the appraisals is collected by a committee. In addition to each team member evaluating all other team members, each person provides a self-evaluation. The team members at Digital respect analysis by peers and are willing to accept the system.[10]

The mechanics of peer evaluation are worth mentioning. The typical method of peer evaluation is for co-workers to complete the same form that managers complete. Under a pure peer evaluation system, the ratings and observations made by peers are combined, or averaged, to achieve a summary evaluation. A modified approach is for the manager to evaluate team members and combine his or her ratings with peer ratings to achieve a final result.

Several organizations are now experimenting with a new approach to peer evaluation that works as follows: Team members first prepare their own evaluation in essay form. The evaluation period is usually one year. A preliminary draft of each evaluation is submitted in double space to all the other team members. Team members are encouraged to add to the first draft, and point out where they agree or disagree.

The person preparing his or her own evaluation incorporates all the comments made by others into his or her own evaluation. A second draft is then sent to team members to make sure that their input has been fairly incorporated into the final report. Additional changes are made as needed.

The output from this peer evaluation method is a one-page "global essay" describing the team member's most important accomplishments and areas for improvement. Figure 6-3 presents a sample global essay. Teamwork is enhanced as the members busily evaluate each other. After reading the first draft of one peer's evaluation, a team member returned it with the following note, "After years of dreaming about it, I've finally met Superwoman. I'm glad to know she's my teammate."

FIGURE 6-3

Global Essay Peer Evaluation

NAME: Jennifer Briggs

JOB TITLE: Marketing Specialist on Process Team

PERIOD UNDER REVIEW: Current Calendar Year

My overall contribution to the team effort was considerably above average. Our process team was able to reduce cycle time by 50 percent for three of the products we handle. We were able to reduce cycle time by 10 percent for two other products. The final product showed a cycle-time reduction of 5 percent. During the year we only had three customer complaints. Our sales volume for six products was up 17 percent.

Although individual contribution is hard to measure, I did considerably more than what was required. Six of my ideas were incorporated into product improvement. I suggested we conduct a focus group composed of our customer's customers to uncover how we could improve product. Whenever the occasion warranted, I willingly worked at night and on weekends to achieve deadlines. To my knowledge, I created no conflict on the team.

I still have a ways to go to become a full contributor to a cross-functional team. In particular, I need more knowledge of finance and engineering. This would help me make a more significant contribution to our process of improving products. It would also benefit the team if I were a little less hesitant to criticize ideas that I think are off base.

I want to thank Al, Betty, Frank, Maggie, Jeff, Lois, Pete, and Ram for their useful input into my report. I hope I have faithfully captured the spirit of their suggestions.

5. Conveying a Sense of Team Stability

Team building and attrition work against each other. A spirit of cooperation is fostered when team members recognize that they will be working together for a long period of time. This approach is one of the pillars of the Japanese strategy for achieving work-group harmony. (Yet during the recent Japanese business recession, long-term employment was less a reality than previously.) Team members should be organized so that they can perceive themselves spending the foreseeable future together. The result is greater commitment to the team. When new members are brought into the team, they are advised that the work team values stability in membership.

Stability has importance in proportion to the complexity of the activities carried out by team members. Members of the process team mentioned in Figure 6-3, for example, are involved in highly skilled work. An important requirement for success in such a team is the development of a sophisticated multidisciplinary perspective. Developing such broad knowledge takes time. A new member who replaces a knowledgeable member may require a while to be perceived as a full contributor to the group.

6. Supporting Outdoor Training

Another option available to organizations for enhancing teamwork is to send members to outdoor training. Wilderness training is closely associated with outdoor training, except that the setting is likely to be much rougher—perhaps in the tundra of northernmost Minnesota during the winter. Some forms of outdoor training can take place in city parks. Both outdoor and wilderness training are forms of learning by doing or experiential learning. Participants acquire leadership and teamwork skills by confronting physical challenges and exceeding their self-imposed limitations. All of these challenges are faced in teams rather than individually, hence the development of teamwork.

Program participants are placed in a demanding outdoor environment. The experience has significance for the revamped workplace, because participants have to rely on skills they did not realize they had, and upon each other, to complete the program. Building the self-confidence necessary for teamwork and leadership is emphasized. Lectures on teamwork, self-confidence, and leadership precede the outdoor activity.

Rope activities are typical of outdoor training. Participants attached to a secure pulley with ropes will climb up a ladder and jump off to another spot. Sometimes the rope is extended between two trees. Another activity is a "trust fall." Each person takes a turn standing on a low platform and falling backwards into the arms of co-workers. The trust fall can also be executed with the participants standing on ground level.

Outdoor training enhances teamwork by helping participants examine the process of getting things done through working with people. Going through the exercises, such as rappeling down a cliff, teaches participants to be better communicators. Participants practice their communication skills by issuing precise instructions to each other about such issues as scaling a cliff safely. At the same time they have to learn to trust each other because survival appears to be dependent upon trust.

Outdoor training has another potential benefit for the revamped workplace. The emphasis on calling on inner resources people did not know they possessed can come in handy after a downsizing. Rather than feel crushed because of job loss, a person might rise to the challenge and find a new career opportunity. The combination of enhancing self-confidence and trusting others helps in a job search, too.

BECOME A TEAM PLAYER YOURSELF

Another important strategy for fostering teamwork is to become a good team player yourself. By being a good team player, you establish a model of teamwork, and you will win the admiration of others. There are ten suggestions of ways to be a good team player yourself.[11]

Be Cooperative

Cooperation is the essential ingredient for effective teamwork. Not all your co-workers are concerned about the smooth functioning of the total organization, but they do want cooperation from you. By being conspicuously cooperative, you gain the edge in terms of your boss's evaluation and bank of goodwill you create with co-workers.

Kenny Chang, an information systems specialist, discovered a novel way to be cooperative with team members that earned him high praise from his peers. Kenny has an extraordinary talent for solving software problems, including computer viruses. To cooperate fully with his co-workers, Kenny gave them permission to call him anytime to help fix a software problem. After he had unsnarled a few problems over the phone after midnight, his co-workers took him seriously. When a team leader position was created in the group, Kenny was the natural choice. He had gained the edge by being supercooperative.

Make the First Move to Gain Cooperation

Achieving a cooperative team spirit is often a question of making the first move. Instead of grumbling about poor teamwork, take the initiative to launch a cooperative spirit in your department. For example, volunteer to help an overloaded team member.

Be a Team Player Even When It Hurts

Do what is best for the team even if it causes you immediate displeasure. Inconvenience and aggravation in the present may give you an edge in the intermediate term. Rich was a team leader for a service team that maintained photocopiers in downtown Richmond, Virginia. In a company effort to boost productivity, Rick's boss was replaced by another manager. Rick was pressured by the new manager to relinquish his team leader title and return to being a full-time specialist.

Although hurting from the potential loss in status, Rick told his boss and his co-workers that he wanted to do what was best for the team. Rick worked cooperatively and cheerfully with his new boss and his teammates. Six months later, Rick had the opportunity to interview for a supervisory position within the company. The hiring manager was generally impressed by Rick but was concerned that his technical qualifications were light. Rick's boss intervened on his behalf and talked glowingly about Rick's ability to learn technical information. The hiring manager was convinced and Rick did get the new position. The coopera-

---

DO WHAT IS BEST
FOR THE TEAM EVEN
WHEN IT HURTS.

---

tive attitude he displayed when he relinquished his team leader position became an investment in his future.

Share the Glory

Share credit for your accomplishments with the team. Glory-sharing is not just a manipulative ploy. If you work in a group, other members of the team usually have contributed to the success of a project. Jim, a process team member, was recognized at a company meeting for reducing the production time on a critical component by 25 percent. Even though Jim had originated the productivity-improvement idea, he immediately mentioned several other members of the process team who assisted him. By acknowledging the contribution of other team members, Jim improved his status as a team player. Later that day, a production engineer on the team gave Jim a handshake of appreciation.

Help Co-Workers Do Their Jobs Better

Take the initiative to help co-workers make needed work improvements. Make the suggestions in a constructive spirit, rather than displaying an air of superiority. Liz, a software development specialist, suggested to the group that they make their overview charts more exciting. She suggested that they add a logo and produce the charts in color. The change dramatically improved the presentations to user groups. People stayed more alert and interested during briefings. Liz received many words of appreciation for dedication to the group cause.

Engage in Mutually Beneficial Exchanges

Exchange favors with co-workers. You explicitly or implicitly promise that the other person will benefit later if he or she complies with your request. A more coercive way to use exchange is to remind the co-worker that he or she "owes you one." A spirit of teamwork develops as group members engage in mutually beneficial exchanges. Here are a few workplace exchanges that can foster teamwork:

- You agree to take care of an angry customer because one of your co-workers is too stressed today to absorb one more hassle.
- You cover for a co-worker who needs a few hours off to speak to his or her divorce lawyer.
- You agree to attend the Little League hockey game of a co-worker's son, providing he or she will attend one of your daughter's Little League soccer games.
- You help a team member prepare an overdue report, recognizing that you are now owed a favor.

Rarely Turn Down a Request from a Co-Worker

Granting requests for help from co-workers is governed by the motivation theory of reinforcement. If you comply with a request from a co-worker, he or she will find it rewarding and return soon with another request. If you turn down more than a couple of requests, that co-worker will stop making requests. If you want to be left alone, just turn down more than a few requests. However, if you want to be perceived as a team player, accept any reasonable request. For example, a co-worker might ask you to draw a process map even though he or she is more experienced with process maps. By accepting the request you have made a big deposit in the favor bank.

Lend a Hand During Peak Workloads

A natural opportunity for being a good team player arises during peak workloads. If you have any slack time, volunteer to help a peer who is overloaded. Even an hour or two of assistance to take some pressure off a co-worker will strengthen your role as a team player.

Be Dependable

A cooperative team spirit is essential for these groups. An important way to keep the team spirit alive is for each member to be highly dependable. Absenteeism, for example, is frowned upon. Jerry Katona, a team member at Xerox manufacturing plant, notes: "We have a spirit of brotherhood and sisterhood working in our Team Xerox unit. Anyone who lets us down is regarded as a poor team player. It would be the same as if a member of a basketball team decided to goof off the night of an important game."

Keep Up the Team Spirit When Things Are Going Poorly

Take on the role of the motivator when the team hits a snag. Keep the group focused on possible favorable outcomes, even if the situation appears bleak. Jason was a copywriter at an advertising firm that was hard hit by a decrease in client advertising. His message to the group was that advertising always runs in cycles. Jason also noted that the bottom point had already been reached.

He encouraged the team by reminding them that management was attempting to increase advertising activity outside of the usual channels. Jason proved to be right. The firm soon landed a few big contracts to conduct direct mail advertising. The payout to Jason was that team spirit had not deteriorated, and two colleagues told Jason that they appreciated his support.

A Checklist for Fostering Teamwork

The new workplace places a premium on teamwork skills. A checklist follows of key tactics for developing teamwork and becoming a team player.

- ☑ Ensure that team members understand and are committed to group goals.

- ☑ Establish a sense of urgency within the group, and give them demanding performance standards.

- ☑ Develop a teamwork culture as reflected in group norms favoring teamwork.

- ☑ Facilitate honest criticism of each other's ideas.

- ☑ Encourage cross-functional thinking

- ☑ Minimize micromanagement of team members.

- ☑ Be a cooperative team member yourself.

Empowering Others Successfully

7

Today's workplace innovations grant workers more authority and responsibility than the traditional workplace ever did. Workers are freer to make decisions and take actions that previously were the prerogative of management. Lower-level managers are also freer to make decisions that were previously the prerogative of higher-level management. Empowerment also extends beyond individual contributors and managers. In the revamped workplace teams are granted more power than traditional work groups.

Empowerment means that higher-level managers share power with lower-ranking workers. As a result of empowerment, individuals and groups are more heavily involved in decision making, planning, and thinking.

Empowering others also means giving them the resources and authority to make things happen. An empowered marketing specialist in a process team within a horizontal organization won't feel empowered if she has to beg for a budget to conduct a customer satisfaction survey. When the same specialist is empowered, she is given a budget to invest wisely in purposes that support the team's mission. Notice that the marketing specialist is assigned a budget. Empowerment does not mean that every worker has unlimited authority.

It's important to understand how empowerment works because the revamped workplace is dependent upon giving more

> # EMPOWERING OTHERS MEANS GIVING THEM THE RESOURCES AND AUTHORITY TO MAKE THINGS HAPPEN.

employees more power. Empowerment is also important because it contributes to what is known as the New Productivity. As Paul A. Allaire, the chairman and chief executive officer of Xerox Corporation explains it, old productivity is accomplishing things cheaper and faster; adding value for the customer is neglected. New Productivity, in contrast, is value-driven. It seeks to create knowledge, eliminate waste, and abandon unproductive work.[1] (Reengineering, process redesign, and the horizontal organization are direct contributors to the New Productivity.)

Allaire explains that New Productivity is achieved by empowering workers to do what they know is right—using their own innovation, judgment, intuition, and brainpower. In the Xerox executive's words, "Management must simply lead, set clear direction, provide the right training and tools—and get out of the way as we liberate the people who can create value. We see it as a universal challenge and common pursuit for all business."

Without empowering others, the workplace cannot be revamped. Yet empowering others requires more serious thought and planning than would appear on the surface. Saying "Poof, you're empowered" to an individual or team is not sufficient.

A model of how empowerment can contribute to useful outcomes in the new workplace is shown in Figure 7-1. The model posits that because employees are empowered, they make continuous improvements (including streamlining work) and their job satisfaction increases. As a consequence, they make quality products and provide good customer service.

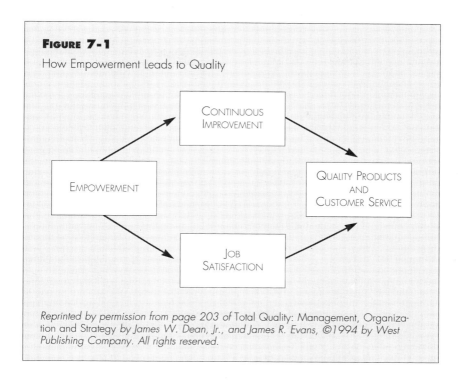

FIGURE 7-1

How Empowerment Leads to Quality

Our purpose in this chapter is to give you some thoughts and tools to make effective use of empowerment. Like other management strategies and techniques, empowerment can help an organization achieve its goals or create turmoil. Much depends on how empowerment is applied.

WHAT EMPOWERMENT REALLY MEANS AND INVOLVES

Empowerment means giving someone else power. Although the meaning seems straightforward, as one digs into the true depths of empowerment, it becomes much more complicated. You can begin to personalize the meaning of empowerment by working the exercise in Figure 7-2. The exercise pinpoints behaviors and attitudes necessary to be an empowering leader or manager. To the extent that you have those attitudes and are willing to en-

FIGURE 7-2

Becoming an Empowering Leader

DIRECTIONS: To empower employees, leaders and managers must convey appropriate attitudes and develop the right interpersonal skills. The following list of attitudes and skills will help you become an empowering leader. To the best of your self-evaluation, indicate which skills and attitudes you have, and which ones require development.

EMPOWERING ATTITUDE OR BEHAVIOR	CAN DO NOW	WOULD NEED TO DEVELOP
1. Believe in the ability of team members to be successful.	____	____
2. Be patient with people and give them time to learn.	____	____
3. Provide team members with direction and structure.	____	____
4. Teach team members new skills in small, incremental steps so that they can easily learn those skills.	____	____
5. Ask team members questions that challenge them to think in new ways.	____	____
6. Share information with team members, sometimes just to build rapport.	____	____
7. Give team members timely feedback and encourage them throughout the learning process.	____	____
8. Offer team members alternative ways of doing things.	____	____
9. Exhibit a sense of humor and demonstrate caring for workers as people	____	____
10. Focus on team members' results and acknowledge their personal improvement.	____	____

Source: Based on Richard Hamlin, "A Practical Guide to Empowering Your Employees," Supervisory Management, April 1991, p. 8.

gage in those behaviors, you are well suited to empower others. Similarly, the attitudes and behaviors you lack can suggest areas for professional development.

Empowerment is familiar to many people because it is an extension of participative management and employee involvement. Empowered employees are not only heavily involved in making decisions, they make decisions themselves and are accountable for the results.[2] An empowered employee on a process team

What Leaders Must Do to Empower Employees

- Identify and change those conditions that make employees feel powerless.
- Boost the confidence of employees so that their efforts to accomplish something consequential are successful.

might decide—without management approval—to eliminate a report that he or she thought added no value to the company. Empowerment thus lies at the extreme end of employee participation. When employees are empowered, they will often take the initiative to solve problems and strive hard to reach objectives.

To empower employees, leaders and managers must take two key initiatives. First, the manager must identify and change organizational conditions that make employees feel powerless. Workers often feel powerless because they are too tightly governed by rules, regulations, and restrictions. An employee working at an eyeglass manufacturing plant said she thought she knew the source of quality problems in her work area: "I'm convinced our lens-grinding machine isn't up to snuff. I've explained the problem to my supervisor. He told me to forget about getting the machine replaced or repaired for now. We can't spare the down time to fix the machine now."

If the above employee were fully empowered, she would have the authority to shut down the lens-grinding machine and have it inspected. If her diagnosis that the machine is defective were correct, the machine would be repaired before being put back into operation. Admittedly, this degree of empowerment would be too shocking for many companies to absorb. An alternative would be for the employee to be empowered enough to be taken seriously.

Employees also feel powerless when their boss is authoritarian or heavy-handed. If the boss makes all the decisions, or is quick to criticize, employees feel that they lack authority to do any significant task. Having a job over which one has little control is an important contributor to feeling powerless.

A second key empowerment initiative is for leaders to increase employees' confidence so that their efforts to accomplish something consequential will be successful. Managers must be willing to boost the self-confidence of team members. A starting point is to delegate to the member the authority to accomplish a relatively easy task. When the team member succeeds, the leader offers praise. Next, the person is delegated a more difficult task, and is praised again. Feelings of self-confidence develop as the team member performs well on successive tasks.

Building egos and self-confidence is important because many workers have hidden doubts that they can perform well without the support of close supervision. The empowering leader must convince team members who need their self-confidence boosting that they can indeed handle responsibility.

Empowerment builds on the principle of job enrichment because jobs become "vertically loaded." Vertical loading means that team members assume some of the responsibilities normally assigned to a person one step up the hierarchy. Ordinarily, this means the team member performs the managerial tasks of planning, organizing, and controlling.

> **BUILDING EGOS AND SELF-CONFIDENCE IS IMPORTANT BECAUSE MANY WORKERS HAVE HIDDEN DOUBTS THAT THEY CAN PERFORM WELL WITHOUT THE SUPPORT OF CLOSE SUPERVISION.**

> ## EMPOWERMENT SUPPORTS THE BEDROCK PRINCIPLE OF TOTAL QUALITY THAT WORKERS SHOULD BE RESPONSIBLE FOR THEIR OWN QUALITY CONTROL.

Vertical loading does not mean that the team member replaces the manager. Yet he or she does perform managerial tasks. An empowered member of a quality-improvement team, for example, might have the authority to schedule which work is performed at what time of day.

Empowerment supports the bedrock principle of total quality that workers should be responsible for their own quality control. An empowered worker searches for errors after work is completed. Of greater significance, the worker improves the process of work to the point that few quality errors occur. This principle of self-control is limited by an important fact about human behavior: It is easier for an outsider to catch your errors than for you to catch your own.

People have a perceptual tendency to gloss over their own errors because their minds create a completed, error-free image. This is why it is difficult to do an outstanding job of proofreading our own reports, or to find errors in our budget proposals. An outsider has the capacity to look more objectively at another's work. It therefore makes good sense for a second party to review the quality of a complex piece of work performed by another person. The spirit of the review should be quality enhancement rather than inspecting or second-guessing.

Empowerment can also be understood in terms of what it is not. Management consultant Peter Block explains that empowerment should not be confused with entitlement.[3] The empowerment movement does not mean that everybody gets what they want. Group members should not use empowerment as a weapon against the company. In the name of empowerment,

Block has heard employees ask for the following:

- More pay
- Larger budget
- More people, bigger empire
- Freedom to pursue strictly personal projects
- Greater recognition and privilege
- Immunity from disappointment from superiors
- A risk-free environment

As Block sees it, these demands in the name of empowerment are out of line. Just because people are encouraged to make many important decisions on their own, it does not mean they can have all their demands met. Nor does empowerment mean that people can be protected from disappointment and risk.

In one company, a group of empowered employees demanded that top management exempt them from an imminent downsizing. The employees argued that as empowered workers they had decided that layoffs were an unacceptable alternative to cost-cutting. A member of senior management told the employee group bluntly that they were expecting too much from empowerment.

At IBM Kingston, the concept of empowerment is described in the following:

- Shared responsibility
- Confidence and trust
- Knowledge/experience building
- Working toward common vision/goals
- An exciting environment where you feel everyday, "It's my business. I do make a difference."
- Challenging the status quo
- Learning from mistakes
- Authority to make decisions
- Accepting ownership

The comprehensiveness of the IBM Kingston list suggests that a variety of activities taking place in healthy work environments have been called empowerment. For example, building knowledge and experience, challenging the status quo, and learning from mistakes were taking place long before somebody labeled them as empowerment.

A final point about the meaning of empowerment can be stated in terms of its objective. As expressed by management professor M.J. Kiernan, the objective of empowerment is to tap the creative and intellectual energy of everybody in the organization—not only members of top management. At the same time, all employees should be provided with the responsibility and resources to exercise leadership within their areas of competence.[4]

TWO COMPANY EXPERIENCES WITH EMPOWERMENT

Empowerment programs are a systematic method of granting more authority and responsibility to workers, and encouraging them to make and implement decisions on their own. Empowerment programs can be integrated into workplace innovations such as reengineering or total quality management, or they can stand alone. The two case histories presented here include some elements of process redesign.

Eaton Corporation

A continuing challenge faced by Eaton Corporation, a manufacturer of gears, engine valves, truck axles, and circuit breakers, is to reduce costs. Reducing costs is crucial because Eaton's major customers are automobile manufacturers that are committed to paring down expenses. An important part of Eaton's cost-cutting strategy is to empower employees to make suggestions for reducing costs and to pay bonuses for achieving results. Teams of workers are empowered to identify opportunities for cost reduction and then to implement these suggestions. Carrying such names as "The Hoods" and "The Worms," the teams ferret out bottlenecks and ways to save money.

Eaton management encourages workers to take thousands of minor steps that incrementally improve the products they manufacture and the processes they use. Such small, continual steps are part of the Japanese philosophy of *kaizen*, which has become an underpinning of quality improvement. Office workers also are invited to uncover ways to trim costs.

In one year at Eaton's Lincoln, Illinois, plant, workers formally presented to management 193 ideas for improving operations. Just three of the 193 were the following:

- One worker explained how sandblasting rather than machining the welding electrodes would save $5,126 per year.
- A team of maintenance workers grew weary of fixing equipment and machines that broke down repeatedly. The alternative they offered management was to build two automated machines to perform tedious functions. Management accepted the idea, and the team built the machines for about one-fourth the price that outside vendors would have charged.
- Another team discovered that one press operator was preheating dies before using them, thus extending the life of the dies. The same practice has been adopted throughout the plant, leading to a $50,000 annual savings.

The savings resulting from suggestions such as these totaled $1.4 million in one year, enabling the Lincoln plant to increase its profit 30 percent over the previous quarter. As a consequence, the employees earned $44,000 in "Eaton bucks," coupons they can exchange for merchandise in the company store. Employees also receive cash bonuses based on total plant performance. In the past decade, Eaton's productivity, measured as output per hour, rose 3 percent a year. This increase exceeds the 1.9 percent average for all U.S. manufacturing. Seeking still further improvement, the company goal is now a 4 percent annual productivity increase.

At the unionized Lincoln plant, productivity increased 10 percent in one year. The company rewarded the gains by offering to relocate 70 low-wage-rate jobs from Mexico. The union workers hired to fill them at half the typical company pay have advanced up the salary scale quickly.[5]

Prudential Insurance Company

The Northeastern Group Operations of the Prudential Insurance Company faced a perplexing dilemma. Surveys indicated that their customers were demanding faster responses, lower prices, and more flexible product designs. At the same time, top management demanded significant and immediate cost cutting. A consulting firm hired to help resolve this dilemma advised the group that a bigger staff was not a prerequisite for improved service. Instead, they were told that the key was to unleash the power of the existing staff. Empowerment of this type would spark the innovation needed to run operations more cost-effectively.

Studies made by the consulting firm indicated that a lack of information and authority prevented employees from responding quickly to customer requests. They also noted that a system of checks and counterchecks dampened productivity and added to higher costs. Overall, the study revealed an organizational culture in which the employees who were closest to the customer and to cost-reduction opportunities were powerless to resolve them. By empowering these workers with greater decision-making authority, company management believed they could enhance both customer satisfaction and market success. It was also thought necessary to emphasize the existence of both external and internal customers.

Top management at Prudential's Northeastern Group Operations began the empowerment process at the top of the organization. Management had to be convinced that it was safe to relinquish power and delegate more authority to lower-ranking team members. Employees who were to be involved in the empowerment program were offered extensive training in customer service, team management, and problem-solving. Forty employees were appointed as customer satisfaction representatives. Another 16 were appointed as operational improvement consultants, whose full-time responsibility was to promote cost reduction.

Much of the empowerment centered around cross-functional groups of staff members and first-line supervisors. Each team was empowered to resolve a critical problem or provide service to a particular customer. So far, these teams have enabled management to delegate authority to lower levels, break down functional barriers, and cultivate ideas for improving service and decreasing costs.

At one location the average claims-processing time has dropped from 10 to 3 days through forming teams of clerical support, processing, and technical and quality control specialists. Each team is empowered to approve certain types of claims, up to a dollar amount that covers 95 percent of all claim submissions. By physically locating members of the claim team in one area, claim-related decisions can be made on the spot.

Another team launched a pilot program that allows employees to process claims at home. Given the freedom to set their own hours, these claims specialists are setting new records for productivity. By processing claims 50 percent more rapidly than their office-based counterparts they are contributing to cost reductions.

Since the empowerment program was implemented, operating costs have been reduced about 12.5 percent. Customers are noticing a substantial improvement in the quality of service and are responding with new business. Gross revenues surged 40 percent over the previous year. Company officials believe that the empowerment program has been instrumental in improving customer satisfaction, which in turn has increased sales revenues.[6]

WHO QUALIFIES FOR EMPOWERMENT?

Who becomes empowered is a critical consideration. As we discussed in Chapter 2 (and will touch upon later in this chapter), which employees are empowered is important. In general, look for employees who are a cut above average at their level of responsibility. Capability and motivation are both major factors in recruiting employees for inclusion in a process redesign or quality-improvement team. Figure 7-3 provides some suggestions for interviewing prospects for empowerment.

SUCCESS FACTORS FOR EMPOWERMENT

As with any management intervention, employee empowerment works best under certain conditions. When these conditions are present, the probability increases that employee empowerment will increase productivity, quality, and satisfaction. Above all, top management has to believe in employee involvement and empowerment and support the program in many ways.

Management researchers Richard J. Magjuka and Timothy T. Baldwin conducted a study of 68 employee involvement administrators and 72 employee involvement teams to identify factors contributing to the effectiveness of these programs. (Employee involvement programs empower workers by getting them involved in decision making about important matters.) Actual productivity and quality data were rarely available, so effectiveness was defined in terms of how the program operators perceived the program to be functioning. The results showed that employee involvement programs are perceived to make the most contribution to organizational performance when:

1. The teams operate under open and unrestricted access to business information.

FIGURE 7-3

Conducting an Empowerment Interview

To be an effective empowering manager it is essential to understand the capabilities of team members. By understanding their capabilities, you will develop a clearer picture of how much decision-making and problem-solving authority you can extend to them. For example, if a team member knew very little about creditworthiness, you would not want to grant him or her considerable leeway in granting credit. You might conclude that this person would be empowered to grant more credit after he or she acquired more knowledge about creditworthiness.

Conducting empowerment interviews has another benefit. As implied here, such an interview communicates the message that you are interested in the growth and development of team members.

Practice conducting empowering interviews with a co-worker, office assistant, or friend. Rely on interview techniques you may have learned through study or experience. As a general guideline, aim toward conducting a conversation with the other person, **but do most of the listening**. The questions that follow can help you learn about the empowerment capabilities of a team member. Choose from among them to conduct a productive interview.

1. What type of problems do you like to work on?
2. What decisions would you like to make that you are not making now?
3. Tell me about your best job skills.
4. What job responsibilities have you handled in the last three years?
5. What work problems have you spotted on your own recently?
6. How closely do you like to check with your boss before making a decision?
7. Tell me about any ideas for improvement you have made on the job in recent years.
8. How much responsibility do you think you can handle?
9. How would you feel if you acted on your own and then made a big mistake?
10. How do you feel when your boss delegates responsibilities to you?

2. The team's membership is represented by diverse job functions and administrative backgrounds.
3. The team has a higher-than-average number of members to draw upon to accomplish the program objectives. (In this study, teams ranged from 8 to 46 members.)[7]

In addition to these tangible factors, the organizational culture should favor employee involvement and empowerment. Two employee involvement consultants, Robert W. Barner and

> ## LOOK FOR EMPLOYEES WHO ARE A CUT ABOVE AVERAGE AT THEIR LEVEL OF RESPONSIBILITY.

J. Jackson Fulbright, contend that certain values pervade companies in which employee involvement is successful. These values are:

- *Employee ownership.* Employees should see themselves as owners in their companies' successes and challenges.
- *Employee self-direction and personal growth.* Employees should take the initiative to establish their own career plans.
- *Open communication.* Fluid communications should exist between team members and managers and across work functions. Workers should have open access to the information they need to accomplish their jobs. The organization should be information-rich, in that there is ample information available for sharing. Influential members of the organization should be willing to pass along information not yet recorded. (For example, a process owner asked a senior executive bluntly, "How important is this customer to us? They give us a hard time about everything. We then have to chase them to get our money." The executive's response: "We had hoped you could salvage this customer. If you can't, just drop them. I don't think they are worth our time.")
- *Risk-taking and innovation.* Team members should assertively look for ways to improve team performance and question outmoded or ineffective methods and procedures.
- *Teamwork.* Team members and managers should support each other, and cooperate with each other and with members of other work groups.[8]

> ## AN AXIOM OF ANY SUCCESSFUL WORKPLACE INNOVATION IS THAT IT RECEIVES TOP-MANAGEMENT SUPPORT.

In addition to the empowerment success factors identified by these two groups of consultants, many additional success factors are worth mentioning. As described next, they include sincere and complete implementation, and maintaining appropriate control measures.

An axiom of any successful workplace innovation is that it receives top-management support. A closely related consideration is that senior management should lead by example. Executives should be the first to relinquish the micromanagement style and involve group members in the entire management process. Workers do not feel empowered unless they carry out activities that were previously the province of management.

Explaining Empowerment

It may be necessary to explain to employees that they are empowered. Granting power and authority to team members is not as obvious as transferring them to a different department or preparing new job descriptions. A manager might say, for example, "From now on you will be recommending pricing for new products. It's not that we've fired our pricing specialists, but that you're empowered."

A member of a process redesign team at an insurance company explained how she became convinced that she was empowered: "Our team was trying to better serve a large manufacturer. We decided on our own that one of us should make an on-premises visit to the customer. I was elected to make the visit, and I scheduled the trip without seeking approval from the next level of management."

Being Patient for Results

After employees are empowered, top management must be patient for results. Turning over managerial responsibility rarely achieves an immediate payout in increased profits, decreased costs, improved quality, or better customer service. A retailing executive decided to empower the cashiers to accept checks for $500 higher than their previous limit. Asked how this act of empowerment was proceeding, a cashier replied, "So far I've seen a few more happy customer faces and a lot more bounced checks." Perhaps in the long run the retailer will benefit from more satisfied customers. In the interim, management has to absorb a few rubber checks as its investment in empowerment.

Empowering Sincerely and Completely

To be successful, empowerment must be done sincerely and completely.[9] Superficial empowerment to create a positive image for management may backfire. It is not unusual for company executives to introduce a small empowerment program for the political purpose of looking modern, thereby hoping to placate employees. Empowerment meetings that are simply gripe sessions or general discussions about work improvement exemplify such superficiality.

   If senior management promises that an era of empowerment is forthcoming, and then does not follow through, employee alienation may occur. Patricia McLagan, the CEO of a consulting and training firm, says, "One of the worst things to do is to tell people you're going to empower them, and then don't do it. That only increases anger and hostility."[10]

   Related to superficial empowerment is the practice of granting workers responsibility for a work process, then taking back the responsibility when trouble or uncertainty occurs. Managers should carefully evaluate whether to implement empowerment. Changing directions on empowerment is confusing and demoralizing, assuming the employees wanted to be empowered in the first place. Many employees are content to let competent managers continue to manage their work.

Setting Limits to Empowerment

Although empowerment must be sincere, the limits of empowerment should be made explicit. Empowered employees need to know the limits to their authority in such matters as budgets, modifying work procedures, hiring and firing workers, training workers, and allocating salary increases. Empowerment does not mean that data-entry technicians gain control of the executive suite.

Reserving Job Security

In one manufacturing plant, each member of a self-managing work team received a key to the plant as a symbol of management trust. Management researchers James W. Dean Jr. and James R. Evans point out, however, that symbols of trust are less important than guarantees of job security.[11] Employees often fear that if workplace innovations lead to productivity improvements, jobs will be cut. A local official of the Communications Workers of America was asked his opinion of employee empowerment. His reply: "Empowerment is fine with me if it gives real power to employees—job power. What good does empowerment do if it means my people work themselves out of a job?"

Workers can demonstrate that they trust management by showing a willingness to take on responsibility without expressing suspicion. It is helpful for empowered workers to directly or indirectly express the attitude, "Yes, we want to be empowered. We have faith that being empowered will benefit us as well as top management and the stockholders."

Empowering Competent Employees

A cornerstone principle of successful empowerment is to empower competent employees. Employees need good technical, interpersonal, and problem-solving skills to be able to make a contribution to the revamped workplace. And as we have noted, high motivation is also an important requirement. Untalented workers are rarely in a position to solve problems sufficiently well to be able to handle empowerment. Notice that the word *untalented* makes no presumptions about experience, education, or training.

Some employees are talented despite having limited credentials. A careful review of past performance appraisal results, and discussion with former supervisors, can help identify those with sufficient talent to handle empowerment. Candidates for empowered positions should be carefully screened through interviews, personnel testing, and, if possible, work simulations. In a simulation, the worker might be given a problem to solve while observers rated his or her performance. Screening outside applicants is even more important than screening already known company employees.

Training Employees

Training can be instrumental in helping employees upgrade their talents, particularly in skill areas such as problem solving. Interpersonal skills can also be taught, but the process takes longer. In addition, a worker's personality exerts a strong influence on the level of his or her job skills. Attending training sessions is no guarantee that a worker will acquire the skills required to become a successful member of an empowered team. The candidate should be screened after training to see if it has made a difference.

As one worker who took a training course in statistics said, "I hated statistics before the class. I hated statistics during the class. I still hate statistics, and I learned nothing." It would be prudent to keep this employee off the quality-improvement team whose members need to solve a problem statistically!

A positive case history of selecting and preparing workers for empowerment took place at Rosenbluth Travel. The nationwide travel firm conducted extensive research into predictors of success in positions such as reservationist for corporate travel. The primary predictors of success were personality type and mix of skills. Newly hired employees attend a two-day orientation session at corporate headquarters. During orientation they are immersed in Rosenbluth's philosophies and values with a special emphasis on the company's concept of customer service. To hammer home this point, company officers serve the new employees afternoon tea on the second day.

The orientation program is only the beginning of training. Travel reservationists must complete up to 320 hours of classroom instruction. The instruction emphasizes the mechanics of reservations and how to provide quality service. A brief anecdote will describe the quality of service Rosenbluth employees are empowered to offer clients.[12]

A regular client called his Rosenbluth Travel agent to book his first trip to the French Riviera. The client knew that a friend had flown from Philadelphia to Nice (the location of the Riviera airport) with a plane change in Paris, so he asked for two tickets to Nice, going through Paris. With her client's best interests in mind, the agent told him, "Your choice of flying through Paris will cost you and your companion several hundred more dollars. Besides that, it will take eight hours longer. Would you prefer that I book you on a direct flight that costs less money and is considerably shorter?"

In this situation the agent was empowered to give a client the best service even if it meant smaller commissions for Rosenbluth Travel. The fact that Rosenbluth is a long-term dominant player in the travel agency business suggests that quality service is an asset to the firm.

Updating the Reward System

Another significant point about successful empowerment is that the reward system should be updated to make empowerment worthwhile for those empowered. The most direct way of modifying the reward system would be for members of the empowered team to receive salary increases and bonuses based on the extra money their units saved or earned.

If a process redesign team reduced the cost of handling credit applications by 75 percent, for example, team members should be entitled to some financial reward beyond a cost-of-living increase. To emphasize teamwork, most of the bonus should be allocated to the team, yet there should also be some provision for outstanding contribution by individual members. The teams might be asked to identify their most outstanding contributors.

Some companies now offer skill-based pay in which team members receive additional compensation for learning new skills. Under such a pay-for-knowledge system, managers calculate starting pay based on the knowledge and skill level required for a given job. Subsequent increases depend on the worker's mastering additional skills and knowledge specified by the firm. Skill-based pay is gaining acceptance for work teams because members must be multiskilled. But provision needs to be made to avoid substantially increasing the pay of workers who upgrade their skills by continually taking courses. A big gap exists between acquiring a skill and actually using it for the betterment of the firm.

Nonfinancial rewards, such as stories run in the company newsletter about exceptional team accomplishment and celebrations, can also support empowerment. Individuals who distinguish themselves on a team can be invited to join teams with more urgent assignments as opportunities permit. A person who finds good work self-rewarding (intrinsic motivation) is rewarded with the opportunity to do more good work.

A final point about the success factors for empowerment concerns how to reap its benefits without inciting a free-for-all.[13] A starting point is to ask probing questions about what the individual or team wants to do. Listen carefully to answers about how the empowered people will spend their time and do their planning. Ask if and how routine work will be accomplished by the individual or teams.

Avoiding a Free-For-All

Empowerment turns over considerable control to workers, but a manager should not abdicate control. Suppose empowerment leads to activities of questionable value (such as too many trips to visit customers and suppliers). You must stand ready to redirect the empowered team or individual. One empowered group in a health-care center scheduled twice-weekly meetings to confer with each other. As a result the average time patients spent in the waiting room increased. Top-level management then met with the team to discuss the problem of patients being neglected because of team meetings, and the issue was resolved satisfactorily.

Demand high quality from empowered groups by setting high standards and deadlines. Turn back work to employees who have failed to meet the rigorous standards you have established.

FOUR LEVELS OF RESPONSIBILITY FOR TEAM EMPOWERMENT

Another useful way of understanding how empowerment fits into the revamped workplace is to specify the activities performed by empowered work teams. Some activities connote more empowerment than others. Being empowered to fix a leaking faucet is much less impressive than being empowered to set a starting salary for a new team member. A team of consultants and researchers, Richard S. Wellins, William C. Byham, and Jeanne Wilson, studied empowered teams for several years. In addition to conducting a survey of 500 organizations, they interviewed officials from 28 companies, and helped dozens of firms implement self-directed work teams. As a result of their investigations they were able to arrange empowerment on a continuum with four anchor points.[14] A careful look at their findings helps to operationalize the meaning of empowerment.

Level 1 is the lowest level of responsibility and authority. The activities are ranged in increasing order of responsibility and authority, beginning with housekeeping, then training each other, followed by equipment maintenance and repair, and production scheduling. Many production departments were performing such activities before empowerment became a buzzword.

Level 2 begins with quality responsibilities, followed by continuous improvement in work methods, managing suppliers, external customer contact, and hiring team members. The amount of empowerment at this level is already impressive in terms of the traditional organization.

Level 3 begins with cross-functional teaming, or forming teams of people from different functions. The next step higher is vacation scheduling, choosing team leaders, equipment purchase, and facility design. An empowered team functioning at this level would experience strong feelings of self-management.

Level 4 begins with budgeting, followed by product modification and development, team-member performance appraisal, handling the disciplinary process, and making compensation decisions. An organization would have to be truly committed to empowerment for teams to be able to achieve level 4 of responsibility and authority. A process team responsible for a major organizational process such as new product development or sales and order fulfillment would qualify for level 4.

Whether or not the activities within the levels are in precise rank order of significance, the empowerment continuum deserves careful attention. You can use it as a sensible index of the extent to which *your* team is empowered.

HAMPTON INN: A CLASSIC EXAMPLE OF EMPOWERMENT AT THE INDIVIDUAL LEVEL

Empowerment is so frequently associated with teams that it is easy to overlook the fact that the focus of empowerment can also be individuals. Even within team structures in the revamped workplace, individuals are still the major unit of change.

In 1989, the Hampton Inn hotel chain initiated a formal policy of guaranteed customer satisfaction. Its *100% Satisfaction Guarantee* states that if guests are not completely satisfied with their stay at a Hampton Inn, they are not expected to pay. To implement this policy, individual employees are empowered to give refunds. The policy requires trust. Skeptics, for example, say that employees could easily take advantage of the policy by treating friends and relatives to free stays at the hotel. Upon checking out, the friend or relative would be instructed to complain to their hotel contact about poor service. The Hampton Inn friend would then use empowerment to reimburse the allegedly disgruntled guest or guests.

In reality, the Hampton Inn empowerment program to support the 100% Satisfaction Guarantee policy has been successful. Employees at every level of hotel operations, including housekeepers, are empowered to use the guarantee as a tool to deliver total guest satisfaction. Advance permission from the hotel general manager is not required. All employees are extensively trained in understanding and implementing the 100% Satisfaction Guarantee.

Company research suggests that the guarantee positively influences customer satisfaction and loyalty to Hampton Inn. Guests who have taken advantage of the guarantee are more likely to become guests again at a Hampton Inn. Top management also believes that the empowerment program has increased job satisfaction and the feeling of ownership among the company's 7,000 employees. A first-hand report from a Hampton Inn employee illuminates what empowerment can mean to the individual worker. Rhonda Thompson's story follows.

CASE STUDY

An Employee's View of Empowerment

A few years ago, while working as a guest service representative at a Hampton Inn hotel, I overheard a guest at our complimentary continental breakfast complaining quite loudly that his favorite cereal was not available. Rather than dismiss the person as just another disgruntled guest, I looked at the situation and saw an opportunity to make this guest happy. I gave him his money back—not for the continental breakfast, but for the cost of one night's stay at our hotel. And I did it on the spot, without checking with my supervisor or the general manager of our hotel, and without making the guest fill out a long complaint form.

Some people might be surprised to hear this story, or they might not believe it could happen. After all, how could a front-desk employee give a guest his or her money back without getting permission from the boss? And why would the hotel support this action for something simple like a bowl of cereal?

The answer is Hampton Inn's 100% Satisfaction Guarantee. This guarantee is a promise the hotel makes to every guest. It states that if guests are not completely satisfied with every aspect of their stay, they're not expected to pay. What's more, the guarantee empowers every Hampton Inn employee to do whatever it takes to satisfy guests, including giving them their money back.

The reason behind our guarantee is simple. If a guest walks away from our hotel dissatisfied, chances are that he or she will tell friends or business associates. And these people might spread the story around to other people. But with the guarantee, guests can walk away impressed with the way Hampton Inn handled the situation.

A NEW CORPORATE CULTURE

When I joined Hampton Inn six years ago, before the 100% Satisfaction Guarantee, my job was like most other jobs in the hotel industry. My responsibilities were outlined in my job description, and I was evaluated on how well I fulfilled those duties. There wasn't much room to express my own

continued

CASE STUDY *continued*

An Employee's View of Empowerment

Many employees—including myself—were skeptical at first. Although we were proud of our hotels and the service that we offered, we thought that guests might take advantage of the guarantees as a way to get something for nothing for free. But the training emphasized that, although any reason given by a guest is a valid reason to invoke the guarantee, most guests would not take advantage of us. The company even provided research to back up this claim. Still, we felt we would have to find out for ourselves.

Now, after more than three years of experience with the 100% Satisfaction Guarantee in place, I believe that our entire corporate culture has changed for the better.

A GUEST'S PERSPECTIVE

By empowering every employee with the authority to implement the guarantee, Hampton Inn basically threw out its old job descriptions. Of course, a housekeeper's duties still include cleaning and preparing guests' rooms. But the housekeeper's real job is to satisfy guests, and this is typically accomplished by cleaning the room to perfection. For example, if a housekeeper sees a guest having a problem with the lock on her room door, the housekeeper has the authority to stop what he or she is doing and take whatever action is necessary to correct the situation.

It is important to point out that the real focus of empowerment is to correct a situation in order to make a guest happy—not simply to refund money. But if a refund is what it takes, that's what we do. In the housekeeper's situation, he or she should first help the guest operate the lock. If that doesn't work, the housekeeper should contact Engineering to fix the lock, offer to move the guest to another room, or—if the guest is still not happy—refund the cost of the night's stay at the hotel.

Because each guest will judge our hotel in a different way, the guarantee makes employees more aware of each guest's needs. We've learned to think like a guest, and look at our hotel the way a guest sees it. That, in turn, has kept the quality of the hotel higher than it would have been if we

continued

CASE STUDY *continued*

An Employee's View of Empowerment

---

had kept to our narrow job descriptions. The guarantee also keeps all employees on their toes, and challenges them to work more closely together as a team.

A MOTIVATED WORK FORCE

While the goal of the 100% Satisfaction Guarantee is to give every guest a satisfying stay, the guarantee has made employees' jobs more satisfying as well. When Hampton Inn tells employees that they can do whatever it takes to make a guest happy—without needing approval from a manager—they're telling employees that they trust them to do their jobs. Most employees have never worked for a company that will unconditionally back them up for refunding a guest's money, no matter how small the problem was to begin with.

This type of trust motivates employees to do a better job, and makes them try harder to deliver excellent customer service. Employees know that they don't have to wait for their once-a-year review to find out if they're doing a good job. They find out every day from the guests staying at the hotel.

A CHECKLIST FOR EMPOWERING OTHERS SUCCESSFULLY

Empowering others is a major component of the new workplace. Teams and individuals are empowered by granting them more authority and responsibility than they might have had in a traditional organization. Adhering to these suggestions for empowerment will increase the chances that empowerment lives up to its expectations.

☑ An important part of empowerment is to encourage workers to use their own innovation, judgment, intuition, and brainpower.

☑ Identify and change organizational conditions that make employees feel powerless, such as overly restrictive regulations.

☑ Look upon empowerment as a way of tapping the creative and intellectual energy of everybody in the organization.

☑ The organizational culture should favor empowerment. The values of such a culture include employee ownership, employee self-direction and personal growth, open communication, risk-taking and innovation, and teamwork.

☑ The limits of empowerment should be made specific by explaining the limits to the authority of empowered workers.

☑ A cornerstone principle of successful empowerment is to empower competent employees. Employees need good technical, interpersonal, and problem-solving skills to be able to make a contribution to the revamped workplace.

☑ Training can be instrumental in helping employees upgrade their talents, particularly in skill areas such as problem solving.

8

Managing Cross-Functional Teams and Projects

*I*n the revamped workplace, teams of people with different functional backgrounds often pool their efforts to achieve an important goal. Cross-functional teams have increased productivity and innovation for many firms.

A trend closely related to the rise of cross-functional teams is the ascending importance of project leadership and management. Many top-performing managers function as project leaders. Today these managers are called process owners, case managers, project managers, or team leaders. Although the new thinking is to emphasize the leadership aspects of a manager's role, the job title *manager* remains in vogue. The term *leader* more often refers to a capability rather than a job title. An exception is that the term *team leader* is a widely used job title.

We have described the contribution of cross-functional teams at several places in this book. Here we expand on the theme and present information that managers and leaders need to successfully direct project-oriented teams. The same information is useful for team members because they share managerial responsibility. This is especially true for the self-managing teams now proliferating in the new workplace.

Managing a cross-functional team creates several formidable challenges. The leader of the cross-functional team must facilitate people working together whose perspectives, interests, and educational backgrounds are substantially different. Furthermore, cross-functional jealousies and rivalries may underlie some of the conflict within the team.

In the Beginning: Project Form of Organization

Cross-functional teams receive much better press these days than project teams because of their newness. Yet cross-functional teams are offshoots of project structures that sprang up in the 1960s. Because of their utility and flexibility, project structures have remained an important part of the fabric of organizations. We describe the nature of projects first because they are the foundation for the structures that support today's workplace innovations. If you understand the inner workings of a project structure, you will have an edge in managing a cross-functional team, task force, or a multiskilled team. You will also understand the basic structure used to accomplish the mission of a virtual corporation.

The project structure developed from departmentalized (or functional) organizations in order to accomplish new tasks and special-purpose missions. Project members work together as a team to accomplish a specific purpose, such as introducing a new product or launching a space station into orbit. In overview, a project organization is a temporary group of specialists working under one manager to accomplish a fixed objective. The project organization is used extensively in high-tech firms because their external environment is so volatile. Project structures also abound in the aerospace, construction, and motion-picture industries. Putting up an office tower, for example, is literally a giant project.

Project management has several distinguishing characteristics. Project managers operate independently from the normal chain of command and usually report directly to a member of top management, often an executive in charge of projects. Project heads negotiate directly for resources with the head of the line and staff departments whose members are assigned to a given project. A project head might have to "borrow" a specialist in expert systems from the information systems department. If the head of the information systems department thinks she cannot spare the expert systems specialist, the project manager might face a conflict. Good negotiation skills are therefore needed to be successful as a project manager.

Project managers act as coordinators of the people and material needed to complete the project's mission. They are accountable for the project's success or failure, yet they are not always accountable for the performance of the personnel assigned to it. Sometimes the functional manager may evaluate the performance of the project team member, using input from the project manager.

The life of the project ends when its objectives are accomplished, such as launching a new product. In contrast, most functional departments are considered permanent. Cross-functional teams such as process teams are also considered permanent unless the firm's mission changes. For example, a core process at Compaq Computer is order fulfillment and delivery. We suspect that this core process will not change as long as Compaq stays in business.

Some form of project organization is found in almost every large and medium-sized firm. Whenever a special project arises, either a formal project group is organized to accomplish the work, or a task force is appointed. Project team members are usually relieved from their regular assignments for the duration of the project. A task force is a group of people who are called on to solve a problem such as conducting a search for a new CEO or helping develop a strategic plan. Members of the task force usually do not give up their regular jobs during the assignment.

The authority of project managers varies considerably. At one extreme, a project group may operate basically as a coordinating body for the major departments. In this situation, the project manager exerts minimum influence in obtaining the resources needed to accomplish the project's mission. In addition, the project management may have difficulty in leading project members. A process owner could not operate effectively under these conditions. At the other extreme, top management may announce that the project manager has been granted full authority to accomplish the mission. He or she then can readily obtain resources from departments and can lead project members.

An example of full authority for a project manager took place in a home furnishings business. The company had lost much of its market share in the baby furniture business. Top management formed a project group to find a new field for the firm to enter. The president wrote a memo to all managers explaining that this project represented one of the most important undertakings in the company's history. The project manager subsequently received remarkable cooperation from other managers in obtaining needed resources. Such top-level support facilitated that project's success. The company is now a major player in the garden furniture market.

To help understand project structures and their evolution, it is useful to compare the project and traditional modes of operation.[1]

Line Versus Staff Organization

From the project viewpoint, vestiges of the hierarchical model remain, but line functions are now in a support position. The manufacturing function, for example, provides manufacturing expertise to the project. A web of authority and responsibility relationships exists that is quite complicated. From the traditional viewpoint, line functions have direct responsibility for accomplishing objectives. Line managers command, while staff members advise.

Vertical Chain of Command

From the project viewpoint, elements of the vertical chain exist, yet the primary emphasis is placed on a horizontal and diagonal work flow. (The vertical chain of command is also known as the scalar principle.) Important business is conducted as the urgency of the task requires. You contact who you want when you need that person, and do not unduly worry about violating the chain of command. In a project structure, talent is given more emphasis than organizational rank.

From the traditional viewpoint, the chain of authority relationships runs from superior to subordinate throughout the organization. Important business is conducted up and down the vertical hierarchy. The primary user of most people's output is the boss. In the extreme, a visit from a high-ranking executive creates more excitement than a visit from a customer.

Manager-Group Member Relationships

From the project viewpoint, much of the salient business is conducted from peer to peer, and from manager to technical specialist. Lateral relationships are emphasized. From the traditional viewpoint, superior to subordinate relationships dominate. If these relationships are kept healthy, success will follow. All important transactions are conducted through a pyramiding structure of superiors and subordinates. (Notice that the terms *superior* and *subordinate* are falling into disuse in nonhierarchical structures.)

Organizational Objectives

From the project viewpoint, management is a joint venture of somewhat independent organizational units. The objective becomes multilateral, often leading to high commitment. From the

FROM THE PROJECT VIEWPOINT, MUCH OF THE SALIENT BUSINESS IS CONDUCTED FROM PEER TO PEER, AND FROM MANAGER TO TECHNICAL SPECIALIST.

traditional viewpoint, organizational objectives are established by a central administrative group, and the project is given a written charter. The objectives are often perceived as unilateral, leading to weaker commitment. (A charismatic leader, however, may foster commitment even in a rigidly hierarchical organization.)

Parity of Authority and Responsibility

From the project viewpoint, considerable opportunity exists for the manager's responsibility to exceed his or her authority. Support people within the project frequently report to functional managers outside the project for pay, performance appraisals, and promotions. From the traditional viewpoint, line-staff relationships are clearly specified. Support personnel report directly to line personnel and thus are under their control. In this way, parity of authority and responsibility is maintained.

Time Duration

In the project organization, the project has a fixed time limit with some opportunity for extension if the task is not completed on time. In the traditional organization, the organizational units tend to perpetuate themselves. (Reengineering and downsizing are organizational initiatives that challenge the permanency of functional departments. As one CEO said as his company embarked upon a program of reengineering, "No department is sacred around here, including the office of the president.")

The overall advantage of the project organization is that it overcomes most of the disadvantages of the traditional functional (or departmentalized) organization. Project organizations help overcome tunnel vision and allow project members to broaden their experience. Projects also speed up decision making and help reduce the problem of overspecialization.

Project organizations offer other advantages as well. First, the project structure encourages identification with the project, which often leads to high morale and productivity. A frequently observed attitude is "We can get the job done right, and on time." Second, project organizations are well suited to dealing with unpredictable situations. They are flexible because so few employees are permanently attached to a project. If a project proves not to be worthwhile, the project group can quickly disband. For instance, a major food retailer based in Los Angeles attempted to reengineer the process of serving customers. After two months of hard work, the redesign team decided it had no productivity enhancers to offer the company.

Despite their advantages, though, project organizations also have some notable disadvantages. One problem is that people assigned to the project may be underutilized once the project is completed. Unless there is another project that requires restaffing, some of the project members may be laid off. (The application of project structure to the horizontal organization usually overcomes the displacement problem. The reason is that the horizontal structures concentrate on core processes that are likely to be around for as long as the firm stays in business.)

Another problem with project organization is that project managers often are not given the authority needed to accomplish their mission. Unless the project manager has been granted substantial authority by top management, he or she has to rely on personal influence to obtain needed support from other managers.

PROCESS OWNERS, TEAM LEADERS, AND CASE MANAGERS: THE NEW BREED OF PROJECT MANAGERS

The importance of project management has escalated because the revamped workplace has so greatly expanded opportunities for managing projects. Process owners, team leaders, and case managers perform work very similar to that of project managers. A key difference is that instead of having a visible project with time limits, a process owner, for example, may work on a continuing process such as order fulfillment. A process owner responsible for new product development, however, may face a time limit for developing a specific product. When one new product is developed, the process team might move immediately into working on another product.

The players on a process owner's team vary with the purpose of the process. A new product development process might include representatives from analysis, strategy, design and engineering, marketing, and manufacturing. Members of the sales and order fulfillment team might include representatives from pricing, sales, shipping, and production. Team members of the customer support process might come from research, advertising, and service.

Few readers of this book are working as case managers, but many of you will be in the future. *Case manager* is an emerging term for a process owner who is responsible for order management. The term will quite likely also be used for people who are responsible for other processes such as research and development or product development. Whatever process a case manager might have total responsibility for, he or she is truly a project manager and leader. (In the new lingo, the person is also a process owner.)

The case manager's "project" is to handle an entire customer transaction from start to completion. Like other project managers, the case manager works with a group of specialists from various disciplines to accomplish a mission. Figure 8-1 illustrates an all-encompassing version of case management. Observe that specialists from four different functions (sales, manufacturing, finance, and logistics) contribute to serving the customer. This

> ## PROCESS OWNERS, TEAM LEADERS, AND CASE MANAGERS PERFORM WORK VERY SIMILAR TO THAT OF PROJECT MANAGERS.

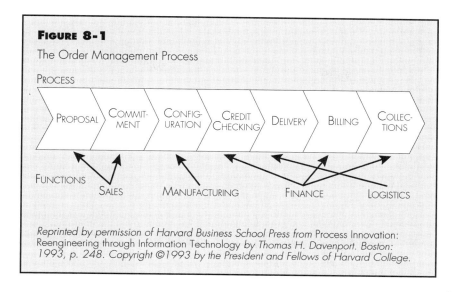

FIGURE 8-1

The Order Management Process

PROCESS

PROPOSAL 〉 COMMIT-MENT 〉 CONFIG-URATION 〉 CREDIT CHECKING 〉 DELIVERY 〉 BILLING 〉 COLLEC-TIONS

FUNCTIONS

SALES   MANUFACTURING   FINANCE   LOGISTICS

Reprinted by permission of Harvard Business School Press from Process Innovation: Reengineering through Information Technology *by Thomas H. Davenport. Boston: 1993, p. 248. Copyright ©1993 by the President and Fellows of Harvard College.*

form of case management would make sense for an industrial company but would be too cumbersome for a retail store. Yet perhaps by the year 2005, the greeters at your local Wal-Mart will be replaced by case managers!

As observed by process innovation consultant Thomas H. Davenport, successful case management has four essential components.[2] First, there is a closed-loop work process that involves the completion of a product or service that can be delivered to the customer (is customer-deliverable). A case manager therefore must stay focused on the goal of getting the product or service to the customer. The case manager must also keep the team members focused on the same goal instead of confusing means with ends. For example, when a team member talks about trying out some exciting new software, the case manager might ask: "How will this help our customer?"

Second, there is role expansion and empowerment to make decisions and address customer issues. Team members are given more authority to take the necessary steps to satisfy a customer demand. A member of one order fulfillment team sent a small electronic motor to a customer by Fedex on a Saturday morning. The case manager was curious as to why the team member did not wait until Monday instead of paying the weekend premium rate. The team member replied, "Because the customer wanted to get the machine running on Sunday afternoon that we shipped him last week." The case manager accepted the team member's decision.

Third, members of the process team have access to information throughout the organization. As was discussed in relation to successful work teams, an effective team needs ready access to information. The team might need to know, for example, manufacturing's track record on shipping parts on time. Such knowledge would enable the team to deal more honestly with external customers.

Fourth, the case manager has a visible location in the organization. Horizontal organizations take care of this requirement effectively because the team might consist of the chairman, the chief operating officer, the vice president of strategy and planning, and the vice president of support services.[3]

If any one of these four components are missing, case management will be ineffective. Davenport reports from his consulting files the case of a high-tech manufacturer that had created a position similar to that of case manager. The case manager's role was to handle order fulfillment for key accounts. Managers of relevant functional groups insisted that a nonexempt employee should be case manager. Because the nonexempt employee had low organizational status, the person was denied access to the key information that she was supposed to coordinate. As a result, the case management system failed.

> ## THE ROLE OF THE CASE MANAGER SATISFIES ONE OF THE KEY PRINCIPLES OF JOB ENRICHMENT— ALLOWING A JOB INCUMBENT TO HANDLE A TOTAL TASK.

Case management, well handled, is beneficial to employees as well as to customers. The role of the case manager satisfies one of the key principles of job enrichment—allowing a job incumbent to handle a total task. The case manager, along with team members, will usually find processing an entire order very satisfying. In essence, every customer order is another small project with a beginning, end, and completion. As long as the company stays in business, there will be another project ready to be processed.

Team members may also receive a boost in self-esteem because they have been trusted by their employer to take the right action to satisfy customers. The case manager must use an empowering style of management to ensure that team members feel that trust. Workers feel trusted when they are granted authority. Yet the case manager must not neglect to monitor performance while concentrating on empowerment.

THE NEW CROSS-FUNCTIONAL TEAMS

Today's cross-functional teams are an extension of yesterday's cross-functional project groups. Almost all the information presented earlier about the nature of project groups applies equally to cross-functional teams.

Workplace innovations in the 1980s increased the demand for cross-functional coordination. The total quality movement and time-based competition (speed is your competitive advantage) both required cross-functional thinking. Then came demands for product design with a cross-functional perspective. Among the battle cries were "design for quality" and "design for manufacturability."[4]

In the 1990s came demands for "design for re-use" and "design for re-manufacturing." Design for re-manufacturing, for example, has been championed by Mercedez Benz. Instead of melting down an old Mercedes (one with 300,000 miles!), the firm has designed its cars to be dismantled by salvage technicians and readily recycled. The design team for a Mercedes would therefore include an auto salvage specialist and an environmentalist.

Designing with another function's requirements in mind has another important cross-functional consequence. The design of manufacturing methods, training programs, vendor selection, marketing strategies, and so forth all occur simultaneously with the design of a product. Considerable coordination and decision making across functions is required to accomplish simultaneous design. As a consequence, cross-functional groups for new product development have burgeoned. Approximately one-half of new product development groups have cross-functional membership. Organizations going through process redesign usually select new product development as a core process, which has further strengthened the move to cross-functional teams.

A major advantage of cross-functional teams is that they enhance communication across groups, often leading to savings in product development time. In 1988, AT&T began developing a cordless telephone. A major obstacle the company faced was a tightly formed hierarchical structure. John Hanley, the vice president of product development, hoped to cut product development time in half. He knew that the company would have to make major changes to accomplish this goal. In the past, the AT&T approach to product development resembled a relay system: The product development group would hand a design over to manufacturing. Next, manufacturing would hand the product over to marketing, who would then sell it to consumers.

Hanley revamped the process by forming teams whose membership included engineers, manufacturers, and marketers. Team members were granted the authority to decide how much the product would cost, how it would work, and what it would look like. Rigid speed requirements were established before design requirements were fixed. Partly because they did not have to send decisions up the hierarchy for approval, the team achieved tight deadlines. As a result of the shift to cross-functional teams, AT&T cut development time down from two years to one year. Equally significant, the manufacturing cost was lowered and product quality improved.[5]

Charles Garfield, a psychologist and a scientist on the Apollo 11 mission team, sheds additional light on the nature of cross-functional teams. He says that such teams can essentially be built by getting people from different functional areas into a room with a facilitator. The facilitator helps break down departmental barriers. Garfield questions the wisdom of having one department work for months, then tossing its plan over the wall to another department (like the AT&T relay system). The problem is that a representative from the next department will often say, "That won't work!" And to emphasize his or her point, the plan will be tossed back over the wall.

It is better for the facilitator to gather people from the different functional areas coordinating efforts from the beginning, and then turn them loose. The facilitator or leader must trust the wisdom of the group. If you are a leader, contribute your views but act mostly to reconcile conflicting opinions.[6]

Another key point in getting started, or chartering the cross-functional team, is to select its members carefully. The criteria for selecting team members we described in Chapter 2 are relevant here, too. It is vital to choose people who think broadly and who are not drum-beaters for their own discipline. Explain to team members that they are pathfinders and part of the new workplace where many departmental borders are blurred.

THINKING CROSS-FUNCTIONALLY

In Chapter 6 we suggested ways for team leaders to use cross-functional thinking as a way of developing teamwork. We introduce the topic again here with a new focus on using analogies, anecdotes, and multifunctional development to foster cross-functional thinking.

The objective of the horizontal corporation is to change the narrow perspectives of functional managers who have spent their careers climbing the proverbial ladder in their areas of expertise. Terry Ennis, a DuPont executive, describes the goal of the horizontal organization in these terms: "Our goal is to get everyone focused on the business as a system in which the functions are seamless."[7]

In the traditional functional organization only a handful of people have the mandate to think cross-functionally. This handful of people includes general managers (such as CEOs and plant managers) and strategic planners. Division and department heads are lauded for their ability to take an overall point of view ("see the big picture"). Yet their jobs rarely depend on developing a general manager perspective. In a cross-functional team, however, each member is expected to develop an overall or systems perspective.

A systems perspective refers to the idea that the individual comprehends how a change introduced in one part of the system creates changes in other parts of the system as well. Assume, for example, that the director of marketing pushes for total customer satisfaction. One change initiated in the organization triggers another change, resulting in the type of chain reaction that follows:

> Upgraded product development → Tighter manufacturing standards → Hiring high-quality employees in manufacturing and customer service → Widespread employee training in customer satisfaction → Increased product cost → Need to reduce costs by reengineering.

The quiz in Figure 8-2 provides you with insights into the current level of your cross-functional thinking. It would be illuminating for other members of your work group to take this quiz, too. In this way you might be able to achieve a team measure of cross-functional thinking.

FIGURE 8-2

To What Extent Are You a Cross-Functional Thinker?

Indicate the extent to which you agree with each of the following statements: strongly disagree (SD); disagree (D); neutral (N); agree (A); strongly agree (SA). Circle the number 1 through 5 under the most accurate answer for each question.

	SD	D	N	A	SA
1. It is best to stick to your specialty and not comment about the work done by people from other disciplines.	5	4	3	2	1
2. I enjoy learning about the contribution made by other departments in my firm.	1	2	3	4	5
3. I rarely talk to people on the job whose work is much different from mine.	5	4	3	2	1
4. When I take on an assignment for the company, I think first of how well the assignment will help my career.	5	4	3	2	1
5. An excellent philosophy is, "It's not what your company can do for you, but what you can do for your company."	1	2	3	4	5
6. Getting people together from different specialties to discuss a technical problem is usually a waste of time.	5	4	3	2	1
7. The best business judgments are likely to stem from talking over the problem with people from different departments.	1	2	3	4	5
8. CEOs have limited perspectives because they no longer concentrate in one area of expertise.	5	4	3	2	1
9. Talking over business problems with people from different areas often leads to a superior solution.	1	2	3	4	5
10. It would suit my interests to work almost exclusively with people doing the same type of work as me.	5	4	3	2	1

SCORING AND INTERPRETATION: Add the totals for the numbers you have circled. A score of 45 to 50 means you have the right mental set to think cross-functionally on the job. A score of 25 to 44 suggests that you have an average tendency to think cross-functionally. A score of 10 to 24 suggests that you think heavily in functional terms. To be fully effective in the revamped workplace you will need to broaden your outlook about the importance of cross-functional collaboration.

A key method for developing cross-functional thinking among team members is for the leader to use the venerable analogy about wearing different hats. From time to time, the leader can casually talk about the importance of each team member owning a functional hat and a cross-functional hat. The team member can then choose which hat to wear on a given day. For most assignments in process redesign and the horizontal corporation, team members must wear their cross-functional hats.

Ennis, the Dupont executive, contends that casting aside functional hats is difficult for most people. "It's very unsettling and threatening for people. You find line and functional managers who have been honored and rewarded for what they've done for decades. You're in a white-water zone when you change."[8]

A team leader can sometimes stimulate cross-functional thinking by asking team members to assume a general-manager perspective on a given issue. Suppose that you are the leader of a process redesign team and your group is about to recommend eliminating outside sales representatives for a particular product line. From a self-interested point of view, the marketing representative would ordinarily think, "There goes our outside sales group right down the tubes." The representative from human resources management might say, "There goes my program for recruiting, selecting, and training outside sales representatives."

To head off self-interested, functional thinking from snow-balling, the head of the design team might comment, "Let's look at our redesign plan as if we were all general managers. What redesign solutions will benefit the organization as a whole? For now, let's forget about whose ox will be gored. What counts most is the long-term health of the entire organization." Repeated pleas to develop a general-management perspective may help bring about the required shift in thinking.

A manager can also make use of anecdotes to deliver the message that cross-functional thinking is a useful way to resolve organizational problems. We recommend anecdotes because they are effective communication devices. Transformational and charismatic leaders in particular make extensive use of anecdotes. Here is an anecdote for communicating the importance of cross-functional thinking:

A hospital was facing the problem of patients getting their dinners later. A cross-functional team of nurses, dietitians, and other nursing unit and food services staff was formed to tackle this problem that so aggravated the patients. Hospital management was concerned that if the problem were addressed only by the nursing unit, the food services department would mostly take the blame. Management was also concerned that if the problem were addressed only by food services, nursing would likely take the blame. In either case, little would have been accomplished.

A cross-functional team unraveled the web of complex scheduling and delivery issues associated with the problem. A small part of the problem was delaying food services receiving an accurate and prompt patient count from nursing. Another small piece of the problem, uncovered through cross-functional thinking, was that kitchen personnel were not working on special orders early enough in the food-preparation cycle.[9]

An elegant way to develop cross-functional thinking is to grant employees the opportunity to participate in multifunctional development or cross-training. Multifunctional development is typically reserved for managers, but professional and technical employees could also benefit from it. Multifunctional development is an intentional effort to enhance the capacity of selected individuals by exposing them to multiple functions within the organization.

A few major corporations already emphasize such cross-training, including Hewlett-Packard, 3M, American Express, Exxon, and Disney Productions. Many other firms emphasize multifunctional management development by rotating management trainees through different departments shortly after they join the firm. Early development of this type will often form the foundation for a career in general management. Cross-functional thinking is, of course, essential for general management.

Small and medium-sized firms sometimes intentionally develop their managers by lending them to different functions as the need permits. A manufacturing manager said that one of his best developmental experiences occurred when the purchasing manager was on medical leave for two months. "The company couldn't spare anybody else, so they threw me in as the acting purchasing manager. I learned quite a bit about another important part of our business."

As researched by Daphna E. Raskas and Donald C. Hambrick, a continuum of five options exists for multifunctional management development.[10] the options are laid out on a continuum of commitment to multifunctional development, as shown in Figure 8-3. At the low end of the continuum, the organization invests the least time and money into development.

The various options are not necessarily trade-offs. Many companies combine approaches. Firms that offer complete mobility across functions also tend to engage in lower-commitment, low-cost approaches. Individuals seeking to develop a multifunctional perspective should seize the opportunity to participate in an assortment of these developmental experiences.

Encouraging employees to study other business functions may not reflect much organizational commitment, yet the technique has merit. Studying other organizational functions helps to develop an appreciation of what other functions entail. Reading a current introduction to business text, or taking such a course, is the quickest way of developing an understanding of the various business functions. Understanding will sometimes lead to empathy.

Higher-level options reflect more extensive organizational commitment to multifunctional development. Exposure to other functions as part of a task force is one of the most practical vehicles for developing a multidisciplinary viewpoint. A computer scientist who had spent the first five years of her career working only with computer scientists was placed on a multidisciplinary task force. The task force was charged with searching for applications of process redesign with the company.

FIGURE 8-3

Continuum of Practical Options for Multifunctional Managerial Development

- HIGH COMMITMENT
- COMPLETE MOBILITY ACROSS FUNCTIONS, I.E., "CAREER MAZE"
- TEMPORARY (SIX MONTHS TO TWO YEAR) ASSIGNMENTS OUTSIDE THE PERSON'S "HOME FUNCTION"
- BRIEF, ORIENTATIONAL ROTATION THROUGH FUNCTIONS
- EXPOSURE TO OTHER FUNCTIONS ON TASK FORCES/PROJECT TEAMS
- CLASSROOM EDUCATION ABOUT OTHER FUNCTIONS
- LOW COMMITMENT

Reprinted, by permission of the publisher, from "Multifunctional Managerial Development: A Framework for Evaluating the Options" by Daphna R. Raskas and Donald C. Hambrick, Organizational Dynamics, Autumn 1992, ©1992. American Management Association, New York. All rights reserved.

After two months on the task force, the computer scientist commented, "Working with people from different disciplines was a real eye-opener. Before I joined the task force I used to refer to people from other areas as 'non-computer scientists.' I now realize that I had a very narrow viewpoint. It humbled me when I tried to explain to others how my work as a computer scientist could really help them."

An intermediate commitment to multifunctional management development is reflected in brief rotations through several functions, often in succession. The individual retains identity in a primary functional area, or a home base. Rotations of this nature are akin to management training programs for newcomers into the firm. The new employee gains firsthand exposure to various functions, and seeks a permanent assignment where the fit appears best. A good fit then leads to a long-term career track.

A just-below-top level of commitment to multifunctional development might encourage individuals to have a "home function" in which they have primary expertise and career goals. At the same time, the employee rotates through periodic assignments in other areas of about six months to two years. A newly hired information systems specialist might work in that capacity for two years, in marketing for one year, and then return to information systems for two more years. Next, the person might receive a six-month assignment in manufacturing, and then go back again to information systems.

The home-function approach to development results in a T-shaped experience profile, which is highly valued in today's workplace. The person develops a deep groove of professional identity (the stem of the T). At the same time the person crosses over into other business functions (the horizontal line on the T).

Visualize a financial manager who develops expertise in optimizing cash flow from accounts receivables. Because most organizations value getting paid promptly, this man has a marketable skill (squeezing cash out of receivables). The same financial manager develops a working knowledge of other functions. He works as a credit analyst in marketing, manages a company store for two years, and also obtains a tour of duty in the employee benefits department. This finance manager has a spike in his experience profile (optimizing cash from accounts receivables), yet also develops breadth based on his assignments outside the finance area.

At the high end of the continuum is a systematic program that affords people complete mobility across organizational functions. Hewlett-Packard is an exemplar of high commitment to multi-functional management development. As part of a "career-maze" program, an employee may receive a first assignment in product design. The employee then moves in succession to marketing, manufacturing, customer service, and so on. Many different combinations of sequencing of assignments are possible, all with the same objective—helping a person develop cross-functional skills and attitudes.

We have presented the various levels of multifunctional development in detail because multifunctional experience is a primary vehicle for learning to think cross-functionally. Take the initiative to develop cross-functionally rather than waiting for a company assignment. Read, study, and volunteer for task forces and rotational assignments. Encouraging others to do the same will enhance cross-functional thinking in the organization.

A FRAMEWORK FOR EFFECTIVE PROJECT MANAGEMENT

The skills and knowledge you already possess for managing others are distinct assets for project management. Whether you are the process manager for reengineering a nationwide system of improving the patent-application process, or for running a blood drive for your company, certain basic management principles apply. You will always need to plan, organize, lead, and control. To establish these universal principles of management, four methods are particularly appropriate for project management.[11] Following them will enhance your effectiveness as a project manager in the revamped workplace. (Project managers, you will recall, include case managers, process owners, and team leaders.)

1. Establish Project Goals and Objectives

Surprise! Effective project management begins with setting project goals. Although goal setting may appear straightforward, setting meaningful goals requires hard work. The project team has to satisfy both external customers and company management. Two project management experts, W. Alan Randolph and Barry Z. Posner, urge that you conduct a dialogue with relevant others to establish goals.[12]

One challenge is that many projects are being done for the first time, so a quantifiable goal may not be immediately apparent. The organization might begin with best estimates of time and cost, based on similar projects completed in the past. At a consumer electronics company, a task force was given the assignment of shortening the time it took to order out-of-stock merchandise for customers. The company's suppliers varied so widely in their cycle times that it was difficult to set a goal immediately. Goal setting became increasingly complicated when the team realized that they would have to incorporate the individual capabilities of the vendors in their goal setting.

The most effective goals are established in terms of the requirements of the end user. In the project for ordering out-of-stock merchandise, a weak goal would be to "establish a new ordering system." A more effective goal would be to "satisfy customer demand for rapid delivery on out-of-stock merchandise."

To condense decades of accumulated knowledge about what constitutes an effective goal statement, keep the following in mind: Specify what is going to be accomplished, who is going to accomplish it, when it is going to be accomplished, and how it is going to be accomplished.

Establishing the "what," "who," "when," and "how" in project goals reduces the chance for misinterpretation. A sample effective goal statement, supported by two objectives (or subgoals) is shown in the accompanying box.

The terms *goals* and *objectives* are often used interchangeably. Yet planners and managers sometimes regard objectives as subgoals that support the larger goals. Objectives for the task under consideration would include developing reliable measures of customer satisfaction with the out-of-stock ordering process. For example, customer satisfaction might be measured by an increase in the percentage of customers who actually purchase the out-of-stock merchandise when it arrives. Another objective for the program would be to work with suppliers in adapting their shipping methods to the store's requirements.

All goals and objectives should be backed by action plans. Ironically, setting an objective (or subgoal) often constitutes the action plan for achieving a goal. For example, to fill out-of-stock orders more quickly, objectives have to be established for getting better cooperation from suppliers.

EFFECTIVE GOAL STATEMENT SUPPORTED BY OBJECTIVES

Goal Statements
The project team working on the out-of-stock project will increase customer satisfaction with receiving merchandise currently out of stock. The project will be completed by December 31 of this year, by working with the six employees assigned to the project.

Objectives
1. Develop a reliable measure of customer satisfaction with the out-of-stock ordering process.
2. Work with suppliers in adapting their shipping methods to the store's requirements.

In setting goals and objectives, avoid one of the shortcomings of many management-by-objectives programs: Creating so much paperwork and electronic work that accomplishing the task becomes more complicated rather than simplified.

2. Establish Checkpoints and Activities

To keep the project running smoothly, establish checkpoints. Checkpoints act as control devices. If progress is monitored at a particular time, and the project is behind schedule, take corrective action. Let's assume that the retailing process team was to hold discussions about prompt deliveries 30 days into the project. If decisive action has not been taken, the project leader must investigate why this activity has fallen behind schedule.

Activities are the actual tasks that must be carried out to achieve events and milestones. Action plans consist of a series of activities to be carried out to reach the objectives. All activities are important because, when pooled together, they constitute the completion of a project. One of the many activities in retailing process redesign is measuring the percentage of customers who come back to the store to pick up out-of-stock merchandise they ordered.

A basic, yet still popular, method for keeping track of progress on a project is the milestone chart. It provides a listing of the subactivities that must be completed to accomplish the major activities listed on the vertical axis. A milestone is the completion of one phase of an activity (such as collecting out-of-stock merchandise slips from the store managers). Each milestone serves as another progress checkpoint. Figure 8-4 presents a milestone chart developed for the complicated project of opening a nightclub.

Flow charts are another important technique for monitoring progress on a project, and are especially relevant in the revamped workplace. The process maps presented in the Appendix are a variation of a flow chart used to understand a work process. A flow chart helps a person visualize progress on a project because it arranges activities in a sequence. In the nightclub example shown in Figure 8-4, the site of the club must be specified and a lease drawn before the owner can apply for a liquor license. The reason for this sequencing is that the liquor commission will grant a license only after approving a specific location.

Scheduling projects is a subject within itself. Project managers rely on advanced scheduling techniques such as program evaluation and review technique (PERT). Software is widely available for preparing PERT diagrams, and for even more advanced scheduling techniques.

3. Coach Individuals and Develop Teamwork

A project manager, acting as a true leader, fits the new mold of the leader as facilitator and coach. Projects are more egalitarian

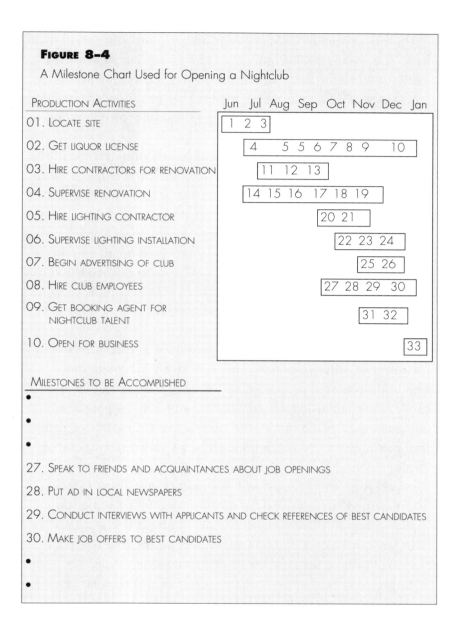

FIGURE 8-4

A Milestone Chart Used for Opening a Nightclub

PRODUCTION ACTIVITIES	Jun Jul Aug Sep Oct Nov Dec Jan
01. LOCATE SITE	1 2 3
02. GET LIQUOR LICENSE	4 5 5 6 7 8 9 10
03. HIRE CONTRACTORS FOR RENOVATION	11 12 13
04. SUPERVISE RENOVATION	14 15 16 17 18 19
05. HIRE LIGHTING CONTRACTOR	20 21
06. SUPERVISE LIGHTING INSTALLATION	22 23 24
07. BEGIN ADVERTISING OF CLUB	25 26
08. HIRE CLUB EMPLOYEES	27 28 29 30
09. GET BOOKING AGENT FOR NIGHTCLUB TALENT	31 32
10. OPEN FOR BUSINESS	33

MILESTONES TO BE ACCOMPLISHED

-
-
-

27. SPEAK TO FRIENDS AND ACQUAINTANCES ABOUT JOB OPENINGS

28. PUT AD IN LOCAL NEWSPAPERS

29. CONDUCT INTERVIEWS WITH APPLICANTS AND CHECK REFERENCES OF BEST CANDIDATES

30. MAKE JOB OFFERS TO BEST CANDIDATES

-
-

than hierarchical structures. Team members therefore expect the project manager (or process owner, case manager, or team leader) to act as a facilitator and coach. The suggestions for coaching presented in Chapter 5 are directly relevant for successful project management.

Closely related to coaching is properly motivating team members. A combination of individual and group incentives are likely to work the best. Few professional and technical people are so devoid of ego and self-interest that group incentives alone are sufficient. Because teamwork is valued in projects, group incentives are also effective.

Every reader of this book understands the importance of motivation, and most readers have a working knowledge of motivational approaches. One of the most practical approaches to motivating rational people is to reward them for doing things right. Keep the following list of incentives, or motivators, in mind when attempting to motivate your team members. Incentives can be used in two basic ways. One is to reward the right performance or behavior *after* it occurs. The second is to explain *in advance* which reward a person will receive should he or she deliver a good performance.

The process owner has to understand the preferences of team members in order to use rewards effectively. Through conversation and observation, determine which reward would be a good fit for a particular individual. For example, many people enjoy being complimented in front of others, yet a minority of people find this motivational technique to be patronizing and embarrassing.

Motivation on a project will sometimes lag after the initial excitement wears off. The mission soon develops some routine aspects. A team leader might be excited about being chosen to help reengineering a company. Completing the first few process maps is likely to trigger a surge of professional pride. Yet by the 35th process map, some of the glamour begins to wear thin. The process owner can help with this problem by reminding teammates of the important mission they are undertaking. An occasional statement such as "We are part of a revolution taking place in this company" can help team members remember the broad purpose of their daily activities.

Building teamwork is another major success factor for a project manager. All the techniques described in Chapter 6 will help

MOTIVATORS THAT WORK

Monetary
Salary increase
Bonus or profit sharing
Stock options
Time off from work with pay
Gift certificates

Social and Pride Related
Compliments
Encouragement
Access to confidential information
"Attaboys" and "Attagals"
Expression of appreciation in front of others

Recognition and Status Symbols
Elegant job titles
Bigger work area or office
Fancier personal computer
Company-paid cellular phone
Wall plaque indicating accomplishment
Special commendation (e.g., professional of the month)
Company recognition pin, watch, or ring

Job and Career Related
Challenging work assignments
Favorable performance review
Freedom to choose own work activity
Promotion
Rotation to higher-prestige project
Improved working conditions
Opportunity to perform more of preferred tasks
Opportunity to be acting project leader when boss is away

> ## ONE OF THE MOST PRACTICAL APPROACHES TO MOTIVATING RATIONAL PEOPLE IS TO REWARD THEM FOR DOING THINGS RIGHT.

you build an effective project team. When a team is composed of willing volunteers, a giant stride has been taken toward developing teamwork. Volunteers are normally eager to work collaboratively. An important exception is that a few people are eager to join teams so that they can loaf and let others carry much of their share. Such loafers can be spotted early in the history of the project and confronted.

4. Deal Assertively with Conflicts and Political Clashes

Project organizations breed conflict and political infighting. Matrix structures (a project superimposed on a functional organization) are even more susceptible to conflict. A major contributor to conflict is that the project manager may engage in squabbles with functional managers over resources. Seven factors are especially important contributors to conflict and political struggles in projects and task forces.[13]

Project Priorities. Team members may have different views as to which tasks are most important. Groups supporting the project also may have different opinions about which tasks should be accomplished first.

Administrative Procedures. Disagreement may arise over how the project will be managed, such as through agreements with other departments about the level of assistance available. Managers of functional departments and other projects may be upset because a high-priority project gets such a large share of company resources.

Technical Opinions. Project members are usually highly trained and highly opinionated. Disagreements may arise over technical procedures, choice of software, and scheduling techniques. Two team members on a quality-improvement team haggled for a month over which statistical procedure was best suited for analyzing data on customer complaints. (One argued for parametric statistics and the other for nonparametric.)

Staffing and Resource Allocations. Team members may argue over what is a fair distribution of work within the project. Most of the project members would prefer to conduct the more technologically sophisticated work and leave the grunt work to others.

Costs and Budgets. Typically, an agreement is reached about costs and budgets before a project begins. Nevertheless, there is ample room for squabbling over categories within the larger budget. One team member assigned to a project took several expensive out-of-town trips. She consumed so much of the travel budget that another team member was told to conduct a telephone interview rather than take a trip. He accused the first team member of being irresponsible and self-centered.

Schedules. Although project members use advanced scheduling techniques, problems still exist with meeting schedules. The project manager may enter into conflict with top management over schedules. Yet the problem might be attributed to the difficulty in predicting contingencies. One process redesign project fell behind schedule because so many of the people feeding data to the project were laid off throughout the firm.

Interpersonal Clashes. Project members usually are competitive people who value their own opinion and status. When their opinion is challenged, they sometimes become defensive and attack the criticizer. Clashes over whose area of technical expertise is the most relevant also arise. An industrial engineer assigned to a process redesign team informed other members that his background made him the most professionally qualified to make recommendations about simplifying work. Several other members said that everyone is a technical equal in a new area like process redesign.

An effective project member must be willing to assertively handle the conflicts and political clashes that arise during the life of a project. The most highly recommended, general-purpose way of resolving conflict is confrontation followed by problem solving. This method helps a person identify the true source of a conflict and resolve it systematically. The confrontation in this approach is gentle and tactful rather than combative and abusive. Reasonableness is important because the person who takes the initiative in resolving the conflict wants to maintain a harmonious working relationship with the other party. Confronting and problem solving a conflict involves six steps:

Step 1: Awareness. Party A recognizes that a conflict exists between himself or herself and Party B, such as the process owner conflicting with the industrial engineer who believes that his opinion about process redesign issues should count the most.

Step 2: The decision to confront. Party A decides that the conflict is important enough to warrant a confrontation with Party B and that such a confrontation is preferable to avoiding the conflict.

Step 3: The confrontation. party A decides to work cooperatively and confronts Party B. At this point, Party B may indicate willingness to accept the confrontation or may decide to gloss over its seriousness. Often the conflict is resolved at this step, particularly if it is not of a serious and complicated nature.

Step 4: Determining the cause of the conflict. The two parties discuss their own opinions, attitudes, and feelings in relation to the conflict and attempt to identify the real issue. For example, the real issue with the industrial engineer might be that he feels he is not being given sufficient professional recognition for his expertise. From the other side, the process owner is unwilling to create a status hierarchy within the group.

Step 5: Determining the outcome and further steps. In this step the parties attempt to develop specific means of reducing or eliminating the source of the conflict. If the cause cannot be changed (such as the industrial engineer's professional pride), a way of working around the cause is devised. If both parties agree on a solution, then the confrontation has been successful. In this situation, the industrial engineer might be invited to demonstrate an advanced technique of work simplification to the group. He might also be considered an internal resource. Both offers, however, are contingent upon his willingness to work on an equal-status level with other project members.

Step 6: Follow-through. After the solution has been implemented, both parties should check periodically to ensure that their agreements are being met.[14]

A Checklist for Managing Cross-Functional Teams

Effective project management is a major requirement for the revamped workplace because so much of the new work is organized into projects, teams, and task forces. Furthermore, most of these groups are composed of people from different disciplines. The successful modern manager must therefore do a first-rate job of managing a cross-functional team. Implementing the following suggestions for the effective management of cross-functional teams will increase your chances of managing successfully in today's workplace.

- ☑ The modern manager must possess the important ability to manage horizontally across projects instead of vertically via functional experts.

- ☑ Cross-functional thinking is one of the major requirements of the revamped workplace.

☑ A key tactic for developing cross-functional thinking among team members is for the leader to use the analogy about people wearing different hats. Each person has a functional hat and a cross-functional hat, and chooses which one to wear on a given day.

☑ To stimulate cross-functional thinking, the team leader can ask team members to assume a general-manager perspective on a given issue.

☑ An important strategy for developing cross-functional thinking is to grant people the opportunity to participate in multifunctional development.

☑ Effective project management begins with setting project goals. In establishing goals, specify what is going to be accomplished, who is going to accomplish it, when it is going to be accomplished, and how it is going to be accomplished.

☑ An effective project member must be willing and able to deal with the conflicts and political clashes that arise during the life of a project. The most highly recommended general-purpose way of resolving conflict is confrontation and problem solving.

Effective
Downsizing

9

Whether you choose to use the term *downsizing*, *rightsizing*, *resizing*, or *restructuring*, trimmed-down organizations predominate in the revamped workplace. The downsizing movement began in the late 1970s, and snowballed in the 1980s and early 1990s. About 6 million corporate jobs were eliminated during this period. From 1991 to early 1994 1 in 10 workers, on the average, have been laid off by half of America's leading business firms.[1]

Despite improved business conditions in the mid-1990s, the downsizing movement has retained some of its momentum. Trimming down the work force has become standard even for profitable companies such as Procter & Gamble. Although the company achieved record earnings in 1993, top management announced plans to cut 13,000 jobs. Trimming down during good times helps a company remain competitive now and in the future. A 1993 American Management Association survey indicated that in 1993, 10.4 percent of the U.S. work force was working for employers who were downsizing.[2]

As reengineering and process redesign gain momentum, the downsizing movement will continue. Although layoffs may decrease in magnitude, the trend toward slimmed-down organizations will not lessen. One of senior management's primary motives for reengineering is to reduce costs through payroll reduction. Conceivably, many executives look to reengineering as a way of improving customer service and modernizing operations. Yet these executives do not suffer from color blindness. Reengineering has the distinct green glow of money saved and increased profits.

Reengineering, process redesign, and the horizontal corporation lead to downsizing because they reduce the number of people needed to carry out business transactions. Total quality management sometimes leads to downsizing. The team emphasis leads to a smaller demand for first-level supervisors and middle managers. If virtual corporations develop as fast as predicted, they, too, will be a force for trimmer organizations. Instead of creating large staffs of specialists, a virtual corporation basically borrows talent for special needs. In its pure form, the virtual corporation can operate with virtually no employees.

Downsizing has improved the financial position and competitiveness of many firms. Unisys Corporation went through a major restructuring in 1986, cutting its work force in half to 56,000. Within five years the company had reversed its pattern of losses. Many small businesses have eliminated the jobs of unproductive people and emerged as more profitable. But despite many successes, downsizing fails to consistently achieve its goals of improved earnings and overall company effectiveness.

Severe downsizing can create financial loss rather than gain. Confusion, inefficiency, costs of paying out early retirement and severance packages, and legal expenses in defending against lawsuits all combine to offset the gains of reduced payroll costs. A 1993 survey by the American Management Association of 547 companies that had downsized during a six-year period found that profits improved for only 43.5 percent. For example, 12 months after substantial downsizings, the following firms showed much poorer return on equity than 12 months before the layoff: Eastman Kodak, Zenith Electronics, Sears, Westinghouse, and American Express. To IBM's chagrin, shedding 100,000 jobs did not improve its intermediate-term profitability.[3]

In a 1992 survey, 1,000 companies were questioned about their success with downsizing. Among the findings were that only 50 percent actually reduced their expenses, and only 22 percent achieved productivity increases. Other indices of downsizing success also came up short, among them the hoped-for improvements in cash flow and speeded-up decision making, rarely took place.[4]

Our intent here is not to bash downsizing but to point toward managerial practices and strategies that lead to successful downsizing. Another purpose is to provide information that will help you manage your career in response to downsizing.

DEVELOPING A DOWNSIZING GAME PLAN

Downsizing is so pervasive today that useful guidelines for its proper execution are readily available. Managers no longer have to rely on intuition to downsize their organizations. Instead, a game plan can be developed to increase the chances that downsizing will produce bottom-line gains yet minimize human suffering. An effective game play will also prevent some of the confusion and disruption that accompany most downsizings. Before laying out recommended components of such a plan, let us look at a carefully planned downsizing that exceeded its intended results.[5]

Bill Ryan, the vice president of human resources for Sea-Land Service, recalls that in 1989 his company was troubled. Sea-Land, a cargo-shipping company based in New Jersey, was

> 1,000 COMPANIES WERE QUESTIONED ABOUT THEIR SUCCESS WITH DOWNSIZING . . . ONLY 50 PERCENT ACTUALLY REDUCED THEIR EXPENSES, AND ONLY 22 PERCENT ACHIEVED PRODUCTIVITY INCREASES.

bloated and inefficient, yet still earning a profit. Ryan knew the company would have to undergo downsizing of up to 15 percent of its work force if it were to remain competitive in the international cargo business.

The first step in developing a downsizing game plan was to conduct a nine-month study that examined virtually every operation of the company. A new job description was created for every position. Next, a zero-based staffing system put all employees at risk of losing their jobs. (Under zero-based staffing, each position has to be justified for retention after downsizing.) Employees at all levels from senior executives to custodial workers were rated against the new job descriptions and matched with the new positions. When a new work force emerged, it heavily emphasized abilities and skills to support the demands of the new organization.

As a result of downsizing, Sea-Land eliminated more than 800 positions and five layers of management. Operating expenses were reduced by about $300 million. Productivity increased beyond what was thought possible. Since 1989, revenues for Sea-Land have climbed by 30 percent to $3.3 billion. Profits have increased 35 percent to $151 million. Of particular significance, Sea-Land achieved these results in an environment of recession and cutthroat overseas competition.

The systematic look at every position in the company inspired many Sea-Land managers and individual contributors to approach their jobs more creatively. Too many employees had become complacent during the boom times of the 1980s. Few companies going through downsizing will achieve the same magnitude of results as Sea-Land. Yet developing a sensible game plan will increase any firm's chances of achieving some of the potential gains from downsizing.

Eliminate Low-Value/No-Value Activities

An essential component of a successful downsizing game plan is to eliminate low-value and no-value activities. Zero-based

> # HOW TO
> # DOWNSIZE EFFECTIVELY
>
> 1. *Eliminate low-value and no-value activities:* This is called activity-based reduction—a new term for systematically comparing the costs of a firm's activities to their value to the customer.
> 2. *Keep the future work requirements in mind:* The answer to bloat is not to let go of people who will be an important part of the firm's future.
> 3. *Identify the tasks that retained employees will perform:* Then prepare and train these employees.
> 4. *Decide which workers will be let go:* Use seniority, position, function, employment status, voluntary resignation, early retirement, and performance as criteria.

staffing, as used by Sea-Land, is a way to eliminate low-value activities. Doing away with unnecessary work fits the spirit of reengineering and process redesign. Note the differences between low-value workers and low-value activities. Many talented, hard-working employees efficiently carry out useless work. An example would be a corporate planner who prepares a 25-page report on a potential strategic alliance. Her report might reflect extraordinary skill, yet the CEO has no interest in forming an alliance and therefore doesn't even read the report.

Activity-based cost reduction is the new term for systematically comparing the costs of a firm's activities with their actual value to the firm. The ultimate question is whether the organization will suffer competitively if the function or task is eliminated. If the answer is no, the function can be eliminated. If the function does contribute to the firm's competitive strength, an-

> ## MANY TALENTED, HARD-WORKING EMPLOYEES EFFICIENTLY CARRY OUT USELESS WORK.

other question must be answered. Is the value of the activity worth its cost?

As explained by consultant Paul Firstenberg, the lowest value-added activities should be the first ones scaled back or eliminated.[6] The underlying principle is that a cost-reduction program is anchored by cutting back on low-value work. Staffs are then cut to reflect the reduced workload, as was done at Sea-Land. In short, downsizing is an outcome of reducing low-value work. A more frequently practiced approach to cost reduction is to eliminate some workers, then expect those people remaining to get all the work done as before. Unless the people eliminated were bunglers and time wasters, the survivors become overloaded.

Under activity-based cost reduction, certain functions might be assigned additional staff during a downsizing because of the value they contribute to the firm. One company going through downsizing, for example, found that the telemarketing staff was highly cost-effective. Although only 5 percent of their unsolicited phone calls resulted in a sale, this closing ratio was profitable. Adding more telemarketers was a good investment.

Activity-based cost reduction is not as easy as it sounds. The cost-reduction team has to make astute judgments as to the value of activities and tasks. During a downsizing in an insurance company, the cost-reduction team came across the job title of "insurance miner." The head of the team was immediately suspicious and wanted to eliminate the position. In reality, the job was cost-effective. The position involved a sales trainee reviewing long-standing inactive accounts and contacting these former policy holders. Many of the former clients welcomed the attention and placed at least part of their insurance coverage with the firm.

Several examples of where value to the organization does *not* justify costs:[7]

- An internal auditing staff was identified whose cost exceeded the savings the group was able to identify. Furthermore, the staff's control function duplicated the work of the firm's external auditors.
- A weekly financial report took the efforts of several full-time staff professionals to prepare. Unfortunately, the report was rarely read by executives.
- An item-by-item review of expense accounts was conducted by an expense control unit. The amount of money their reviews uncovered was miniscule in comparison to the total compensation paid the unit. Instead of the expense-control unit, the company instituted a comparison of expense accounts against formulas based on prior experience. Using these formulas was just as effective as the expense-control unit in keeping such expenses in line.

Keep Future Work Requirements in Mind

An important part of an effective downsizing game plan is to downsize in such a way as to fit the firm's future requirements. The present organization might be bloated, yet an answer to the bloat is not to lay off people who will be an important part of the firm's future. Companies making the transition from an old-line to a modern corporation often face the challenge of meeting future requirements while downsizing. The employees most needed for the future are those who can adapt to change and high technology.

After NYNEX separated from AT&T in the mid-1980s to become a separate company, it had to cut 9,000 positions from its managerial staff of 25,000. NYNEX implemented a voluntary separation program that included generous severance pay, pensions, and other incentives. Bill Coffey, the NYNEX corporate director of human resources, said: "We were successful in getting raw numbers of people to leave, but we were very unsuccessful in retaining some of the best minds. We wound up with too many people in certain divisions and not enough in others."

As a result of many of the wrong people leaving, NYNEX had to hire back people to fill 4,000 positions. The lesson carried over to a downsizing undertaken in 1991. NYNEX developed a workplace plan that kicks in automatically when hiring patterns warrant intervention in any organizational unit. Staffing decisions are now made by the head of each business unit rather than by the CEO or chairman. The implication is that while one division may be shrinking during a downsizing, another may be growing.

In 1992, the New York Telephone division needed to trim the number of engineers from 500 to 400. The company presented a formal business case which included the rationale for the staff reductions. All 500 employees were notified that a reduction in force would take place. A task force established updated criteria and requirements for engineering positions within the next few years. Managers then compared engineers to the new job descriptions. Three categories of engineers were created: retained, eligible for voluntary severance, and at risk.

After the evaluations were completed, New York Telephone management reviewed the downsizing plan from a legal and human resources perspective. Staff attorneys checked for Equal Employment Opportunity violations, and human resources professionals ensured that downsizing was administered correctly and fairly. Engineers were then informed of their status and told that downsizing would be completed within 60 days.

Engineers in the at-risk and voluntary categories received severance and bonus packages ranging in value from $50,000 to $500,000. In addition, they received outplacement counseling. Any engineer in the retained category who decided to leave did so on his or her own without receiving separation benefits.

The workplace-management plan used by NYNEX was effective in retaining those engineers who could fit with the modern culture of a telephone company that no longer held a monopoly.[8] Some engineers who had worked for the company when it was a monopoly could not understand that customer satisfaction was given so much importance.

Another vital part of a downsizing game plan is to identify the tasks and functions that retained employees will perform. The tasks and functions at issue here are those deemed worthy of being continued. Before assigning these extra tasks, it is important to assess the capabilities of the remaining staffers. Employees at all levels vary in their capacity to handle additional work. People who are already stretched to their limits are poor candidates for additional responsibilities. Assigning them additional tasks after downsizing is complete may result in incomplete and shoddy work. An overloaded middle manager put it this way:

> Bit by bit the firm is trying to put me into an emergency cardiac unit. Two years ago, we lost practically all our secretarial support in a cutback. I make all my travel reservations, type my own letters, and place all my phone calls. Now I'm supposed to handle the work of three managers, including doing 25 performance appraisals.

A task related to identifying the work to be assumed by the retained employees is training and preparing them to take it on. Management often assumes that co-workers in the same department can perform each other's work quite readily. In reality, co-workers sometimes do not understand each other's jobs. Ordinarily, an employee who is leaving will help train his or her successor. Sometimes a downsized employee is not so eager to train the replacement. Furthermore, some companies march downsized workers out the door the very day of the layoff announcements, making it logistically impossible for the laid-off employee to train a replacement.

Decide Which Workers Will Be Downsized

Establishing the right criteria for who gets placed on the downsizing list is essential for successful downsizing. A hastily composed list of highly paid workers within their job category can backfire. The problem is that pay is closely related to age. Dismissing the more highly paid workers may result in laying off mostly older workers. The potential would therefore be high for lawsuits based on age discrimination. In fact, most lawsuits related to downsizing involving age discrimination. The following criteria for selecting candidates for downsizing, either singly or in combination, are used by many companies:[9]

Seniority. Length of service with the employer is probably the most frequently used criterion. "Last in, first out" is particularly applicable to unionized companies where seniority is highly respected. Layoff policies in educational settings also respect seniority. Employees usually perceive seniority to be a fair criterion for layoff decisions, and the process is objective and easy to administer.

A serious disadvantage of seniority as criterion is that management loses control over which employees are retained. Job performance and skills portfolio—two very important criteria—are largely ignored. Some most productive employees might be dismissed and unproductive ones retained. An exception is that senior employees tend to be competent because in many cases less competent workers are weeded out earlier in their careers.

Position or Function. Dismissing workers who are carrying out nonessential functions is sensible. Such dismissals fit squarely with activity-based cost reduction. Most employees will interpret the decision as impersonal. At times, several of the high performers in nonessential functions can be retained to fill openings in the downsized organization.

Dismissing workers by position or function also has its disadvantages. Some workers will interpret the decision as political. Cries of favoritism are most likely when several workers are performing the same type of work, yet not all of them are eliminated. In one company, five of the middle managers who supervised first-level managers were dismissed, yet two other middle managers performing the same activity were retained. The story circulated that the CEO had formed personal friendships with the two middle managers who kept their jobs. Another problem is that many competent workers who are performing nonessential work will be dismissed while many marginal employees who are performing essential work will be retained.

Employment Status. An easy hit during a downsizing is to lay off part-time and temporary workers. Many employers hire contract workers as a buffer against having to lay off permanent workers during a business downturn. Full-time employees heartily endorse laying off part-timers and temporary workers because it preserves their own job security. Unfortunately, employment status is not an infallible downsizing criterion. At times, creative and talented people engaged in critical work may be terminated. One company, for example, hired contract workers to carry out advanced information systems projects. The company finally compromised by offering full-time employment to two of the information systems specialists working on key projects.

Laying off part-time workers can lower productivity in two other important ways. Part-time workers are less expensive because their pay is relatively low and their benefits package small. Also, part-time workers are sometimes used to meet weekly demand cycles such as handling peak work loads on Mondays and Fridays. If these workers are laid off, departments with peak loads will be understaffed on peak demand days and overstaffed during the other days.

Voluntary Resignations and Early Retirements. A widespread downsizing practice is to ask employees to leave the firm voluntarily, often with an inducement for leaving. The criterion here is that people are selected for layoff if they volunteer. Many of these voluntary resignations and early retirements fall into the category of an offer too good to refuse. Numerous people are told that they can accept an early-retirement package now or face the possibility of a layoff later. Voluntary quits and early retirements are generally popular with employees. Many of them take their retirement bonuses to help them start a small business. Armed with retirement benefits, certain employees can afford to pursue a lower-paying but more satisfying occupation. A former bank vice president in Cleveland now works full time teaching adults to read. She observes, "I always thought my work as a banker was socially useful and valuable. But the impact was indirect. Now I feel I am helping people directly."

The voluntary criterion must be controlled by management or it can backfire, with too many high-talented people leaving. Volunteers should be accepted only with the approval of top management. The company cannot stop people from quitting, but they can refuse to give them a generous separation package. DuPont was one of the first companies to experience the hazards of voluntary retirements. The company wanted to eliminate 6,500 jobs but twice that number of people left. Eastman Kodak Company had a similar experience, but of approximately half the magnitude. During a downsizing many talented people leave without financial inducements because they choose to leave an organization that is on an apparent decline. We'll pick up on this theme later in the chapter.

Performance. A generally productive criterion for dismissal during a downsizing is work performance. The poorest performers within each organizational unit scheduled for downsizing are placed on the termination list. If the firm wants to trim the work force by 10 percent, the bottom 10 percent of performers are targeted for dismissal. A major reason for using performance measures is to decrease the political element in downsizings. It is widely observed that the people most likely to stay are those who are liked by people in power. When poor work performance is used as a primary criterion for dismissal, the downsizing becomes an ideal opportunity for getting rid of employees the company does not want. An executive at a gas and electric company said, "After downsizing in our region we got rid of two-thirds of our whiners and freeloaders."

Conducting performance appraisals for the purpose of downsizing may appear too political: those workers the company wants to retain receive high evaluations, and vice versa. Existing performance evaluation results are more important because they record performance over a longer period of time. Measuring performance over time helps to develop a fairer evaluation of a person's ability. Exceptionally good or bad chemistry with just one boss can result in a skewed evaluation.

In making final decisions about which employees are dismissed, it is best to use a combination of criteria. The ideal candidate for dismissal might be a recently hired temporary doing nonessential work and receiving atrocious performance reviews! Another is the person who asked to be placed on the dismissal list so that he or she can grab some severance pay.

MINIMIZING THE DISRUPTIONS OF LAYOFFS

The macro purpose of downsizing is to increase organizational effectiveness. Despite this noble purpose, downsizing may create so much disruption that its potential gains are obscured. Costs may be substantial, morale and productivity may suffer, and employees may feel unmotivated. Motivation always suffers when employees develop negative perceptions of their employer. Many workers become understandably preoccupied with thoughts of being caught in the next round of layoffs. As a result, they put less effort into their jobs. Confusion and insecurity are rampant, leading to high levels of job stress. Employees spend time conducting job searches rather than concentrating on their work.

During a downsizing, many capable employees leave voluntarily, sensing they might be next. Often, too many people accept early retirement, including some top performers. This places the firm in the embarrassing position of having to recruit to fill certain positions. A long aftermath of employers distrust may follow a downsizing.

Adding to the disruption, many fearful, insecure workers worry that just one mistake will lead to job loss. Such employees are reluctant to suggest new ideas or programs for fear of making a mistake that could jeopardize their jobs. A form of disruption unique to consumer products companies is that many laid-off employees are also customers. As disgruntled former employees they may no longer buy from the firm. Even worse for the firm, they may request all their families and friends to do likewise.

The game plan previously described will curtail some disruption. An activity-based cost reduction plan will help decrease the chances that remaining employees will be overloaded with work. Anticipating future organizational needs will lessen the possibility that employees will have to be hastily recruited in the future. Carefully choosing the criteria for who gets dismissed is another way of minimizing disruption. Suggestions for minimizing the human suffering associated with downsizing are presented in the next chapter. Here we suggest a few additional ideas for preventing and treating the disruption that downsizing creates.

Sharing Information

An important strategy for getting survivors refocused on their jobs is for management to share information with employees. Information sharing helps quell rumors about further reductions in force. Employees should always understand the rationale for downsizing. Following this approach, a Bank of America manager noted, "We had senior managers showing how our changes trended with the downturn in the economy. We showed with key internal business indicators where our business was in trouble and why we just could not continue operating with the same number of people."[10]

Make Changes Quickly

The argument continues whether in times of layoffs to make the cuts all at once or over a protracted period. If alternative placement is not available for the workers affected, reductions in staff are much less disruptive if done all at once rather than gradually. A key argument for making the changes quickly is that the survivors deal better with the downsizing if they are reasonably assured that no further cuts will be forthcoming. The ambiguity of not knowing who will be eliminated creates considerable stress. As many managers have said after an initial period of restructuring, "We are all waiting for the other shoe to fall."

Another human resource problem stemming from gradual cuts is that the organization may lose many competent employees who are concerned about job security. Rather than wait to be terminated, some of the more qualified employees may look for better opportunities in another firm. Less competent employees also spend work time conducting a job search and worrying about losing their jobs.

To counter the risk of losing competent people, top executives should personally contact the most valuable employees to assure them that they are valued by the firm. If the organization is particularly rank-conscious, top management can request that the valued person's immediate superior deliver the message. Shortly after Louis V. Gerstner became CEO of IBM, he found himself faced with an exodus of many highly skilled people who were not targeted for layoffs. Gerstner held face-to-face discussions with several talented workers who were vacillating about

> TO STEM THE TIDE OF LOSING COMPETENT
> PEOPLE, TOP EXECUTIVES SHOULD
> PERSONALLY CONTACT THE MOST
> VALUABLE EMPLOYEES TO ASSURE THEM
> THEY ARE VALUED BY THE FIRM.

leaving IBM. In several instances, his intervention succeeded in retaining key people.

IBM also took other steps to hold onto valuable personnel during the company's downsizing phase. One of Gerstner's first decisions was to offer 1,200 key managers a swap of their devalued stock options for cash exceeding their value. Another initiative was to travel around the country with the head of human resources and administration to assure employees that IBM cared about them.[11]

The call for quick action during downsizing does not mean that laid-off employees should be rushed out the door, with barely enough time to collect their belongings. Being given an hour to clear out one's desk is a stress-provoking indignity.

Listen to Employees

Listening to employees is another strategy for dealing with the potential disruptions stemming from downsizing. After the Bank of America downsizing, brown-bag lunches were held between executives and employees throughout the firm. Managers gave employees the opportunity to discuss their feelings about the layoff and concerns about their place in the firm. A caution is that this approach can backfire when angry employees are looking for the opportunity to tear into management.

Use Task Forces to Solve Special Managerial Problems

After downsizing, fewer managers are present to solve problems. An antidote to this concern is to set up task forces, composed of managers and professionals, to solve special problems. Once the problem is solved, task force members return to their regular assignments full time. The task force can function part-time or full-time, according to the magnitude of the problem.

The task-force approach makes it possible for an organization to operate efficiently with fewer managers occupying full-time, permanent positions. Special problems suitable for the task force might include:

- developing policies for dealing with sexual harassment
- gathering cost-reduction suggestions
- searching out new markets for an existing product line
- creating better career opportunities for the physically disabled
- responding to an organizational crisis such as a product recall

The task forces are also useful because they help staffers stay mentally prepared for the revamped workplace. Task force membership is usually multidisciplinary and lateral relationships are emphasized more than vertical relationships. Members of the task force therefore look upon each other more as teammates and equals rather than deferring to one person as the boss.

Be Honest

An underlying theme in most approaches to minimizing the disruptions of layoffs is that top management should be honest with employees. According to consultant and business professor Oren Harari, the biggest mistake management can make during a downsizing is not to be straight with people.[12] Managers should inform people ahead of time if layoffs are imminent or even a possibility. Workers should be told why layoffs are likely, who might be affected, and in what way. Employees will want to know how the layoff strategy will help strengthen the firm and facilitate growth.

To appear (and be) honest, it is important to tell the same version of the truth to various groups. In one company, the CEO hinted to manufacturing personnel that most of the cuts would come from the ranks of white-collar workers. The following day, he hinted to office workers that most of the cuts would be made in manufacturing. Shortly thereafter, these two versions of the hit list were exchanged by workers from manufacturing and white-collar groups. As a result, the CEO lost credibility in a hurry and rumors about the depths of the cuts escalated.

As implied by this anecdote, the alternative to telling the truth can produce drastic consequences. When people suspect that major decisions about their futures are being formulated in secrecy, negative rumors are sure to increase, with employees meeting to exchange doomsday scenarios.

Another form of dishonesty concerns public announcements of downsizing. When employees learn about downsizings in their own company through the media, morale is dealt a severe blow. This is how a marketing analyst from a large office products firm described his own experience:

> I picked up the morning newspaper to read with shock that the company was laying off 10,000 people during the upcoming year. Things got worse as the day progressed. When I reached the office there was a letter from my boss awaiting me. The grim message was that I had lost my job. Three days ago I had had a career planning discussion with my boss. During our session I heard not even a hint about layoffs.

MANAGING IN A LEANER ORGANIZATION

Managing effectively in a trimmed-down organization requires many adjustments. Managers who survive have to become more self-sufficient, form partnerships with people, and continually look for ways to streamline work. The burden for most of these

> THE BIGGEST MISTAKE MANAGEMENT
> CAN MAKE DURING A DOWNSIZING IS NOT
> TO BE STRAIGHT WITH PEOPLE.

shifts lies with the surviving middle managers and supervisors. Senior executives count heavily on others to make the adjustments. For example, few CEOs cut back on their secretarial support after a downsizing.

Strive for Self-Sufficiency

Becoming more self-sufficient after downsizing usually involves the manager in operating with fewer staff to take care of administrative details. In a downsized organization, middle managers often write their own memos through word processing and electronic mail, and they answer their own phones. Other signs of self-sufficiency include making your own travel arrangements, photocopying brief documents, placing your own long-distance calls, ironing out billing problems with suppliers, and setting up for meetings.

To show that you fit in with the times, it may be necessary to cheerfully carry out many chores that were previously done by a personal assistant or the department secretary. If you gripe about doing clerical work, you might be pegged as a poor team player. The constructive behavior is to upgrade your clerical skills, and attempt to batch as many of these tasks together as possible. For example, some managers do most of their clerical work in the late afternoon or early evening, or at home.

Form Partnerships with Co-Workers

Executives in de-layered companies often make a subtle shift in attitude toward the manager's role. The new-style leader, as described in Chapter 5, works as a coach and a facilitator. Another important dimension of this new role is for the surviving manager to work as a partner with team members. Consultant Rick Maurer recommends that managers in trimmed-down organizations get team members up to speed and then turn them loose.[13] The wide span of controls in the de-layered organization are one reason that partnering is so important. Managers simply do not have time to closely supervise team members.

A necessary aspect of adapting one's leadership style to the downsized organization is to avoid leadership approaches that will brand you as not fitting the times. Among these negative traits and behaviors are:

- Using over-controlling, hands-on leadership (micromanaging)
- Pursuing your own agenda, making it difficult for supervisors, peers, clients, and group members to work for you
- Lacking the ability to tune in to the needs and subtle messages of supervisors, peers, clients, and group members
- Intimidating others and being unaware of your impact[14]

Streamline Your Work

Earlier we described how in the period preceding downsizing an external or internal consultant engages in activity-based cost reduction. In a similar manner, those managers who survive downsizing must look for ways to streamline work—both the manager's and that of team members. A worker who previously had just his or her position to take care of winds up responsible for the equivalent of two or three positions. Nobody is around to handle correspondence or answer phones other than through voice mail. Many individuals work 12-hour days. To intensify the hardship, they see no opportunities for promotion in the trimmed-down firm. If work isn't eliminated, the result can be substantial productivity losses and burnout.[15]

Managers must eliminate as much low-value work as possible. Justify whether every work procedure, memo, meeting, or ceremonial activity is contributing value to the firm. Group luncheon meetings away from the office might be cut in half, giving staff members more time during the day to conduct urgent work. Earl Landesman, a principal in the consulting firm of A.T. Kearney, expresses the problem this way:

> Too often, people focus on trying to do the same work better or more efficiently. What they should be doing is fo-

cusing on streamlining their work processes to include only those things that are necessary to meet customer requirements.[16]

A growing approach to streamlining work, as we have seen, is to outsource activities to firms that can handle certain services at low cost and high quality. Departmental candidates for outsourcing include payroll, benefits claim processing, printing, custodial services, and food services. But the cost of outsourcing services must be well below what was previously paid to full-time employees to deliver them. If you recommend outsourcing and it proves to be cost-ineffective, you have made a giant political blunder.

Motivate Fearful People

Many employees are fearful before, during, and after downsizing. An obvious worry is job loss, even if they have survived the first round of cuts. The ambiguity of not knowing how long one's job will last creates anxiety in all but the most self-confident employees. Employees also fear making mistakes during downsizing because they believe the company is looking for reasons to get rid of people. During a Kmart downsizing, one store manager said, "I feel like I'm playing Russian roulette. My heart pounds whenever I receive a letter or phone message from my regional manager. I look at each day's receipts and pray they are outstanding. My husband says I'm a nervous wreck. He's right. I look tired, and I'm suffering from dermatitis for the first time in my life."

> **JUSTIFY WHETHER EVERY WORK PROCEDURE, MEMO, MEETING, OR CEREMONIAL ACTIVITY IS CONTRIBUTING VALUE TO THE FIRM.**

The most effective strategy for overcoming fear of unemployment is to convince people of your personal confidence that the storm will blow over. (Of course, you must believe this yourself to be convincing.) Explain that if people act like winners, they will be winners and survivors. Emphasize the accomplishments of your organizational unit. Underscore the fact that the vast majority of employees have not lost their jobs. Let staffers talk about their anxieties, but then translate that energy into action plans for improved performance. If you are fearful yourself, communicate these fears to somebody other than the people in your unit.

MANAGING YOUR CAREER IN A DOWNSIZED ENVIRONMENT

Career management in a downsized firm contains all of the elements of effective career management in general. You need to set goals, develop action plans, and maintain an effective network, among dozens of other tactics. In a downsized environment you need to pay particular attention to forming political alliances, developing critical skills, and becoming a free-agent manager. Developing answers to the questions in Figure 9-1 will help you manage your career in a downsized environment.

Forming Political Alliances

A widely observed reality about who escapes the hit list during a downsizing is that being liked by people in power makes a major contribution to holding your job. In a pure meritocracy, the best performers would have the highest job security. Unfortunately, most organizations are not pure meritocracies. Meritorious performance is extremely important, but it is not sufficient. How to form alliances with powerful people is a book-length subject, but it is worth mentioning a few basic principles.

FIGURE 9-1

Preparing Now to Cope with Downsizings in the Future

Downsizings, rightsizings, and restructurings have become a corporate way of life. Begin preparing now to prevent a downsizing from derailing your own career. Answer each of the following questions in a couple of sentences.[17]

1. Do I keep an ongoing file of all my work accomplishments? (Give a couple of examples.)

---

2. Am I prepared for any contingency by maintaining a constantly updated résumé? (Also, write down the two most important skills that will be included in your résumé.)

---

3. Are my communication skills (oral, written, and nonverbal) impressive? (If your answer is negative, explain how you intend to improve these skills.)

---

4. Do I keep records of people I meet in business, as well as socially, who could be a source of job leads or who might hire me? (If your answer is negative, indicate when you intend to get your Rolodex into gear.)

---

5. Do I strive toward becoming indispensable? (If your answer is yes, jot down what you are doing that makes you so valuable. If your answer is negative, explain how you can work toward becoming indispensable.)

---

6. Do I persist in my professional education? (If your answer is no, indicate what steps you can take to acquire important job skills and knowledge.)

---

7. Am I pleasant and courteous? (If your answer is no, describe your action plans for becoming more socially skillful.)

---

8. What back-up plans do I have if I were told that I would be losing my job in 30 days from now?

---

9. How much of a financial cushion have I developed to tide me over while conducting a job search? (If your answer is less than six months' pay, describe how you are going to begin developing a bigger cushion.)

Do anything you find morally acceptable to be noticed in a positive way by key people. Choose from among tactics such as the following that you believe are honest: Compliment senior management publicly, write a letter to the editor of the local newspaper defending your company, and write memos about how your work contributes to corporate strategy. Make statements in meetings about how you believe strongly in the company's rightsizing (a more palatable term than downsizing) efforts. Send key people newspaper and magazine articles supportive of top management's positions on key issues. Send a book to the CEO that supports his or her business philosophy. Befriend workers who are close friends and relatives of key people.

Develop and Market Critical Skills

A highly professional and meritorious way of retaining your job during a downsizing is to develop skills that are closely tied to the organization's new thrust. The same strategy might even result in a promotion during a downsizing. If your firm is committed to customer satisfaction, acquire new skills and knowledge geared toward providing exceptional customer service. If your company is going the route of reengineering and process redesign, immerse yourself in the topic. After you have upgraded your skills, let key people know you are ready to apply them. Announce your new competence via electronic mail to people who might be interested.

By upgrading your skills to meet current organizational needs, you will position yourself to work on problems of central interest to your firm. For example, many people have been pro-

> **DURING A DOWNSIZING BEING LIKED BY PEOPLE IN POWER IS A MAJOR CONTRIBUTOR TO HOLDING YOUR JOB.**

moted to quality manager because they upgraded their skills in quality management. The promotion came about because the topic of total quality management was perceived as an excellent vehicle for achieving high quality.

Become a Free-Agent Manager

In today's turbulent corporate environment it may be necessary to place your own interests above those of the organization. If every manager and professional is entirely self-interested, self-centered, and self-aggrandizing, their employers may suffer, thus becoming less competitive. As a consequence, every employee and stockholder will suffer. Nevertheless, if you are ready to jump ship before being shoved overboard, you will soften the blow to yourself of a downsizing.

Management professor Paul Hirsch labels this being-prepared approach "becoming a free-agent manager." Free-agent managers and professionals have developed skills very different from those taught in traditional MBA and executive development programs. (An exception is that today many of these programs offer a seminar in organizational power and politics.)

First, free-agent managers are loyal primarily to themselves, because sacrificing personal goals for the organization is no longer rewarded or appreciated by the organization. During a restructuring, even the most loyal company person might be put on the hit list.

Second, free-agent managers and professionals protect themselves and learn to survive in their own environment. Previously guaranteed perks such as pension plans and fringe benefits are no longer automatic. As a result, managers must develop their own protection plans.

Third, the new breed of managers are still committed to their careers, but they see the company as a temporary arena in which to apply their skills and knowledge. This attitude is imperative because the organization will not hesitate to fire managers in order to reach its financial objectives—particularly a good return to shareholders.

Fourth, free-agent managers and professionals regard temporary setbacks, such as being fired, as challenges. They realize that downsizing decisions are made by people who do not know them personally and who have little concern for human welfare. "Remote-control management," says Hirsch, "is inevitable as mergers and acquisitions place a greater emphasis on efficiency (as measured by headcount) than on effectiveness."[18]

Finally, free-agent managers strive to take control of their own destiny. Proactive rather than reactive strategies and tactics are required to increase their visibility in the organization and in their industry. If you want to become a free-agent manager or professional, take the following steps:[19]

1. *Maintain your mobility.* Because jobs are only temporary, assume that you will move on your own terms should the need arise.

2. *Avoid long-term or group assignments where your accomplishments cannot be clearly defined.* Today's team environment makes it difficult to cut back on group assignments. Yet strive for some individual problem-solving assignments and avoid attempting to solve the unsolvable.

3. *Become a generalist rather than a specialist.* Usually, you need to build your reputation as an expert in some area, but once your career is solidly launched, branch out into more general assignments. Overspecialization can hinder movement from one corporation to another. Remember, however, that a delicate balance must be achieved. Strive to become a generalist with a well-defined bag of tricks in your repertoire as well. Executive recruiters usually pursue an executive who has a track record of accomplishing a specific task such as cost cutting, penetrating new markets, or mobilizing distributors.

4. *Return calls from executive recruiters, thus maintaining your marketability.* Not returning calls is a tip-off that you are not willing to test the waters.

5. *Cultivate networks that enhance your visibility outside your organization.* Participation in professional organizations (such as the National Association of Accountants or the Purchasing Managers' Association) and community activities makes you visible as a competent manager or professional.

By following these guidelines you are better equipped to deal with the ravages of downsizings.

A CHECKLIST FOR EFFECTIVE DOWNSIZING

Downsizing itself is one of the workplace innovations. It is also a frequent consequence of reengineering and process redesign. Given that approximately one-half of all downsizings fail to achieve their goals, it is important to recognize factors associated with effective downsizing. A checklist follows to improve the chances of having a successful downsizing from both the organizational and individual perspective.

☑ An essential objective of a successful downsizing game plan is to eliminate low-value and no-value activities. The lowest-value activities should be the first to be scaled back or eliminated.

☑ Downsizing should be done in such a way as to fit the firm's future requirements, such as retaining people with critical skills.

☑ Work performance is a generally productive criterion for dismissal during a downsizing. It is fairest to make use of existing performance appraisal information rather than to evaluate performance for the purpose of downsizing.

☑ To stem the tide of losing competent people departing during a downsizing, top management should personally contact the most valuable workers to assure them that they are valued by the firm.

☑ A manager must learn habits of self-sufficiency after downsizing because clerical support is often in short supply.

☑ A highly professional and meritorious way of retaining your job during a downsizing is to develop skills closely tied to the organization's new thrust.

☑ As a free-agent manager, strive to become in charge of your own destiny through such means as maintaining your mobility, becoming a generalist with at least one area of specialization, and cultivating a network of valuable contacts.

10

Easing the Pain
of Downsizing

After a large public corporation announces a substantial
downsizing, Wall Street stock analysts usually cheer.
From the stock analyst's perspective, layoffs are good
news. Top management has finally wised up. Gone is the bloat
and excess of the past. The firm will now be the right size to
handle its current sales volume. The analysts predict that earnings per share and profits will rise because of reduced payroll
costs. As a consequence, the company's stock receives a "buy"
recommendation. Investors swoop in to buy shares in the downsized company, and the stock price increases.

While the stock analysts are rejoicing, many downsized
workers are facing the most devastating trauma of their careers.
While still in shock they hurriedly put together résumés and send
blanket mailings to prospective employers. Stress-related disorders such as migraine headaches, colitis, dermatitis, and cardiac
disease escalate. Abuse of family members skyrockets. The sui-
cide rate for laid-off workers is 30 times the national average. In
short, the layoffs associated with downsizing create enormous
human suffering.

In addition to these obvious types of suffering associated with
downsizing, a more subtle form of damage also takes place in
the form of disappointed expectations. More specifically, the
downsizing era has violated the psychological contracts between

employees and employers. Such a contract is the set of expectations that are held by the individual. They specify what the employee and employer expect to give and receive from each other in the course of their relationship. A major provision of this contract is that so long as the employee performed well and was loyal, he or she would be "taken care of."

"Being taken care of" meant having a job until retirement, followed by a generous pension from the employer. Many employees are overwhelmed by the fact that this form of psychological contract no longer exists. Because they cannot adjust to the new reality that most jobs are temporary, they suffer when they are forced to find new employment.

Although downsizing appears heartless, steps can be and have been taken to ease the suffering associated with layoffs and dislocation. The purpose of this chapter is to describe some of the initiatives companies have used to reduce the suffering, and also to look at a path-finding process for easing the pain.

CREATIVE DOWNSIZING OPTIONS

"What can we do besides lay off people if profits are down?" many executives ask. In selected situations employers can find creative ways to downsize an organization without laying off large numbers of people. Three such options that have eased the suffering of many people are career redeployment, career redirection, and creation of a temporary worker pool.

> ## THE DOWNSIZING ERA HAS VIOLATED THE PSYCHOLOGICAL CONTRACT BETWEEN EMPLOYEES AND EMPLOYERS.

Redeployment

Although the term *redeployment* is sometimes used as a synonym for *layoff*, there is a big difference in terms of human suffering. In redeployment the company uses inventive means to find jobs for as many people as possible throughout the organization. Significantly, the employer still achieves its intended cost savings. A public utility in Ontario, Canada, provides a good example.

Several years back, Ontario Hydro set out on a new corporate direction to become a world-class energy company. To achieve this goal, the size of the organization had to be readjusted. Hydro, however, had promised employees that none of them would be terminated, even though some jobs might become redundant. Working with a consulting firm, a career center was established. All employees were invited to attend career planning workshops, on company time, to explore career opportunities both inside and outside the firm.

During the same time period, Hydro divulged its plans so that employees would know the status of their positions. Employees whose jobs were redundant were given first consideration for new job openings as they occurred. Generous separation allowances were given to those employees who chose to leave Hydro. During the rightsizing process, consultants provided counseling and guidance to employees at all levels.

The rationale behind Hydro's voluntary rightsizing was straightforward. Employees with sharper insights into their strengths and skills could make informed career decisions. For many, this would mean staying with Ontario Hydro in the same or a new position. Other employees would choose to leave the firm after finding more suitable positions elsewhere. They would be able to accomplish this, however, in a time frame that allowed them to develop the appropriate job search skills.

By combining voluntary separations with normal attrition, Hydro was able to meet its staffing requirements without terminating employees. Furthermore, the company ended up with employees whose skills matched the needs of the evolving organization. As Don Tyler, Hydro's director of redeployment, analyzed the situation: "We had gone through downsizings and major outplacement programs before, and these caused some serious employee relations problems. The difference this time was that this was not outplacement, but redeployment."

Tyler noted that, previously, employees had felt that management controlled almost the entire process of downsizing. "This time, they determined their futures," he said. "That's not to say that everyone found the job they'd always wanted, but they did get a realistic look at where the company was going and how they could fit into those plans."

Hydro's redeployment program achieved excellent results. Within two years of starting the program, 620 out of 650 potentially surplus employees were successfully redeployed. Of this group, 80 percent found positions inside Hydro and 20 percent outside. Employees took an average time of about three months to secure a new position. The company's average cost per employee going through the voluntary rightsizing program was less than one month's salary. Tyler noted that under a forced severance approach used in the past, the cost to Hydro was about one year's salary per employee.

Employee morale, according to Tyler, also benefited from the voluntary program. Surveys conducted prior to and after the project indicated high satisfaction for both managers and the surplus staff. Employees who remained did so with a renewed commitment. Many saw for themselves that Hydro was a comparatively good employer.

"The redeployment program meant a rethinking and flexibility on the part of our managers," said Tyler. "We had to get away from viewing people in terms of narrow boxes but rather according to what they could really do. In some cases this meant taking gambles on people but, by and large, those gambles have paid off. Interestingly enough, we found that most so-called performance problems were really relationship issues which disappeared on redeployment. The career center continues and will likely remain as part of our corporate values and culture."[1]

Career Redirection

After downsizing, many workers are displaced because there appear to be virtually no other job openings for which they can apply with their current skills. In 1993, there were approximately 17 million displaced workers in the United States and Canada. Among the many displaced workers are low-skilled factory workers and telephone receptionists. Many middle managers have also found themselves searching for positions that are in scarce supply. Yet, contrary to widespread publicity, the job loss for middle managers is much lower than for production workers. About 16 percent of middle managers lost their jobs, while about 20 percent of production workers were displaced.

A humane alternative chosen by top management in many companies is to send displaced workers to private industry councils in their states. An important function served by these councils is to provide unemployed people with career evaluation and guidance. A combination of psychological tests and interviews help to identify new career paths for workers sent to the councils.[2]

"We put people on a long-term training program to become a nurse, a truck driver, or anything," says Greg Hilad, a test administrator for the Private Industry Council in Tampa Bay, Florida. "Basically, we try to get a fit between what a person would be suited to do and what jobs are available in Florida for that person."

When an individual comes to the council for help, one of the first steps is diagnostic testing. The tests help point the individual toward the appropriate training. "We don't want to get someone into something that's going to bore him or her to death, or where the person can't figure out what's going on," says Hilad.

A counselor reviews the assessment results and interviews the client about past employment, education, and job training. The client is given a list of schools in the area that might offer the type of training sought. If a match between interests and available training is found, the counselor facilitates the training. The council works closely with community colleges and vocational-technical schools in the area.

"We look at a person's abilities and whether the person can handle the kind of training he or she is interested in," says a counselor. "If the person can, we usually set up an appointment to attend an orientation at that particular school."

Sometimes people lack the mental ability or skill level they need to possess to enter the field they want. In those cases, they are guided into a less challenging position within the same field. For example, a person who did not currently have the skills to enter programming might be routed into data entry. A computerized learning center is available to help people upgrade their skills to match their career interests. The person routed into data entry might qualify for training at a later time in computer programming.

The Private Industry Council is careful not to flood the local job market so that newly trained workers do not compete for the same few job openings. A council staff member first does a labor market survey to uncover the demand for certain jobs and the starting wages. So far, the placement rates for people graduating from vocational schools is excellent. Graduates of these programs acquire skills in demand, such as those required to be an executive secretary or computer service technician. Many of them find jobs with starting salaries higher than those offered college graduates for entry-level positions.

Participating in a Private Industry Council thus helps displaced workers reorient themselves into productive careers. Not every displaced worker can be helped. Nevertheless, each laid-off person who finds a new career is another person spared some suffering. The person with a new-found career is also a contributor to society. Many individuals who were reengineered out of a job now become wage earners who can stimulate the economy. Reengineering is only worthwhile if it does not lower the demand for products and services because so many people have become unemployed.

OFFERING COMPENSATION AND SUPPORT FOR THE DISPLACED PEOPLE

The managers, professionals, and other workers who lose their jobs under restructuring will need various forms of support. The support required may be financial, emotional, or a combination of the two. Middle managers often require more help than other employees in coping with a layoff. "We're not altogether sure that it isn't the white-collar people who suffer more," says Jeanne Gordus, who has designed program to help thousands of unemployed auto, glass, and steel workers. Managers and professionals are often so attached to their jobs that they have greater stress and emotional problems when separating, she believes.[3]

Developing support mechanisms begins with planning for layoffs in order to treat employees with dignity and respect, instead of rushing them out the door. A widely used downsizing practice is to tell an employee that his or her position has been eliminated. At the same time, the employee is told that he or she has one hour to gather personal belongings and leave the premises. One woman, escorted out the door on such a short notice, begged the company representative to let her back in to retrieve a favorite sweater. After pondering her request, the representative demanded that the woman wait in the lobby while he retrieved the sweater.

A generous severance pay guideline is one week of pay for every year of service, plus full retirement and health insurance payments. During one of its downsizings, Eastman Kodak Company even paid the Social Security taxes for qualifying early retirees until they reached age 62. As many a departing Kodak employee has stated, "The company made me an offer too good to refuse."

A study of 407 downsized firms showed that 40 percent of the companies emphasized severance pay and extended health benefits as a way of easing the transition out of the company. Twenty-three percent of the firms encouraged the people to leave through early retirement and voluntary separation. The other 37 percent of firms in the study did the best they could to prevent layoffs by redeploying surplus people.[4]

The next step in providing adequate support to laid-off workers is to offer each person a candid but sympathetic statement of why he or she was laid off. Because *every* worker is not eliminated in a downsizing, the person let go undoubtedly wonders why he or she was targeted for removal. An appropriate statement from the bearer of bad news might be: "We have decided to lay off 90 percent of the managers at your level. Your performance has been above average, but we are only retaining those 10 percent of managers with outstanding performance appraisals who have critical skills that no other managers in the firm possess. You will receive a favorable employment reference."

Outplacement services are by far the most popular form of support offered by companies. The outplacement field in the United States and Canada has grown from a handful of firms with $50 million in sales in 1980 to about 240 firms with total sales of about $750 million in 1994.[5] Outplacement eases human suffering through four basic services: personal evaluation, job-search skills and counseling, institutional support, and job leads.

A counseling-oriented outplacement service provides job seekers with a comprehensive evaluation of themselves. Using personnel and psychological tests, interviews, and sometimes feedback from co-workers and superiors, outplacement counselors identify the job seeker's strengths and weaknesses. Many outplacement firms use certified psychologists to conduct or supervise the personal evaluations. Job seekers are taught to identify their transferrable skills and professional goals so that they can seek positions that will further their careers. A personal evaluation can alleviate human suffering because the job seeker might be given a better foundation for finding a suitable position.

A basic part of all outplacement programs is to both teach job search skills and provide some emotional support. The two are closely related because the outplaced worker will often need strong encouragement to persist in the job search when rejections mount. Job seekers receive coaching and information about writing resumes, cover letters, and thank-you letters. They are also coached on uncovering job leads, using good interview techniques, and creating a positive appearance.

Most people who go through outplacement counseling are aware of how to create a positive appearance, but downsizing victims have a special problem. It is difficult for some people to maintain a healthy, robust appearance when forced to look for a job in an economy where many firms hire sparingly. Among the suggestions to look robust is to engage in physical exercise followed by a shower as close to the interview as possible. Attempt to maintain a body weight appropriate to your height and frame. Another suggestion applies to light-skinned people. Spend time outdoors so you have a healthy glow to your skin.

Should the job search linger on, job seekers may require counseling to deal with their discouragement, despair, low self-esteem, and self-pity. In some outplacement programs, job seekers give each other emotional support as they meet regularly to discuss progress and problems, exchange information about

> THE OUTPLACEMENT FIELD IN NORTH AMERICA HAS GROWN FROM A HANDFUL OF FIRMS WITH $50 MILLION IN SALES IN 1980 TO ABOUT 240 FIRMS WITH TOTAL SALES OF ABOUT $750 MILLION IN 1994.

the job market, and share job-finding tips. At times, the job seekers become part of each other's networks.

The counselor is the heart of the outplacement service because he or she is the person who can do the most to minimize human suffering. One component of the counseling relationship is to offer sympathetic understanding, yet to be stern when the client needs a push. One of the biggest challenges facing the counselor is to get the job seeker to telephone as many people as possible, including former bosses. Job seekers often find this experience uncomfortable.

Another key component of the counseling relationship is giving strategic advice and counsel on conducting a successful job search. Understanding what qualifications employers in a specific industry are seeking is critical. A counselor with in-dustry-specific knowledge might inform a job seeker about which skills he or she should emphasize in the job search. For example, many manufacturing firms are now emphasizing cross-disciplinary skills. The counselor would then instruct the client to emphasize his or her experience in carrying out interdiscipli-nary tasks.

Another standard outplacement service is institutional sup-port in the form of a base of operations for conducting the job search. Institutional support includes office space, clerical sup-port, and the use of telephones, photocopying machines, fax machines, and personal computers. A time limitation is usually placed on this type of support. As the term limitation ap-proaches, the people still seeking jobs are sometimes given sug-gestions on how to use their homes as a base of operation. So

---

COUNSELORS ARE THE HEART OF THE OUTPLACEMENT SERVICE BECAUSE THEY ARE THE PEOPLE WHO CAN DO THE MOST TO MINIMIZE HUMAN SUFFERING.

many people have offices at home today that placing one's job search center at home may not be a difficult transition. Yet the job seeker must still grapple with feelings of isolation and despair.

Some outplacement firms supply job leads to their clients by maintaining contacts with employers and sometimes with employment agencies. Such direct help is the swiftest way to alleviate the suffering of job loss. Finding a job while unemployed supplies a jolt of good feeling and a sudden improvement in mental health. Part of the task of supplying job leads is to point a client toward a geographic area where jobs are plentiful. A New York City bank vice president was laid off. The outplacement counselor advised the vice president to approach banks in Charlotte, North Carolina, based on that city's prosperity. Through letter writing and follow-up telephone calls, the woman lined up five job interviews. She received two job offers, both at more money than she had been earning in New York.

Although outplacement often does alleviate the suffering associated with job loss, the process can backfire. One of the major disappointments of outplacement for some people is that the job seeker is required to rely so heavily on his or her own resources. Early in the outplacement process, the job seeker is asked to compose a list of up to 100 personal contacts. The job seeker is then told to arrange interviews with each one of these people to ask for assistance in the job search, or to "collect information." Asking contacts for personal interviews is fraught with excuse-making and outright rejection.

Another way in which outplacement backfires is that it can increase rather than decrease suffering for some people. Having daily contact at the outplacement firm with so many depressed and anxious job seekers can be emotionally upsetting. A laid-off manager from General Electric put it this way:

> After a couple of weeks of checking in at the agency every day, I had to stop. I couldn't take dealing with the walking wounded every day. It was so depressing. The other job

seekers were supposed to bolster each other's ego, but it had the opposite effect on me. I felt uncomfortable being associated with so many people whose careers were failing. I particularly couldn't take all those horror stories about the rudeness the unemployed managers were facing. One guy told me a story about how people would hang up once they knew he was calling them to look for a job.

PROVIDING JOB SECURITY AND EMOTIONAL SUPPORT TO THE SURVIVORS

The current demographics have been a challenge for many organizations, says organizational planner Robert M. Tomasko. The postwar baby boomers reached middle management age at a time when downsizing of organizations eliminated many of the positions they hoped to occupy. "Companies that have responded to this by pruning back their organizations *and* working hard to provide job security for those selected to remain will be one step ahead of the others in having loyal and committed people to deal with the demographics of the next decade."[6]

One way of shoring up the prospects of job security is to explain to the remaining managers that they are a select cadre of managers upon whom the organization hopes to build its future. Words alone are not sufficient to convince the survivors that their job security is not threatened. It is equally important to manage the company in such a way that job security is high. For example, temporary help can be used to staff certain jobs. The heavy reliance on temporary help suggests to permanent employees that the company considers them to be part of an elite work force. Also, workers believe that if further downsizing is necessary, temporary workers can be readily trimmed, thus protecting the jobs of permanent workers.

Job security can be communicated in another important way. Should the company hire back workers or add new ones from the outside, this fact should be publicized. To many people, any type of hiring connotes growth and organizational health. As a consequence, the survivors will feel that they are with a company that needs every competent person on the staff.

Survivors of a downsizing may need emotional support to help them deal with the distress of seeing their former work associates dismissed. Toward this end, some companies offer survivor workshops that function as support groups. A professional counselor may run a few group sessions where the survivors can talk about their guilt and anxieties and encourage each other.

We recommend that these survivor workshops be limited to several months following the layoffs. If the survivor workshop becomes an ongoing program, it will have the depressing effect of symbolizing continuous layoffs. It is important for the company to provide on-site group support for the survivors. But once they have dealt with their troubled feelings for a while, workers should be tough enough to get on with their jobs. More will be said about the grieving process and layoffs later in the chapter.

A creative way of supporting survivors emotionally is for the company to recognize the heavy demands placed upon them. The remaining employees in a streamlined organization work extra hard because they assume the responsibilities of the downsized workers. To compensate for this extra work, many companies are now creating flexible benefits to help employees blend their family and work lives. Among these benefits are dependent care facilities, job sharing, and part-time work. Dana Friedman, of the Families and Work Institute, says that companies see these work and family programs as survivor benefits. "Those who have survived the layoffs have low morale and feel insecure in their jobs. They've got to keep them happy."[7]

The job satisfaction of middle managers who survive the downsizing should also be addressed. As we have seen, top management can explain to these people that they have been chosen to carry the organization forward. Furthermore, the expanded roles for middle managers can contribute to job satisfaction, providing work has been properly streamlined.

A Four-Level Process for Easing the Suffering of Survivors

Layoff victims suffer substantially and so do many survivors of downsizing. The suffering experienced by the workers who hold on to their jobs has been labeled the *layoff survivor sickness*. The condition consists of a host of negative feelings associated with still having a job while co-workers and friends have been laid off. As uncovered by the in-company research of David M. Noer, layoff survivors experience the following feelings:[8]

- *Fear, insecurity, and uncertainty.* Almost all layoff survivors suffer from these feelings. When people around you are forced out of the company, it is difficult to feel secure.
- *Frustration, resentment, and anger.* Layoff survivors tend to suppress these emotions, and this emotional blockage can create further problems, such as health disorders.
- *Sadness, depression, and guilt.* To appear tough and cool, layoff survivors often attempt to hide their depression and guilt. Nevertheless, these feelings gnaw away inside and often interfere with concentration on work.
- *Unfairness, betrayal, and distrust.* Workers often attempt to cope with these feelings by blaming others for the layoff problems, and demanding more and more information about the layoffs.

If too many people throughout the organization have these disturbed feelings, morale, productivity, and quality will suffer. Noer has developed a four-level process for helping individuals and organizations deal effectively with layoff survivor sickness. Each successive level is a more comprehensive approach to the problem, as shown in Figure 10-1. We describe the approach in

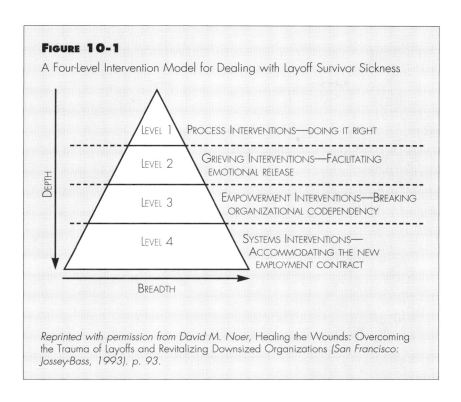

FIGURE 10-1

A Four-Level Intervention Model for Dealing with Layoff Survivor Sickness

LEVEL 1 — PROCESS INTERVENTIONS—DOING IT RIGHT

LEVEL 2 — GRIEVING INTERVENTIONS—FACILITATING EMOTIONAL RELEASE

LEVEL 3 — EMPOWERMENT INTERVENTIONS—BREAKING ORGANIZATIONAL CODEPENDENCY

LEVEL 4 — SYSTEMS INTERVENTIONS— ACCOMMODATING THE NEW EMPLOYMENT CONTRACT

DEPTH

BREADTH

Reprinted with permission from David M. Noer, Healing the Wounds: Overcoming the Trauma of Layoffs and Revitalizing Downsized Organizations (San Francisco: Jossey-Bass, 1993). p. 93.

detail here because in totality it is akin to reengineering. A sweeping overhaul of the process is undertaken instead of making only minor adjustments.

Level 1: Managing the Layoff Process and Damage Control

Immediately after the layoff announcements are made, the suffering begins. The company needs to do something in a hurry to keep feelings under control, much like offering on-site counseling to disaster victims. First-level interventions aim to keep survivors afloat emotionally until more substantial and permanent help can be offered.

Layoff planners typically work out the procedures for severance pay, making the layoff announcements, arranging benefit packages, and referring displaced workers for outplacement services. Layoff procedures also include how desks get cleaned out, how computer files are retained by the company, and how victims are escorted to the door. In some companies layoff announcements are made on Friday afternoon to minimize disruption in the office. All of these routines are often carried out with little thought of their impact on survivors.

A constructive approach at the time of layoffs is for the company to communicate as much information as possible about the subject. Layoff survivors have an insatiable appetite for details about anything to do with the layoffs. An obvious concern is who is going to be terminated, when they are going, and the basis for their selection. In addition, as Noer describes it:

> Workers want to know that the cafeteria will be operational, the paychecks will not bounce, the softball league will continue, the dental plan will stay in effect, the Monday-morning staff meeting will still take place. You name it, they want to know about it.[9]

Written and electronic communication is a good start, but the survivors will need much more. Managers should communicate face-to-face with the survivors, listening to all their concerns. Especially important is to communicate any shred of good news, such as a big customer order, improved profits, or selective hiring in any unit of the company. Communications should be free-flowing, and management should make sure to dispense authentic information only.

Managers should communicate the brutally honest fact that no guarantees can be offered that layoffs have ended. Downsizing has become an ingrained strategy for most businesses worldwide. As long as business conditions fluctuate and the board of directors and top management want to maximize profits, layoffs are a possibility. A chief engineer at a Westinghouse Corporation division said in 1994, "I couldn't believe that my position was terminated. I was led to believe that the worst was over for our company. We were already lean and mean. The rug was pulled out from under me."

Level 2: Facilitating the Necessary Grieving

The purpose of second-level interventions is to help employees unblock suppressed feelings. Some employees have emotional outlets at home, among friends, or with professional counselors. Yet, on the job, cultural norms run counter to employees' admitting or expressing survivor emotions. Among the strongest of these emotions are anger toward the company and guilt for still having a job while friends have been terminated. Many employees slog through endless bleak days, turning their anger inward and sinking deeper into survivor guilt and depression. Many of the incidents of sabotaging computer files in recent years have conceivably been a by-product of survivor anger.

One method of facilitating grieving is for organizational units to hold a retreat, run by a facilitator. At the retreat, group member are encouraged to expressed their angry feelings and then develop some action plans for regaining their concentration and productivity. As part of restructuring, one large firm spun off one of its divisions. The former division manager was appointed as CEO of the new operation. The human resources manager urged the top-management team to hold an off-site retreat to deal with feelings about a 10 percent reduction in force following the spinoff.

At the retreat, the CEO tended to deny any angry feelings. Yet the group members freely discussed their confusion and anger about the 10 percent across-the-board cuts required to help pay for the spinoff of their division. The team described the CEO as the villain for going along with the spinoff.

The retreat was followed by individual sessions with the team members in which they were encouraged to discuss their feelings about the layoffs. Team members were filled with anger toward the parent company for spinning them off without giving them a choice. Blame was laid in many different directions. The president was blamed for selling out the team and for ineffective leadership. Team members blamed each other for not pulling an equal amount of weight. They also blamed employees in general for not being grateful for still having a job, and for not appreciating how hard the team members were working to keep the company afloat. The CEO disliked the negative feedback he received and blamed the team for not understanding his vision.

A third step in the intervention was to meet with the top team as a group and discuss the individual feelings of blame and anger. After considerably angry discussion, the top team developed action plans to deal with layoff survivor sickness. The action plans included managers throughout the company attending revitalization workshops. Managers attended in groups of strangers rather than in those with managers working for a common boss. During the workshop managers learned to recognize their own survivor feelings and to be more supportive toward their own group members. Helping skills included active listening, giving and receiving feedback, and responding to feelings.

After managers attended the workshop, they were required to meet with their team members individually to discuss worker feelings about the layoffs. Although this was an uncomfortable role for some of the managers, it was considered better than having no discussion. The manager-team member sessions gave managers an opportunity to practice listening, thus enhancing their coaching skills.

The grieving program had a promising start, but the program was halted several months later when the board, which included several of the venture capitalists who funded the spinoff, fired the CEO. The CEO's replacement initiated another round of layoffs, including one of the supporters of the grieving program.

Level 3: Breaking the Codependency Chain and Empowering People

Interventions at the third level are more powerful than the previous two. Level three interventions help people shift from being victims of the organization to being controllers of their own fate. Instead of remaining dependent on the organization, people are empowered to use their own creative powers to become independent. The free-agent manager described in the previous chapter would fit this framework.

Third-level interventions are aimed most directly at helping individuals break organizational codependency. The term *codependency* is applied to people who invest so much energy into controlling an addict that they are addicted themselves. If you live with an alcoholic, for example, you spend much of your life adapting to that person's maladaptation. Noer believes that many people are codependent within an organizational system. Such people have enabled the organization to control their own sense of worth and self-esteem. (If the firm fires a codependent person, he or she feels flawed.) The organizational codependent invests considerable energy in attempting to control the system, such as trying to change low performance appraisals or fighting for a promotion based on seniority.

The individual who is not dependent on the organization is less likely to suffer from survivor layoff sickness. Workers who are independent rather than codependent link their self-worth and dignity to their own work rather than the actions of the firm. As a result, they do not get sick when the organization does something disappointing such as downsizing.

A key symptom of codependency is that the codependent person's sense of value and identity is based on pleasing or controlling someone else. Codependent people are permanent victims because they are forever suffering from the tribulations of the addicts they attempt to help or control. Survivor layoff sickness often occurs when workers surrender to organizational values and tie their identities to the firm.

The primary strategy for breaking organizational codependency is to see that pleasing the boss and remaining an employee of a particular firm is separate from a person's own identity. Instead of attempting to please the boss, one should concentrate on doing good work. Pleasing the boss and the organization should be a by-product of doing good work. Some of the saddest layoff victims are long-time employees from paternalistic corporations who have given so much of themselves to the firm. As a plant superintendent said, "After 30 years at IBM (Poughkeepsie), I doubt I could work for any other employer. IBM is my whole life."

Detaching oneself from the organization begins with the decision not to rely on the employer to nurture you in every aspect of life. The plant superintendent from IBM should have been thinking 10 years ago, "What else could I do if the company decides to shut down my plant or eliminate my job? Do I have any identity other than being an 'IBMer'?"

Another important part of detachment is for the codependents to let go and realize that they cannot control the organization. The manager in charge of a secretarial pool may find ample evidence that the demand for secretarial support is shrinking rapidly within the organization. The combination of word processors, e-mail, voice mail, copying machines, and fax machines is eliminating many secretarial jobs. Instead of lobbying for an enlarged secretarial pool, the manager should look for a new role either inside or outside the firm.

The codependency chain can be broken when someone has the courage to talk straight about sensitive issues. For example, a human resources professional might confront the manager of the secretarial pool and say: "What do you intend to do when there is no longer a need for a centralized secretarial pool? So far I have only heard you talk about expanding your department. That seems unrealistic." Talking straight about an issue may help a person make plans to become less dependent upon the organization.

> DETACHING ONESELF FROM
> THE ORGANIZATION BEGINS
> WITH THE DECISION NOT TO RELY ON
> THE EMPLOYER TO NURTURE
> YOU IN EVERY ASPECT OF LIFE.

If you are concerned that you might be an organizational codependent, think through whether you are trying to control the organization to prove how worthwhile you are. If you have to try too hard, it could mean that your present role is not so valuable for this organization at this time. It could be the moment to find another job within your present organization or to take your present job elsewhere.

Another important step in breaking your codependency is to define good work in your own terms. Think of your happiest moments in actually accomplishing work—not necessarily pleasing others. What tangible results have you accomplished that made you proud? Perhaps you developed a crisp marketing plan, prepared a quarterly report, or reengineered a tired old work process. Capture those moments in your mind, and regard them as you at your best. Think of your career in terms of producing more such good work. Who you produce this good work for is less important than the work itself.

Level 4: Building a New Employment Relationship

The highest-level interventions in survivor layoff sickness create systems and processes that help prevent the problem. Such interventions are based on developing new psychological employment contracts between employees and the organization. For new contracts to be forged, it is necessary to contrast old versus new psychological contracts. Figure 10-2 summarizes the major assumptions of the two contracts. Major comparisons of old versus new contracts are as follows:

- Under the old contract the employment relationship is long-term, resulting ultimately in an older work force. Under the new contract, the employment contract is situational, resulting in a flexible work force.
- Under the old contract, promotion is the reward for good performance and often results in a plateaued work force. Under the new contract, the reward for good performance is recognition of the relevance of one's work.

FIGURE 10-2

Implicit Assumptions of Old versus New Employment Contracts

OLD EMPLOYMENT CONTRACT	NEW EMPLOYMENT CONTRACT
Long-term employment relationship	Situational employment relationship
Reward for performance is promotion	Reward for performance is acknowledgment of contribution and relevance
Paternalistic management	Empowering management
Loyalty means remaining with the organization	Loyalty means responsibility and good work
Lifetime career is offered	Explicit job contracting is offered

Source: Compiled from David M. Noer, Healing the Wounds: Overcoming the Trauma of Layoffs and Revitalizing Downsized Organizations (San Francisco: Jossey-Bass, 1993), pp. 156–157.

- Under the old employment contract, management is paternalistic, resulting in a dependent work force. Under the new employment contract, management is empowering. The result is an empowered, self-directing work force.
- Under the old employment contract, loyalty means staying with the firm, often leading to a narrow and homogeneous work force. Under the new contract, loyalty means behaving responsibly and doing good work. The result is a responsible, psychologically mature work force.
- Under the old employment contract, a lifetime career is offered, resulting in a codependent work force. Under the new contract, explicit job contracting is offered. The result is a bond between employee and employer based on good work.

The essence of the Level 4 interventions, according to Noer, are strategies that support the new employment contract. Management practices must change to fit the realities of the modern workplace. Several of these management practices have already been described. Among them are shifting the predominant leadership style in the firm from command and control to coaching and facilitation. Developing teamwork and empowering employees also goes a long way toward developing a new psychological employment contract between employer and employee.

Many specific changes in management practices and policies will also help employees to become less dependent on the organization. Flexible and portable benefit plans will make it easier for workers to shift employers because they will not be sacrificing tenure-based credits should they join another firm. Universities and research laboratories have had such portable pensions for many years. A faculty member or research scientist can therefore switch employers in mid-career without sacrificing hard-earned pension credits. An outside financial services firm holds the pension funds, not the employer.

The most hard-hitting intervention, or strategy, is for organizations to reach explicit new agreements with employees about the nature of the employment relationship. It would include seven clauses:

1. *Task outcomes.* A clear statement is made of the work to be accomplished, along with key indicators of success.
2. *Agreement duration.* An agreement is reached as to how long the task will take, or when a project will be completed. If the task is continuous, such as providing customer service, the agreement is for a specified time period. At that date a renewal agreement will be drawn, if mutually acceptable.
3. *Contingency plans.* Agreement should be reached as to what happens if unanticipated changes take place with either the individual or the organization. For example, what might happen to the mechanical engineering staff if the company shifts to outsourcing most of its manufacturing?
4. *Compensation agreement.* The compensation agreement should be flexible enough to meet the employee's needs. The more risk-tolerant workers might want more stock options and less cash. Some other might want larger salaries and lower pension payments.
5. *Development agreement.* The employment contract specifies how the organization will contribute to the employee's skill

and professional development for jobs inside and outside the organization. Skills are particularly important today because the more sophisticated workers want portability across employers.

6. *Termination provisions.* Specifics are provided about what happens when the contract ends and there is no other work in the organization that is appropriate to the person's background.

7. *Renewal options.* Explicit mention is made of the results that must happen for both the individual and the organization in order to justify a contract renewal.

The seven clauses in the new psychological contract can ward off human suffering because they lower the probability of survivor layoff sickness taking place. No longer will people say or feel, "Charlie was let go. How could they do that to such a dedicated manager with 15 years seniority? I'm in shock." Instead, they will say: "It was great having Charlie with us. He made a real contribution while he was here. Now he is going to apply his skills somewhere else where they are more in demand. Let's celebrate his new career step." If this happens, the new employment contract will have accomplished its goal.

A CHECKLIST FOR EASING THE PAIN OF DOWNSIZING

Easing the pain and suffering associated with downsizing can be one of the most challenging tasks of the revamped workplace. To deny that the problem exists, or to ignore it, can be self-defeating. Building employee loyalty, or at least preventing it from crumbling completely, remains an important success requirement. The checklist that follows will help keep you focused on what can be done to soften the blow of downsizing.

☑ In selected situations, employers can find creative ways to downsize an organization without laying off large numbers of people.

☑ Outplacement services are by far the most popular form of support offered to laid-off workers by companies. A key ingredient in outplacement is the quality of the counselor.

☑ Downsizing survivors may need emotional support to help them deal with the distress of seeing former work associates being dismissed. Toward this end, some companies offer survivor workshops that function as support groups.

☑ Immediately after the layoff announcements are made, the company needs to do something in a hurry to keep feelings under control Humane layoff procedures should be developed that include giving workers as much information as possible about the downsizing. Face-to-face communication is essential.

☑ Interventions should be developed that help employees shift from being overly dependent on the organization to becoming controllers of their own fate. The primary vehicle for breaking organizational codependency is for people to concentrate on doing good work instead of on pleasing the boss.

☑ Detaching oneself from the organization begins with the person's decision not to rely on the employer to nurture him or her in every aspect of life.

☑ A hard-hitting strategy is for organizations to reach explicit new agreements with employees about the nature of the employment relationship. For example, workers should be aware of the task outcomes expected and in agreement on the duration of the task. When one task is completed, a new agreement can be drawn.

Putting It All Together

To help integrate many of the ideas we have presented about the human aspects of reengineering, we conclude with a brief case history of a successful experience. In addition, we will make brief interpretations of how the actions taken by the company relate to key ideas about leading and managing in the new workplace. Top management at the company was particularly sensitive to the human resources issues involved in business process reengineering. The details of the company experience are as follows.[1]

CASE STUDY

CTB Macmillan/McGraw-Hill

It's a fog-shrouded morning in Monterey, California. Inside the conference room of a large office complex, a dozen people are determined to cut through layers of corporate red tape. The group is exploring ideas about the best way to map out a new direction for the corporation. They are trying to deal with a multitude of complex issues, both gut-wrenching and challenging at the same time.

As the discussions continue, the mood shifts from unbridled enthusiasm to genuine skepticism. Yet through all these heavy discussions, the group main-

continued

289

tains its focus and composure. The group feels compelled to stay focused because the future of the company depends on the effectiveness of its decisions.

The scenario taking place is not the board of directors talking about ways to institute a total quality management system. Nor is it a task force devoted to streamlining operations by simply laying off workers. The group includes senior management, line employees, and the vice president of human resources. Its purpose is to tear the company's operations apart systematically and put them back together again, piece by piece. *[Reengineering requires a radical redesign of operations, not a simple modification.]*

Because the company has come to resemble an automobile engine that is too unwieldy and complex from years of modification and additions, the group is designing an entirely new corporate motor. The new motor will either power the firm to greater profit and productivity or stall out on the road to market dominance.

The firm is CTB Macmillan/McGraw-Hill, a provider of standardized achievement tests to schoolchildren in grades kindergarten through 12. The problem is diagnosed as operations so bureaucratic and cumbersome that customer service is slow and unresponsive. *[Reengineering requires creative thinking and incisive analyses of the causes of problems.]*

Group problem solving, aided by an external consultant, pointed to a solution: complete reengineering of CTB's test-scoring division. The group looks upon reengineering as a process that will radically change the way employees work, how projects are handled, and the way employees think about their jobs.

"There's no turning back," says Mary Layman, CTB's vice president of human resources, and one of the key members of the committee planning the change. *"We are totally committed to a vision." [The reengineering task force needs a vision, which can be crafted by the group or the reengineering team leader or process owner. A vision about reengineering articulated by top management is also of prime importance.]*

When CTB began its reengineering effort in June 1993, Mary Layman was determined not to let the human resources group get pushed out of the picture. *[Political skill is required to ensure that the reengineering effort has a balanced cross-functional perspective. Including a human resources perspective is not a thought that comes automatically to every executive responsible for reengineering.]* Senior management knew that it had to make operations more efficient and responsive.

During the previous two years, the firm had embarked on a variety of streamlining and restructuring efforts, but these had realized only minimal results. To maintain the firm's market share it was clear that something more drastic had to be done. *[To repeat, reengineering at its best is a radical departure from present practice.]* CTB is the nation's largest publisher of standardized achievement tests, making the company an easy target for competitors aiming at a share of the market.

CTB decided to initiate a pilot reengineering program to see if it could save money and make its core operations more responsive. *[A pilot program can be an effective method of introducing change. If the pilot program accomplishes its goals, it can trigger a success cycle of a small success followed by a larger success, and so forth.]* The company's initial goal was to decrease the turnaround time on the tests from 21 days to 10 days, and to slash $1 million in operational costs per year.

When CTB pulled together a steering committee to guide the effort, human resources (HR) was not included. The project team, assembled with the help of an outside consultant, had personnel from customer service, finance, information systems, computer operations, and marketing, all making decisions about the firm's future. *[Reengineering efforts always rely on a team structure both in the start-up phase and during implementation. To establish a "reengineering department" would be antithetical to the nature of process redesign.]*

When Layman immediately asked if she too could participate in the meetings, her boss quickly gave her the nod. "I went out of my way to get involved because I knew it was going to incorporate human resources issues. In the beginning, they didn't see that, or they didn't want to address it. They were looking at the reengineering effort in a more technical way. They hadn't begun to look at the organizational changes that were going to be needed. Unfortunately, you can't have one without the other," Layman explains.

continued

[Although this was not stated explicitly in the previous chapters, reengineering practitioners are often accused of paying cursory attention to the human element. Radical change in the scope of reengineering requires gaining commitment—or at least acceptance—from people at all organizational levels. Heel-dragging by people who fear losing their jobs is rampant under reengineering.][2]

Sitting in on the meetings, Layman offered her HR expertise. As the process progressed, she began to establish criteria for new work teams, set up interviews for positions on the teams, and arrange to provide training and help communicate new policies to the scoring division's 250 employees. *[Reengineering is dependent upon selecting capable, flexible people for the teams. After selection comes training. Without training, few employees will develop the insights or skills necessary to redesign a business process.]*

After documenting and studying every step in the scoring process and using focus groups to determine major deficiencies, the project team began determining how cross-functional teams in the new organization would operate and what work could be eliminated altogether. *[Cross-functional teams are necessary for successful reengineering. The multiple perspectives are helpful in identifying wasted steps in a process that might go undetected by a specialist in the process being studied.]*

When the dust had cleared three months later, CTB had reduced the number of steps in the scoring process from 154 to 68. It had also reduced the number of temporary workers needed during the peak scoring season from 450 to 360, and had eliminated several permanent positions. The company now expects profits from the scoring operation to increase by 120 percent. The turnaround time for scoring tests was reduced from 21 days to as few as 5. CTB expects to cut its peak work force by more than 20 percent, a savings of $2.4 million during the next two years. The early successes of the reengineering program encouraged to management to reengineering other processes throughout the firm.

CTB's program incorporates most of the key elements of a successful reengineering effort, including the facts that it is:

- Taking place in a highly competitive arena
- Fundamentally changing the way people work
- Cutting across traditional department lines
- Requiring new technology and training
- Benefiting from the clear vision and total commitment of the CEO and executive team.

[Reengineering is moving along well at CTB. Unlike reengineering at many other firms, the program has not led to massive layoffs of full-time employees. Many of the savings in payroll costs have come from not replacing people who leave by attrition and hiring fewer temporary workers. The emphasis has been on increasing profits by being more responsive to customer needs, thus regaining market share.]

Appendix:
Process Maps

Process maps lie at the heart of reengineering because they specify the steps and activities involved in a business process. A process in this context is a series of definable and measurable tasks, all leading to a useful result for the customer, who can be internal or external. After a process is presented in detail by a process map, nonessential steps can be eliminated. Two versions of process mapping are included here. The first version is representative of process mapping in a large company; the second version is a process map developed by administrative staff members at a college.

PROCESS MAPPING AT A TELECOMMUNICATIONS COMPANY

The steps involved in process mapping are presented, followed by the process map developed by following these steps.

Step 1 is to identify the participants involved in the process. Their names are written on pieces of adhesive notepaper. The notes are arranged in a vertical column on a flip chart or wall. The customer is at the top of the column.

Step 2 is to identify the customer action that triggers the process. The action is written on adhesive notepaper and placed next to the customer notes.

Step 3 is to identify with whom the customer interacts and what activity each person performs. This activity is written on adhesive notepaper and placed to the right of the customer input. The activity should appear on the same row as the participant who generates the activity.

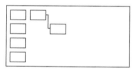

Step 4 is to identify who receives the output of this activity and what activities these people perform.

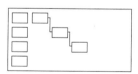

Step 5 is to continue to create the adhesive notes and position them in the same way until the process is complete—when the customer receives the output, such as a project or a proposal.

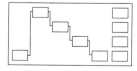

Step 6 is to compile lists of Moments of Truth and of nonessential steps in the process. A Moment of Truth is how well a customer's expectations are met at each service encounter, such as the compassionate hearing of a complaint. If customers' expectations are not met at a particular step, that step must be improved. A nonessential step is one that does not add value. A example might be holding an order for one week in order to search for minor errors that someone in the previous step should have the responsibility for finding. Quality consultant and management professor Gary Bonvillian says he looks to see if a step in the process really helps a customer or is simply a police action. In the spirit of reengineering, "police actions" are eliminated.[1]

Figure 1 presents the type of process map derived from the six steps described above. The process map describes the customer complaint process at the telecommunications company. Starting at the upper left, the process begins with a customer request or complaint. The customer response center documents the customer issue (1). The gray box (2) indicates that the customer issue is handled once again by the customer response center, and then is routed to the customer response manager for review. The customer response manager resolves or escalates the problem. The process continues until the customer issue is finally resolved (the box in the upper right on the process map).

A key feature of the process map are the gray boxes. All of them indicate steps in the process that were identified in building the process map, but that were later eliminated because they appeared to be nonessential. Five steps were eliminated as a result of this process mapping. For example, under Step 5, the marketing manager and branch manager no longer are involved in developing and implementing preventive measures. When a substantial number of steps are eliminated from a process, positions are likely to be eliminated.

Figure 2 symbolizes the difference between major process redesign and minor improvements to the current process flow.

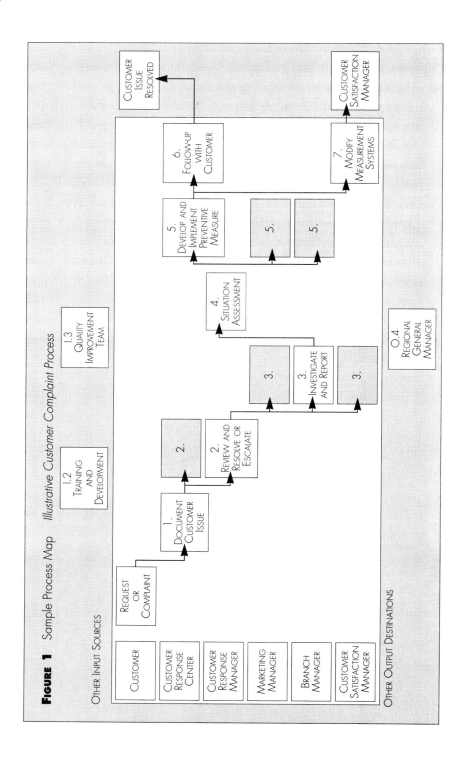

FIGURE 1   Sample Process Map   *Illustrative Customer Complaint Process*

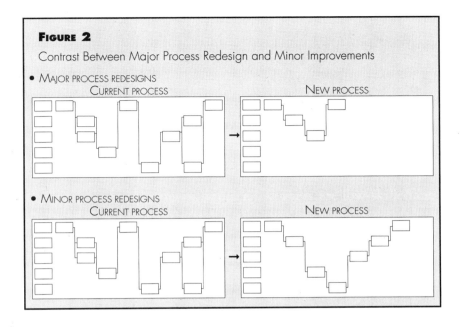

FIGURE 2

Contrast Between Major Process Redesign and Minor Improvements

- MAJOR PROCESS REDESIGNS
  CURRENT PROCESS   NEW PROCESS

- MINOR PROCESS REDESIGNS
  CURRENT PROCESS   NEW PROCESS

Reengineering aims to achieve major process redesign. In the words of many process redesign specialists, "We are building new roads, not just paving cow paths."

PROCESS MAPPING AT A COLLEGE

The Process Mapping Team at the College of Business, Rochester Institute of Technology, set out to simplify the cumbersome process whereby students withdrew from a course. Some students complained that they missed the deadline for withdrawing from a course because the process was so complicated. Figure 3 presents the withdrawal process before the process maps were drawn. Figure 4 presents the withdrawal process after the process maps were drawn. The team responsible for this activity reports that students now report more satisfaction with the course withdrawal procedure.

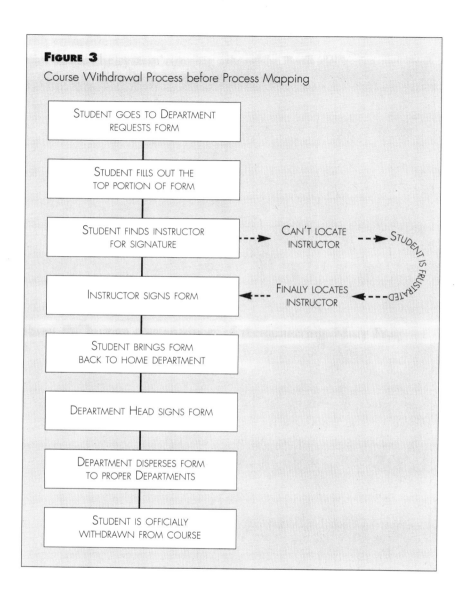

FIGURE 3

Course Withdrawal Process before Process Mapping

STUDENT GOES TO DEPARTMENT REQUESTS FORM

STUDENT FILLS OUT THE TOP PORTION OF FORM

STUDENT FINDS INSTRUCTOR FOR SIGNATURE

CAN'T LOCATE INSTRUCTOR

STUDENT IS FRUSTRATED

INSTRUCTOR SIGNS FORM

FINALLY LOCATES INSTRUCTOR

STUDENT BRINGS FORM BACK TO HOME DEPARTMENT

DEPARTMENT HEAD SIGNS FORM

DEPARTMENT DISPERSES FORM TO PROPER DEPARTMENTS

STUDENT IS OFFICIALLY WITHDRAWN FROM COURSE

This basic example of process mapping illustrates an important point. Although reengineering in its pure form is a radical redesign of the way people work, process mapping itself can often be used to fix problems that do not involve an overhaul of the work system. In this case, two steps were eliminated from a process that contributed to student (a.k.a. customer) dissatisfaction.

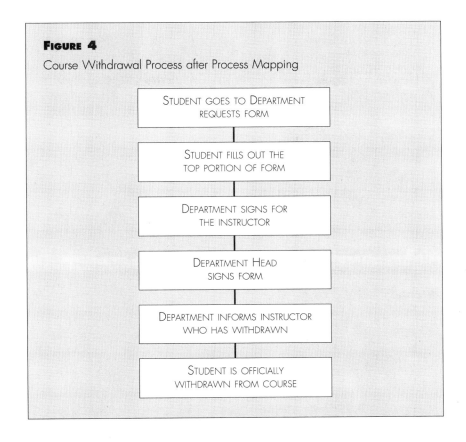

FIGURE 4

Course Withdrawal Process after Process Mapping

STUDENT GOES TO DEPARTMENT
REQUESTS FORM

STUDENT FILLS OUT THE
TOP PORTION OF FORM

DEPARTMENT SIGNS FOR
THE INSTRUCTOR

DEPARTMENT HEAD
SIGNS FORM

DEPARTMENT INFORMS INSTRUCTOR
WHO HAS WITHDRAWN

STUDENT IS OFFICIALLY
WITHDRAWN FROM COURSE

Chapter
Notes

Preface

1. John A. Byrne, "The Pain of Downsizing: What It's Really Like to Live Through the Struggle to Remake a Company," *Business Week*, May 9, 1994, p. 61; "Downsizing Becomes 'Dumbsizing,'" *Time*, March 15, 1993, p. 55.

Chapter 1

1. Michael Hammer and James Champy, *Reengineering the Corporation: A Manifesto for Business Revolution* (New York: Harper Business, 1993), p. 32.
2. The description of reengineering presented here is based on Robert M. Tomasko, "Intelligent Resizing (Part II): View from the Bottom Up," *Management Review*, June 1993, pp. 20–22.
3. Ibid., p. 21.
4. D. Keith Denton, "Customer-Focused Management," *HRMagazine*, August 1990, pp. 66–67.
5. William Patalon III, "Xerox to Cut 800 Jobs," *Rochester Democrat and Chronicle*, December 12, 1991, p. 1.
6. Kirkland Ropp, "Restructuring: Survival of the Fittest," *Personnel Administrator*, February 1987, p. 46.
7. John A. Byrne, "The Virtual Corporation," *Business Week*, February 8, 1993, p. 101. Much of our description of the virtual corporation is based on this source.
8. Erle Norton, "Future Factories," *The Wall Street Journal*, January 13, 1993, p. 1.

9. William Patalon III, "Factories Made to Order," *Rochester Democrat and Chronicle/Times-Union*, January 18, 1993, pp. 1, 6.
10. Several items on the list are from "Tomorrow's Skills: Success in the Virtual Corporation," *Executive Strategies*, June 1993, p. 2.

Chapter 2

1. Gene Hall, Jim Rosenthal, and Judy Wade, "How to Make Reengineering Really Work," *Harvard Business Review*, November-December 1993, p. 129.
2. John E. Hunter, Frank L. Schmidt, and Michael K. Judiesch, "Individual Differences in Output Variability as a Function of Job Complexity," *Journal of Applied Psychology*, February 1990, pp. 28–42.
3. Reprinted with permission from Hall, Rosenthal, and Wade, "How to Make Reengineering Really Work," pp. 124–126.
4. Linda S. Godfredson (ed.), "The g Factor in Employment," *Journal of Vocational Behavior*, Special Issue, Vol. 29, No. 3 (Duluth, MN: Academic Press with the Johns Hopkins University Project for the Study of Intelligence and Society, 1986).
5. Robert J. Sternberg, *Beyond IO: A Triarchic Theory of Human Intelligence* (New York: Cambridge University Press, 1985).
6. Michael Hammer and James Champy, *Reengineering the Corporation* (New York: Harper Business, 1993), pp. 84–101.
7. Thomas H. Davenport, *Process Innovation: Reengineering Work Through Information Technology* (Boston: Harvard Business School Press, 1993), p. 107.
8. Barbara Ettoree, "Benchmarking: The Next Generation," *Management Review*, June 1993, p. 12.
9. John A. Byrne, "Management's New Gurus," *Business Week*, August 31, 1992, p. 45.
10. John G. Belcher, Jr. *Productivity Plus* (Houston, TX: Gulf Publishing Co., 1990).

Chapter 3

1. Michael Hammer, "Reengineering Work: Don't Automate, Obliterate," *Harvard Business Review*, July–August 1990, p. 107.
2. Alan J. Rowe and James D. Bougarides, *Managerial Decision Making: A Guide to Successful Business Decisions* (New York: Macmillan, 1992), p. 172.
3. James M. Kouzes and Barry Z. Posner, *The Leadership Challenge: How to Get Extraordinary Things Done in Organizations* (San Francisco: Jossey-Bass, 1987), p. 33.

4. "Innovative Thinking: Stand Out from the Herd," *Executive Strategies*, November 1993, p. 12.
5. Anne Skagen, "Creativity Tools: Versatile Problem Solvers that Can Double as Fun and Games," *Supervisory Management*, October 1991, pp. 1–2.
6. Teresa M. Amabile and S. S. Gryskiewicz, *Creativity in the R & D Laboratory* (Greensboro, NC: Center for Creative Leadership, 1987).
7. Donald W. Blohowiak, *Mavericks! How to Lead Your Staff to Think Like Einstein, Create Like DaVinci and Invent Like Edison* (Homewood, IL: Business One Irwin, 1992).
8. David Campbell, *Take the Road to Creativity and Get Off Your Dead End* (Niles, IL: Argus Communications, 1977).
9. "Innovative Thinking: Stand Out from the Herd," p. 12.
10. Gareth Morgan, *Creative Organization Theory: A Resourcebook* (Newbury Park, CA: Sage, 1990).
11. Bryan W. Mattimore, *99% Inspiration: Tips, Tales & Techniques for Liberating Your Business Creativity* (New York: AMACOM, 1994, pp. 118–119.

Chapter 4

1. Gene Hall, Jim Rosenthal, and Judy Wade, "How to Make Reengineering *Really* Work," *Harvard Business Review*, November-December 1993, pp. 126–127. Reprinted with permission.
2. Thomas H. Davenport, *Process Innovation: Reengineering Work through Information Technology* (Boston: Harvard Business School Press, 1993), p. 177.
3. James A. F. Stoner and R. Edward Freeman, *Management*, 4th ed. (Englewood Cliffs, NJ: Prentice-Hall, 1989), p. 369.
4. Gary Yukl, *Skills for Managers and Leaders: Text, Cases, and Exercises* (Englewood Cliffs, NJ: Prentice-Hall, 1990), p. 59.
5. Hall, Rosenthal, and Wade, "How to Make Reengineering *Really* Work," p. 131.
6. Davenport, *Process Innovation*, pp. 191–192.
7. "Revive Your Mission Statement," *Working Smart*, April 1993, p. 1.
8. Davenport, *Process Innovation*, p. 119.
9. William M. Cohen, *The Art of the Leader* (Englewood Cliffs, NJ: Prentice-Hall, 1991).
10. "Revive Your Mission Statement, p. 1.
11. Davenport, *Process Innovation*, p. 304.
12. "Poor Attitudes Are Obstacles to Quality," *HRfocus*, January 1992, p. 12.

13. Warren Gross and Shula Shichman, "How to Grow an Organizational Culture," *Personnel*, September 1987, pp. 52–56.

Chapter 5

1. Richard J. Walsh, "Ten Basic Counseling Skills," *Supervisory Management*, July 1977, p. 9.
2. Charles C. Manz, "Helping Yourself and Others to Master Self-Leadership," *Supervisory Management* (November 1991), p. 9.
3. Charles C. Manz and Henry P. Sims, Jr., "SuperLeadership: Beyond the Myth of Heroic Leadership," *Organizational Dynamics*, Spring 1991, p. 18.
4. Adapted from Andrew J. DuBrin, *Participant Guide to Module 10: Development of Subordinates* (McGregor, TX: Leadership Systems Corporation, 1985), p. 11.
5. James S. Kouzes and Barry Z. Posner, "The Credibility Factor: What Followers Expect from their Leaders," *Management Review*, January 1990, p. 30.
6. Michael Hammer and James Champy, *Reengineering the Corporation: A Manifesto for Business Revolution* (New York: Harper Business, 1993), pp. 115–116.
7. Robert M. Tomasko, *Rethinking the Corporation: The Architecture of Change* (New York: AMACOM, 1993), pp. 132–133.
8. Ibid.
9. Ibid., pp. 160–161.
10. Ibid., p. 161.

Chapter 6

1. John R. Katzenbach and Douglas K. Smith, "The Discipline of Teams," *Harvard Business Review*, March–April 1993, p. 112.
2. Katzenbach and Smith, "The Discipline of Teams," p. 119.
3. Lee G. Bolman and Terrence E. Deal, "What Makes a Team Work?" *Organizational Dynamics*, Autumn 1992, pp. 40–41.
4. "Microsoft: Bill Gates' Baby is On Top of the World. Can It Stay There?" *Business Week*, February 24, 1992, p. 63.
5. "Psychology at Work," *Working Smart*, December 1991, p. 8.
6. Samuel Greengard, "Reengineering: Out of the Rubble," *Personnel Journal*, December 1993, p. 48J.
7. Judy Huret, "Paying for Team Results," *HRMagazine*, May 1991, p. 40.

8. "The Search for the Organization of Tomorrow," *Fortune*, May 18, 1992, pp. 95–96.
9. Phil Ebersole, "Kodak Tries Going with the Flow," *Rochester Democrat and Chronicle*, August 26, 1990, pp. 1F–2F.
10. Carol A. Norma and Robert A. Zawacki, "Team Appraisals—Team Approach," *Personnel Journal*, September 1991, p. 102.
11. Andrew J. DuBrin, *Stand Out! 330 Ways for Gaining the Edge with Bosses, Co-Workers, Subordinates and Customers* (Englewood Cliffs, NJ: Prentice-Hall, 1993), pp. 112–117.

Chapter 7

1. Presentation by Paul A. Allaire, Xerox Corporation, February 2, 1993.
2. This section is based on James W. Dean, Jr., and James R. Evans, *Total Quality: Management, Organization, and Strategy* (St. Paul, MN: West, 1994), pp. 198–200.
3. Peter Block, *Stewardship: Choosing Service Over Self-Interest* (San Francisco: Berrett-Koehler, 1993), p. 34.
4. M. J. Kiernan, "The New Strategic Architecture: Learning to Compete in the Twenty-First Century," *Academy of Management Executive*, February 1993, p. 14.
5. Based on Thomas F. O'Boyle, "Working Together: A Manufacturer Grows Efficient by Soliciting Ideas from Employees," *The Wall Street Journal*, June 5, 1992, pp. A1, AF.
6. Based on Peter C. Fleming, "Empowerment Strengthens the Rock," *Management Review*, December 1991, pp. 34–37.
7. Richard J. Magjuke and Timothy T. Baldwin, "Team-Based Employee Involvement Programs: Effects of Design and Administration," *Personnel Psychology*, Winter 1991, pp. 793, 806.
8. Robert W. Barner and J. Jackson Fullbright, "Set the Stage for Employee Involvement," *HRMagazine*, May 1991, p. 76.
9. Dean and Evans, *Total Quality*, pp. 202–207.
10. Bob Smith, "The Dark Side of Corporate America," *HRfocus*, October 1992, p. 8.
11. Dean and Evans, *Total Quality*, p. 203.
12. Hal F. Rosenbluth, "Have Quality, Will Travel," *The TQM Magazine*, November/December 1992, pp. 267–270.
13. "Fine Line Between Empowerment and Chaos," *Working Smart*, January 1993, p. 4.
14. Richard S. Wellins, William C. Byham, and Jeanne M. Wilson, *Empowered Teams: Creating Self-Directed Work Groups That Improve Quality, Productivity, and Participation* (San Francisco: Jossey-Bass, 1991), pp. 24–28.

Chapter 8

1. Adapted and updated from David I. Cleland, "Understanding Project Authority," *Business Horizons*, Spring 1967, pp. 63–70.
2. Thomas H. Davenport, *Process Innovation: Reengineering Work through Information Technology* (Boston: Harvard Business School Press, 1993), p. 261.
3. John A. Byrne, "The Horizontal Corporation: It's About Managing Across, Not Up and Down," *Business Week*, December 20, 1993, p. 76.
4. Jay R. Galbraith, *Competing with Flexible Lateral Organizations*, 2nd ed. (Reading, MA: Addison-Wesley, 1994), pp. 66–67.
5. D. Keith Denton, "Multi-Skilled Teams Replace Old Work Systems," *HRMagazine*, September 1992, p. 49.
6. "Talking with Dr. Charles Garfield about Empowering Your Team," *Working Smart*, June 1992, p. 7.
7. Byrne, "The Horizontal Corporation," p. 79.
8. Ibid., p. 78.
9. Adapted from James W. Dean, Jr., and James R. Evans, *Total Quality: Management, Organization, and Strategy* (St. Paul, MN: West, 1994), p. 179.
10. Daphna F. Raskas and Donald C. Hambrick, "Multifunctional Managerial Development: A Framework for Evaluating the Options," *Organizational Dynamics*, Autumn 1992, p. 8.
11. Randolph and Posner, *Getting the Job Done!*, pp. 19–88.
12. Ibid., p. 8.
13. Ibid., pp. 90–91.
14. D. H. Stamatis, "Conflict: You've Got to Accentuate the Positive," *Personnel*, December 1987, pp. 48–49.

Chapter 9

1. Susan Kleinman, "Is Your Attitude Killing Your Career?" *Cosmopolitan*, May 1994, p. 225; Bernard Baumhol, "When Downsizing Becomes 'Dumbsizing,'" *Time*, March 15, 1993, p. 55.
2. "More Cuts . . . Deeper Cuts . . . and More Help for Employees," *HRfocus*, November 1993, p. 24.
3. "When Layoffs Alone Don't Turn the Tide," *Business Week*, December 7, 1992, p. 101.
4. Robert M. Tomasko, "Restructuring: Getting it Right," *Management Review*, April 1992, p. 10.
5. Based on information in Samuel Greengard, "Don't Rush Downsizing: Plan, Plan, Plan," *Personnel Journal*, November 1993, pp. 64–65.

6. Paul Firstenberg, "Downsizing: What's Your Game Plan?" *Management Review*, November 1993, p. 46.
7. Ibid., p. 50.
8. Based on information in ibid., pp. 66–67.
9. Richard L. Bunning, "The Dynamics of Downsizing," *Personnel Journal*, September 1990, pp. 70–72.
10. Harold P. Weinstein and Michael S. Liebman, "Corporate Scale Down: What Comes Next?" *HRMagazine*, August 1991, p. 36.
11. Laurie Hays, "Gerstner Tries to Stem Flight of Top Talent as He Seeks to Achieve an IBM Turnaround," *The Wall Street Journal*, August 27, 1993, pp. B1, B2.
12. Based on Oren Harari, "Layoffs: An Internal Debate," *Management Review*, October 1993, p. 31.
13. Rick Maurer, *Caught in the Middle* (Cambridge, MA: Productivity Press, 1993).
14. Jerome C. Beam and Howard M. Pines, "Working with Survivors of Downsizings," *HRfocus*, August 1992, p. 12.
15. Greengard, "Don't Rush Downsizing," p. 69.
16. Donna Deeprose, "Managing a Permanently Lean Staff," *Executive Management Forum*, April 1992, p. 1.
17. Based on quotes from Robert Half in "Career 'Insurance' Protects DP Professionals," *Data Management*, June 1986, p. 33.
18. Paul Hirsch, *Pack Your Own Parachute* (Reading, MA: Addison-Wesley, 1987).
19. Ibid.

Chapter 10

1. Based on Robert Harris, "Canadians Replace Layoffs with Voluntary Rightsizings," *Personnel*, May 1991, pp. 15–16.
2. Based on "Testing Leads displaced Workers Into New Careers," *Human Resource Measurements* (A supplement to the January 1993 *Personnel Journal*), p. 8.
3. Quoted in Robert M. Tomasko, "Running Lean, Staying Mean," *Management Review*, November 1987, p. 38.
4. Anne T. Lawrence and Brian S. Mittman, "Downsizing on the Upswing," *HRfocus*, February 1991, p. 14.
5. Peter Crowden, "Outplacement Services Assessment," *HRMagazine*, September 1992, p. 69; updated by interview with representative of Drake Beam Morin, April 1994.
6. Tomasko, "Running Lean, Staying Mean," p. 37; Tomasko, *Rethinking the Corporation: The Architecture of Change* (New York: AMACOM, 1993), pp. 23–32.

7. Judith Evans, "Firms Increasing Flexible Benefits to Offset Longer Hours at Work," *Rochester Democrat and Chronicle*, November 30, 1992, p. 1.
8. The remaining sections of the chapter are based on David M. Noer, *Healing the Wounds: Overcoming the Trauma of Layoffs and Revitalizing Downsized Organizations* (San Francisco: Jossey-Bass, 1993), pp. 87–188.
9. Ibid., p. 97.

Chapter 11

1. Adapted from Samual A. Greengard, "Reengineering: Out of the Rubble," *Personnel Journal*, December 1993, pp. 48B–48H.
2. Personal communication with Donald O. Wilson, May 1994.

Appendix

1. Personal communication with Gary Bonvillian, Rochester Institute of Technology, April 1994.

Index